BOOKS ON

COMMUNICATIONS TECHNOLOGY

HANDBOOKS OF COMPUTER-COMMUNICATIONS STANDARDS

VOLUME 1
THE OPEN SYSTEMS INTERCONNECTION (OSI) MODEL AND OSI-RELATED STANDARDS

A description of the *master plan* for all computer-communications standards, the OSI model. The book also provides a detailed presentation of OSI-related standards at all 7 layers, including HDLC, X.25, ISO internet, ISO transport, ISO session, ISO presentation, Abstract Syntax One (ASN.1), and common application service elements (CASE).

VOLUME 2
LOCAL NETWORK STANDARDS

A detailed examination of all current local network standards, including logical link control (LLC, IEEE 802.2), CSMA/CD (IEEE 802.3), token bus (IEEE 802.4), token ring (IEEE 802.5), and fiber distributed data interface (FDDI, ANS X3T9.5).

VOLUME 3
DEPARTMENT OF DEFENSE (DOD) PROTOCOL STANDARDS

A description of the protocol standards that are mandated on all DOD computer procurements and are becoming increasingly popular on commercial local network products.

All of these books provide a clear tutorial exposition, a discussion of the relevance and value of each standard, an analysis of options within each standard, and an explanation of underlying technology.

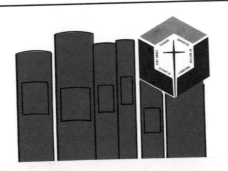

Handbook of
COMPUTER-
COMMUNICATIONS
STANDARDS

The Macmillan Database/Data Communications Series

Jay Ranade, Consulting Editor

Cave/Maymon: *Software Lifecycle Management*
Fadok: *Effective Design of CODASYL Data Base*
Ha: *Digital Satellite Communications*
Ranade/Ranade: *VSAM: Concepts, Programming, and Design*
Singer: *Written Communication for MIS/DP Professionals*
St. Amand: *A Guide to Packet-Switched, Value-Added Networks*
Stallings: *Handbook of Computer-Communications Standards I. The Open Systems Interconnection (OSI) Model and OSI-Related Standards*
Towner: *The ADS/Online Cookbook*
Wipfler: *CICS: Application Development and Programming*

Forthcoming
Azevedo: *ISPF*
Emanuel: *CICS: Designing for Performance*
McGrew/McDaniel: *In-House Publishing in a Mainframe Environment*
Piggott: *CICS: A Guide to Tuning*
Potter: *Local Area Networks: Applications and Design*
Ranade: *VSAM: Performance, Design, and Fine Tuning*
Samson: *MVS*
Stallings: *Handbook of Computer-Communications Standards II. Local Network Standards*
Stallings: *Handbook of Computer-Communications Standards III. Department of Defense Protocol Standards*
Towner: *Automate Plus*
Towner: *IDMS/R*™ *Cookbook*

Handbook of COMPUTER-COMMUNICATIONS STANDARDS

VOLUME 1

THE OPEN SYSTEMS
INTERCONNECTION (OSI) MODEL
AND OSI-RELATED STANDARDS

William Stallings, Ph.D.

Macmillan Publishing Company
NEW YORK

Collier Macmillan Publishing
LONDON

Copyright © 1987, Macmillan Publishing Company, a
division of Macmillan, Inc.

Printed in the United States of America

All rights reserved. No part of this book may be
reproduced or transmitted in any form or by any means,
electronic or mechanical, including photocopying,
recording, or by any information storage and retrieval
system, without permission in writing from the Publisher.

Macmillan Publishing Company
866 Third Avenue, New York, NY 10022

Collier Macmillan Canada, Inc.
Collier Macmillan Publishers • London

Printing: 2   3   4   5   6   7   8

Year: 7   8   9   0   1   2   3

Library of Congress Cataloging-in-Publication Data

Stallings, William.
    Handbook of computer-communications standards.

    (The Macmillan database/data communications series)
    Contents: v. 1. The Open Systems Interconnection (OSI)
model and OSI-related standards.
    Bibliography: v. 1, p.
    Includes index.
    1. Data transmission systems--Standards. I. Title.
II. Series.
TK5105.S732 1987   004.6'2   87-14062
ISBN 0-02-948071-X (v. 1)

For Tricia

Contents

Preface

In the early 1970s, networks that interconnected computers and terminals began to appear. The primary motivations were to share expensive computing resources and minimize data transmission costs. Since that time, the rapid proliferation of minicomputers and personal computers has increased the demand for data communications between computers, between terminals, and between terminal and computer. The generic name for these capabilities is computer communications. Such communication is accomplished by means of protocols. Typically, the task is too complex to be accomplished with a single protocol. Rather, a structured set of protocols, forming a communications architecture, is used.

In recent years, there has been an explosion of activity in the design of standards for computer-communications protocols and the implementation of these protocols. Since the introduction of the *Open Systems Interconnection (OSI)* model, all of the standards work, and most of the development of protocols, has been in the context of that hierarchical, seven-layer, communications architecture.

OBJECTIVES

This book is one of a series of books that provides a comprehensive treatment of computer communications standards, presented within the framework of the OSI model. The series systematically covers all major standards topics, providing the introductory and tutorial text missing from the actual standards. The books function as a primary reference for those who need an understanding of the technology, implementation, design, and application issues that relate to the standards. The books also function as companions to the standards documents for those who need to understand the standards for implementation purposes.

In terms of content, the objectives for this and the other volumes are

- Clear tutorial exposition
- Discussion of relevance and value of each standard

- Analysis of options within each standard
- Explanation of underlying technology
- Manageable and consistent treatment of a variety of standards
- Comparative assessment of alternative standards and options

This volume, Volume 1, introduces the OSI model, which is the master framework for all the standards to be covered. This model specifies a seven-layer architecture with one or more protocol standards at each layer. This volume contains a chapter on each layer, with the exception of the network layer, which warrants two chapters. For each layer, the general functions and services to be included are described. For layers 1 through 3, this material is supplemented with important examples of protocols at those layers. For layers 4 and 5, a unique standard has been developed for each layer, and these standards are presented. For layers 6 and 7, standards for what might be called utility services have been developed and are described; standards for specific applications at these two layers are examined in another volume.

INTENDED AUDIENCE

The book is intended for a broad range of readers interested in computer-communications architecture and protocols:

- **Students and professionals in data processing and data communications:** This book is intended as a basic tutorial and reference source for this exciting area of data processing and data communications.
- **Computer and communication system customers and managers:** The book provides the reader with an understanding of what features and structure are needed in a communications capability, as well as a knowledge of current and evolving standards. This information provides a means of assessing specific implementations and vendor offerings.
- **Designers and implementers:** The book discusses the critical design issues and explores approaches to meeting user requirements.

RELATED MATERIALS

Computer Communications: Architectures, Protocols, and Standards, Second Edition, (IEEE Computer Society Press, 1987) contains reprints of many of the key references cited herein. The IEEE Computer Society Press is at P. O. Box 80452, Worldway Postal Center, Los Angeles, CA 90080; telephone (800) 272-6657.

A videotape course that covers the material of this text is available from the Association for Media-Based Continuing Education for Engineers, Inc., 500 Tech Parkway NW, Suite 200A, Atlanta, GA 30313; telephone (404) 894-3362.

chapter 1

Introduction

1.1 COMMUNICATION PROTOCOLS AND ARCHITECTURE

When computers, terminals, and other data processing devices exchange data, the procedures involved can be quite complex. Consider, for example, the transfer of a file between two computers. There must be a data path between the two computers, either directly via a point-to-point link or indirectly via a communication network. But more is needed. These are the typical tasks to be performed:

1. The source system must either activate the direct data communication path or inform the communication network of the identity of the desired destination system.
2. The source system must ascertain that the destination system is prepared to receive data.
3. The file transfer application on the source system must ascertain that the file management program on the destination system is prepared to accept and store the file.
4. If the file formats used on the two systems are incompatible, one or the other system must perform a format translation function.

It is clear that there must be a high degree of cooperation between the two computer systems. The exchange of information between computers for the purpose of cooperative action is generally referred to as *computer communications.* Similarly, when two or more computers are interconnected via a communication network, the set of computer stations is referred to as a *computer network.* Since a similar level of cooperation is required between a user at a terminal and a computer, these terms are often used when some of the communicating entities are terminals.

In discussing computer communications and computer networks, two concepts are paramount:

- Protocols
- Computer-communications architecture

A protocol is used for communication between entities in different systems. The terms *entity* and *system* are used in a very general sense. Examples of entities are user application programs, file transfer packages, data-base management systems, electronic mail facilities, and terminals. Examples of systems are computers, terminals, and remote sensors. Note that in some cases the entity and the system in which it resides are coextensive (e.g., terminals). In general, an *entity* is anything capable of sending or receiving information, and a *system* is a physically distinct object that contains one or more entities. For two entities to communicate successfully, they must *speak the same language.* What is communicated, how it is communicated, and when it is communicated must conform to some mutually acceptable conventions between the entities involved. The conventions are referred to as a *protocol,* which may be defined as a set of rules governing the exchange of data between two entities. The key elements of a protocol are:

- *Syntax:* includes such things as data format and signal levels
- *Semantics:* includes control information for coordination and error handling
- *Timing:* includes speed matching and sequencing

Having introduced the concept of a protocol, we can now introduce the concept of a computer communications architecture. We make the observation that the task of communicating between two entities on different systems is too complicated to be handled by a single process or module. Figure 1.1 illustrates the file transfer application. Tasks 3 and 4, listed above, might be performed by an application-oriented protocol implemented in a file transfer package. For the two file transfer packages to exchange data, each invokes a network services module, which performs task 2 and exchanges data with its local file transfer module. To perform task 2, the two network services modules employ a system-to-system protocol. Finally, to actually transfer the data, the network services module must perform task 1, by engaging in a network access protocol with the

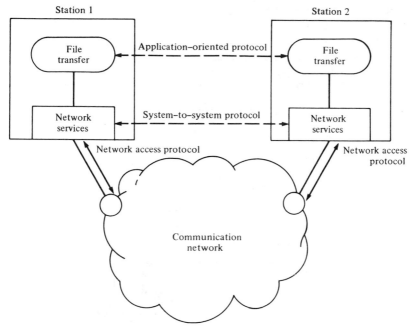

Figure 1.1. Example of computer communications architecture.

boundary node of the communication network. Thus, instead of a single protocol, there is a structured set of protocols that implement the communication function. That structure is referred to as a *computer communications architecture*.

As suggested by Figure 1.1, the various elements of the structured set of protocols are layered, or form a hierarchy. This is even more clearly indicated in Figure 1.2, which depicts the *open systems interconnection* (OSI) model. The OSI model was developed by the International Organization for Standardization in 1984 as a model of a computer communications architecture. Table 1.1 briefly defines the functions performed at each layer. The intent of the OSI model is that protocols be developed to perform the functions of each layer.

1.2 STANDARDS

The Importance of Standards

It has long been accepted in the communications industry that standards are required to govern the physical, electrical, and procedural characteristics of communication equipment. In the past, this view was not embraced by the computer industry. Whereas communication equipment vendors recognize that their equipment will generally interface to and

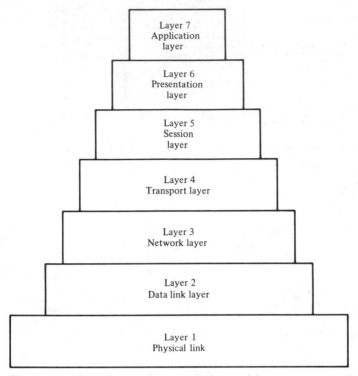

Figure 1.2. Open systems interconnection model.

communicate with other vendors' equipment, computer vendors have traditionally attempted to monopolize their customers. The proliferation of computers and distributed processing has made that an untenable position. Computers from different vendors must communicate with each other and, with the ongoing evolution of protocol standards, customers will no longer accept special-purpose protocol conversion software development. The day is quickly coming when the standards discussed in this book and in the other books in this series will dominate the marketplace.

The key advantages of standardization are:

- A standard assures that there will be a large market for a particular piece of equipment or software. This encourages mass production and, in some cases, the use of large-scale integration (LSI) or very-large-scale integration (VLSI) techniques, resulting in lower costs.
- A standard allows products from multiple vendors to communicate, giving the purchaser more flexibility in equipment selection and use.

The principal disadvantage of standards is that they tend to freeze technology. By the time a standard is developed, subjected to review and

Table 1.1. THE OSI LAYERS

1. Physical	Concerns the transmission of unstructured bit stream over physical medium; deals with the mechanical, electrical, functional, and procedural characteristics to access the physical medium
2. Data link	Provides for the reliable transfer of information across the physical link; sends blocks of data (frames) with the necessary synchronization, error control, and flow control
3. Network	Provides upper layers with independence from the data transmission and switching technologies used to connect systems; responsible for establishing, maintaining, and terminating connections
4. Transport	Provides reliable, transparent transfer of data between end points; provides end-to-end error recovery and flow control
5. Session	Provides the control structure for communication between applications; establishes, manages, and terminates connections (sessions) between cooperating applications
6. Presentation	Provide independence to the application processes from differences in data representation (syntax)
7. Application	Provides access to the OSI environment for users and also provides distributed information services

compromise, and promulgated, more efficient techniques are possible. Nevertheless, the advantages of standards are so great that customers are willing to pay this price.

So far, we have not given a definition of the term *standard*. Although there is no widely accepted and quoted definition, the following definition from the 1979 National Policy on Standards for the United States encompasses the essential concept [NSPA79]:

> A prescribed set of rules, conditions, or requirements concerning definition of terms; classification of components; specification of materials, performance, or operations; delineation of procedures; or measurement of quantity and quality in describing materials, products, systems, services, or practices.

In this book, we are concerned with standards that have been developed to specify services and protocols that are used within the framework of the OSI architecture. These standards have been developed primarily by two organizations: ISO and CCITT. These and other organizations are described briefly later in this chapter.

Standards and Regulation

It is helpful for the reader to distinguish three concepts [CERN84]:

- *Voluntary standards*
- *Regulatory standards*
- *Regulatory use of voluntary standards*

Voluntary standards are developed by standards-making organizations such as CCITT and ISO. They are voluntary in that the existence of the standard does not compel its use. That is, manufacturers voluntarily implement a standard if they perceive a benefit to themselves, and in a legal sense the practical consequences of departing from a standard are minimal. Voluntary standards are also voluntary in the sense that they are developed by volunteers who are not paid for their efforts by the standards-making organization. These volunteers are generally employees of interested organizations, such as government and industrial groups. Voluntary standards work because they are generally developed on the basis of broad consensus and because the customer demand for standard products encourages the implementation of these standards by the producers.

In contrast, a regulatory standard is developed by a government regulatory agency to meet some public objective such as economic, health, and safety. These standards have the force of regulation behind them and must be met by providers in the context in which the regulations apply.

A relatively new, or at least newly prevalent, phenomenon is the regulatory use of voluntary standards. A typical example of this is a regulation that requires that the government purchase of a product be limited to products that conform to some referenced set of voluntary standards. This approach has a number of salutory effects:

- It reduces the rule-making burden on government agencies.
- It encourages cooperation between government and standards organizations to produce standards of broad applicability.
- It reduces the variety of standards that providers must meet.

1.3 STANDARDS ORGANIZATIONS

Throughout this book, we describe key standards that have been developed within the context of the OSI model. Various organizations have been involved in the development or promotion of these standards [RUTK86]. This section provides a brief description of the most important (in the current context) of these organizations.

International Organization for Standardization (ISO)

ISO is an international agency for the development of standards on a wide range of subjects. It is a voluntary, nontreaty organization whose members are designated standards bodies of participating nations and nonvoting observer organizations. Although ISO is a nongovernmental organization, more than 70 percent of ISO member bodies are governmental standards institutions or organizations incorporated by public law. Most of the remainder have close links with the public administrations in their own countries. The United States member body is the American National Standards Institute (ANSI).

ISO was founded in 1946 and has issued more than 5000 standards on a broad range of areas. Its purpose is to promote the development of standardization and related activities to facilitate international exchange of goods and services, and to develop cooperation in the sphere of intellectual, scientific, technological, and economic activity. Standards have been issued to cover everything from screw threads to solar energy. ISO is organized as a group of technical committees chartered to produce standards in various areas. The area of work of relevance to this book is handled by Technical Committee 97 (TC97), Information Processing Systems. As with all ISO technical committees, TC97 is organized into subcommittees and working groups that actually do the work of producing the standards. The work related to OSI is carried on by subcommittees SC6 and SC21. Table 1.2 shows the organization of TC97.

The development of an ISO standard from first proposal to actual publication of the standard follows a seven-step process. The objective is to ensure that the final result is acceptable to as many countries as possible. The steps are briefly described below (time limits are the minimum time in which voting could be accomplished, and amendments require extended times) [LOHS85]:

    1. A new work item is assigned to the appropriate technical committee (TC), and within that TC, to the appropriate working group (WG). The WG prepares the technical specifications for the

Table 1.2. SUBCOMMITTEES OF ISO TC97 CONCERNED WITH OSI

SC 6   Telecommunications and Information Exchange Between Systems
   WG 1   Data link layer
   WG 2   Network layer
   WG 3   Physical interface characteristics
   WG 4   Transport layer
   WG 5   Architecture and coordination of layers 1–4

SC 21   Information Retrieval, Transfer, and Management for OSI
   WG 1   OSI architecture
   WG 2   Computer graphics
   WG 3   Database
   WG 4   OSI management
   WG 5   Specific application services and protocols
   WG 6   Session, presentation, common application service elements, and upper layer architecture

proposed standard and publishes these as a draft proposal (DP). This DP is circulated among interested members for balloting and technical comment. At least 3 months is allowed, and there may be iterations. When there is *substantial support*, the DP is sent to the administrative arm of ISO, known as the Central Secretariat.

   2. The DP is registered at the Central Secretariat within 2 months of final approval by the TC.

   3. The Central Secretariat edits the document to ensure conformity with ISO practices; no technical changes are made. The edited document is then issued as a Draft International Standard (DIS).

   4. The DIS is circulated for a 6-month balloting period. For approval, the DIS must receive a majority approval by the TC members and 75 percent approval of all voting members. Revisions may occur to resolve any negative vote. If more than two negative votes remain, it is unlikely that the DIS will be published as an International Standard (IS).

   5. The approved DIS and revision are returned within 3 months to the Central Secretariat for submission to the ISO Council, which acts as the board of directors of ISO.

   6. The DIS is accepted by the Council as an IS.

   7. The IS is published by ISO.

As can be seen, the process of issuing a standard is a slow one. Certainly, it would be desirable to issue standards as quickly as the technical details can be worked out, but ISO must assure that the standard will receive widespread support.

International Telegraph and Telephone Consultative Committee (CCITT)

CCITT is a committee of the International Telecommunications Union (ITU), which is itself a United Nations treaty organization [HUMM85]. Hence the members of CCITT are governments. The U.S. representation is housed in the Department of State. The charter of CCITT is "to study and issue recommendations on technical, operating, and tariff questions relating to telegraphy and telephony." Its primary objective is to standardize, to the extent necessary, techniques and operations in telecommunications to achieve end-to-end compatibility of international telecommunication connections, regardless of the countries of origin and destination.

   CCITT is organized into 15 Study Groups that prepare standards, called Recommendations by CCITT. There are three areas of activity concerned with OSI matters: data communications, telematic services, and integrated services digital networks (ISDN). Telematic services are user-oriented services that involve information query and update. ISDN refers to a planned worldwide digital telecommunications facility that will eventually replace existing telephone and telecommunications services. Work in these three areas directly involves six study groups (Table 1.3).

Table 1.3. STUDY GROUPS OF CCITT CONCERNED WITH OSI

Study Group I	Responsible for defining the operational aspects of the telematic services, including Teletex (communication among office work processing systems), videotex (interactive information retrieval), and facsimile (image transmission)
Study Group VII	Responsible for interfaces to public data networks, including the X.25 and related standards. Also responsible for the OSI reference model for CCITT applications
Study Group VIII	Responsible for developing terminal equipment recommendations for the telematic services. Their work focuses on protocols at the upper four layers of the OSI architecture
Study Group XI	Primarily concerned with switching and control signaling for telephony. Also working on aspect of the ISDN customer interface
Study Group XVII	Concerned with data transmission over the telephone network, including modem interfaces
Study Group XVIII	Responsible for digital networks in general and ISDN in particular

Work within CCITT is conducted in 4-year cycles [BELL84]. Every 4 years, a Plenary Assembly is held. The work program for the next 4 years is established at the assembly in the form of questions submitted by the various study groups based on requests made to the study groups by their members. The assembly assesses the questions, reviews the scope of the study groups, creates new or abolishes existing study groups, and allocates questions to them.

Based on the questions, each study group prepares draft recommendations to be submitted to the next assembly, 4 years hence. After approval by the assembly, these are published as CCITT Recommendations. If a certain draft recommendation is very urgent, a study group may employ a balloting procedure to gain approval before the end of the 4 years. Again, as with ISO, the process of standardization within CCITT is a slow one.

Within the fields of data communications and information processing, traditionally there has been a split between the interests of CCITT and ISO. CCITT has primarily been concerned with data transmission and communication networks issues. Roughly, these occupy the lower three layers of the OSI model. ISO has traditionally been concerned with computer-communications and distributed processing issues, which correspond roughly to layers 4 through 7. The increasing merger of the fields of data processing and data communications, however, has resulted in considerable overlap in the areas of concern of these two organizations.

Fortunately, the growth of the overlap has been accompanied by a growth in cooperation, so that competing standards are not being issued.

Other Standards-Making Organizations

In terms of standards for data and computer communications, ISO and CCITT are the dominant organizations. Other groups are also involved, and some of the most important of these are:

- *American National Standards Institute (ANSI):* nonprofit, nongovernmental organization composed of manufacturers, users, communications carriers, and other interested organizations. It is the national clearinghouse for voluntary standards in the United States. It is also the U.S.-designated voting member of the ISO. ANSI's interests roughly parallel those of ISO [SHER86].
- *National Bureau of Standards (NBS):* part of the Department of Commerce. It issues Federal Information Processing Standards (FIPS) for equipment sold to the federal government. The Department of Defense (DOD) need not, and frequently does not, comply. The concerns of NBS are broad, encompassing the areas of interest of both CCITT and ISO. NBS is attempting to satisfy federal government requirements with standards that, as far as possible, are compatible with international standards [BODS85].
- *Federal Telecommunications Standards Committee (FTSC):* interagency advisory board responsible for establishing standards (FED-STD) for federal procurements to assure interoperability of government-owned communications equipment. FTSC tends to concentrate on standards corresponding to the lower layers of the OSI model, whereas NBS is more focused on higher layers. However, there is an unresolved area of overlap between the two sets of standards [BODS85].
- *Defense Communications Agency (DCA):* promulgates communications-related military standards (MIL-STD). DOD feels that its requirements in some areas are unique, and this is reflected in DCA standards that are unlike those used elsewhere [SELV85].
- *Electronics Industries Association (EIA):* trade association of electronics firms and a member of ANSI. It is concerned primarily with standards that fit into OSI layer 1 (physical).
- *Institute of Electrical and Electronics Engineers (IEEE):* professional society and also a member of ANSI. Their concerns have been primarily with the lowest two layers of the OSI model (physical and data link).
- *European Computer Manufacturers Association (ECMA):* composed of computer suppliers selling in Europe, including the European divisions of some American companies. It is devoted exclusively to the cooperative development of standards applicable to computer technology. ECMA serves as a nonvoting member of CCITT and ISO and also issues its own standards. Because of the

rapidity of their efforts, they have had considerable influence on OSI work.

Standards-Related Organizations

The success of standards related to OSI depends not only on the development of timely, technically appropriate standards, but on their acceptance by the vendors who supply and the customers who buy equipment that conforms to the standards. One of the most promising developments in recent years is the creation of a number of organizations whose goal is to ensure that acceptance. In this subsection, we briefly mention four of these organizations.

- *MAP*
- *TOP*
- *COS*
- *U.S. Government OSI User's Committee*

The *Manufacturing Automation Protocol* (MAP) is an effort begun by General Motors in 1982, and since has been transferred to the Society of Manufacturing Engineers [KAMI86]. The objective of MAP is to define a local network and associated communications architecture for terminals, computing resources, programmable devices, and robots within a plant or a complex. It sets standards for procurement and provides a specification for use by vendors who want to build networking products for factory use that are acceptable to MAP participants. The strategy has three parts:

1. For cases in which international standards exist, select those alternatives and options that best suit the needs of the MAP participants.
2. For standards currently under development, participate in the standards-making process to represent the requirements of the MAP participants.
3. In those cases where no appropriate standard exists, recommend interim standards until the international standards are developed.

Thus, MAP is intended to specify those standards and options within standards appropriate for the factory environment. This guarantees a large market for products that conform to those standards. To date, hundreds of companies have participated in the MAP effort.

A similar effort, called *Technical and Office Protocols* (TOP), addresses the needs of the office and engineering environments [FARO86]. Like MAP, TOP specifies standards and options within standards, and has received widespread support. TOP was begun by Boeing and is now under the management of SME.

An equally important development is the creation, in early 1986, of the *Corporation for Open Systems* (COS). COS is a nonprofit joint venture of more than 60 of the major suppliers of data processing and data communications equipment. Its purpose is [COS86]: "to provide a vehicle for acceleration of the introduction of interoperable, multi-vendor products and services operating under agreed-to OSI, ISDN and related international standards to assure widespread customer acceptance of an open network architecture in world markets." COS is involved in a number of standards-related activities. Its most important activity is the development of a single consistent set of test methods, test facility, and certification procedures. This will allow vendors to certify that their products do in fact meet the international standards and will interoperate with equipment from other vendors.

A final significant development worth noting is the creation in September of 1986 of the *U.S. Government OSI Users Committee* [HEFF86]. The U.S. government is the world's largest user of computers and thus has a profound impact on the product plans of many of the vendors. The objectives of the committee are to:

• develop implementable OSI specifications.
• coordinate cooperative efforts between government agencies and industry.
• define unique agency requirements and work for OSI incorporation.

In addition, the Office of Management and Budget is developing a policy that would require the federal government to use products for computer-to-computer communication that implement OSI-related standards.

All of these organizations represent forces that virtually guarantee the widespread development and use of products that conform to the OSI-related standards.

1.4 PLAN OF THE BOOK

The purpose of this book is to provide a survey of computer-communications protocol standards within the context of the OSI model. Chapter 2 examines the OSI model in detail. The remainder of the book consists of one chapter for each of the seven layers of the OSI model, with the exception of layer 3, which warrants two chapters.

The choice of standards to examine and the emphasis varies with the chapters. First, let us consider the choice of standards. For layers 1 through 3, much of the protocol development predates the OSI model, and examples of these standards are supplied. In particular, the following standards are emphasized: RS-232 for layer 1, HDLC for layer 2, and X.25 for layer 3. ISO has divided layer 3 into sublayers, with X.25 fitting nicely into the lower sublayer. The upper sublayer of layer 3 deals with a concept known as internetworking, and ISO has issued a single standard for that sublayer. We examine this sublayer, and the ISO standard, in a separate chapter. For layers 4 and 5, ISO has issued a single standard for each layer, and these standards are examined in detail. At layers 6 and 7, ISO has developed standards for what might be called utility services; these standards are described in the last two chapters in the book.

Several important sets of standards have been omitted. At layers 1 through 3, important standards have been developed for local networks, by IEEE and ANSI, and for ISDN, by CCITT. At layers 6 and 7, both CCITT and ISO have developed standards for specific applications, such as file transfer and electronic mail. All of these standards are examined in other volumes of this series.

In terms of emphasis, the reader will note a gradual shift as the book progresses. There are two key aspects of any OSI-related standard. The first aspect is the set of services that a particular protocol provides to users of that protocol at the next higher layer of the architecture. The second aspect is the set of mechanisms and functions by which protocol entities in two different systems cooperate to provide the services. As a general rule, we can make the following statement: At the lower layers of the architecture (approximately 1 to 4), the services to be provided are relatively simple, but the mechanisms required are relatively complex; the reverse is true for the upper layers (approximately 5 to 7). This difference is reflected in the emphasis on mechanisms versus services in the various chapters.

chapter 2

The OSI Model

This chapter has two purposes. First, it introduces the Open Systems Interconnection (OSI) model and describes its key characteristics and conventions. Second, it serves as an overview of the remainder of the book, since the standards to be examined in the next chapters can be described in the context of the OSI model.

We begin with a discussion of a simple 3-layer communications architecture. This allows us to look at some of its essential elements without being bogged down in the details of the 7-layer OSI architecture. Next, we provide an exposition of the concept of a communications protocol. The fundamental mechanisms found in a variety of protocols are described. Finally, we are in a position to introduce and examine the OSI model.

2.1 A SIMPLE COMMUNICATIONS ARCHITECTURE

In very general terms, communication can be said to involve three agents: processes, hosts, and networks. *Processes* are the fundamental entities that communicate. One example is a file transfer operation. In this case, a file transfer process in one system is exchanging data with a file transfer process in another system. Another example is remote logon. In this case, a user terminal is attached to one system and controlled by a terminal-handling process in that system. The user may be remotely connected to a time-sharing system; then data is exchanged between the terminal-handling process and the time-sharing process. Processes execute on *hosts* (computers), which can often support multiple simultaneous processes. Hosts are connected by *networks,* and the data to be exchanged is transmitted by the network from one host to another. From this point of view, the transfer of data from one process to another involves first getting the data to the host in which the process resides and then getting it to the process within the host.

With these concepts in mind, it appears natural to organize the communications task into three relatively independent layers:

- Network access layer
- Transport layer
- Process layer

The *network access layer* is concerned with the exchange of data between a host and the network to which it is attached. The sending host must provide the network with the address of the destination host, so that the network may route the data to the appropriate destination. The sending host may wish to invoke certain services, such as priority, that might be provided by the network. The specific protocol used at this layer depends on the type of network to be used; different protocols have been developed for circuit-switched, packet-switched, local networks, and others. Thus, it makes sense to separate those functions having to do with network access into a separate layer. By doing this, the remainder of the communication software, above the network access layer, need not be concerned about the specifics of the network to be used. The same higher-layer software should function properly regardless of the particular network to which the host is attached.

Regardless of the nature of the processes that are exchanging data (e.g., file transfer, remote logon), there is usually a requirement that data be exchanged reliably. That is, we would like to be assured that all of the data arrives at the destination process and that the data arrive in the same order in which it was sent. As we shall see, the mechanisms for providing reliability are essentially independent of the nature of the processes. Thus, it makes sense to collect those mechanisms in a common layer shared by all process; this is referred to as the *transport layer.*

Finally, the *process layer* contains those protocols needed to support the various applications. For each different type of application, such as file transfer, a protocol is needed that is peculiar to that application.

Figure 2.1 illustrates this simple architecture. Three hosts are connected to a network. Each host contains software at the network access and transport layers, and software at the process layer for one or more processes. For successful communication, every entity in the overall sys-

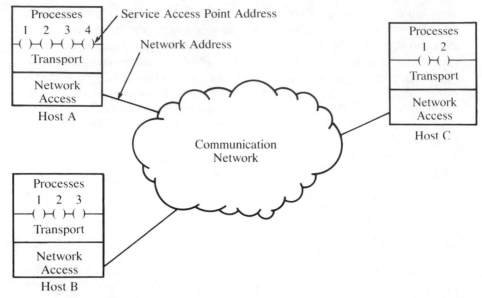

Figure 2.1.   A simplified communications architecture.

tem must have a unique address. Actually, two levels of addressing are needed. Each host on the network must have a unique network address; this allows the network to deliver data to the proper host. Each process within a host must have an address that is unique within the host; this allows the transport layer to deliver data to the proper process. These latter addresses are known as *service access points* (SAPs), connoting the fact that each process is individually accessing the services of the transport layer.

Let us trace a simple operation. Suppose that a process, associated with SAP 1 at host A, wishes to send a message to another process, associated with SAP 2 at host B. The process at A hands the message over to its transport layer with instructions to send it to host B, SAP 2. The transport layer hands the message over to the network access layer, which instructs the network to send the message to host B. Note that the network need not be told the identity of the destination SAP. All that it needs to know is that the data is intended for host B.

To control this operation, control information, as well as user data, must be transmitted, as suggested in Fig. 2.2. Let us say that the sending process generates a block of data and passes this to its transport layer. The transport layer may break this block into two smaller pieces to make it more manageable. To each of these pieces the transport protocol appends a transport header. The combination of data from the next higher layer and control information is known as a *protocol data unit* (PDU); in the case of a PDU created by the transport protocol, it is referred to as a

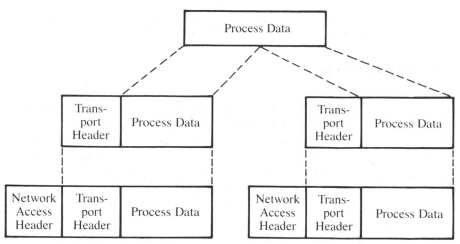

Figure 2.2. Protocol data units.

transport PDU. The header in each transport PDU contains control information to be used by the peer transport protocol at host B. Examples of items that may be stored in this header include—

- *Destination SAP:* When the destination transport layer receives the transport PDU, it must know to whom the data is to be delivered.
- *Sequence number:* Since the transport protocol is sending a sequence of PDUs, it numbers them sequentially so that if they arrive out of order, the destination transport entity may reorder them.
- *Error-detection code:* The sending transport protocol may include a code that is the function of the contents of the remainder of the PDU. The receiving transport protocol performs the same calculation and compares the result with the incoming code. A discrepancy results if there has been some error in transmission. In that case, the receiver can discard the PDU. This concept is examined later in this chapter.

The next step is for the transport protocol to hand its PDUs over to the network layer, with instructions to transmit them to the destination host. To satisfy this request, the network access protocol must present the data to the network with a request for transmission. As before, this operation requires the use of control information. In this case, the network access protocol appends a network access header to the data it receives from the transport layer, creating a network-access PDU. Examples of the items that may be stored in this header include—

- *Destination network address:* The network must know to whom the data is to be delivered.

> • *Facilities requests:* The network access protocol might want the network to make use of certain facilities, such as priority.

2.2 PROTOCOLS

A fundamental aspect of any communications architecture is that one or more protocols operate at each layer of the architecture and that two peer protocols at the same layer, but in different systems, cooperate to achieve the communication function. Before turning to an examination of the rather complex OSI architecture, it will be helpful to consider a rather small set of functions that form the basis of all protocols. Not all protocols have all functions; this would involve a significant duplication of effort. There are, nevertheless, many instances of the same type of function being present in protocols at different levels.

This discussion is, by necessity, rather abstract. It does provide an integrated overview of some of the key functions of protocols and is useful in understanding the relationship between the layers of the OSI model. The remainder of the book examines a number of specific protocols and provides concrete examples of the functions listed here.

We can group protocol functions into the following categories:

- Segmentation and reassembly
- Encapsulation
- Connection control
- Ordered delivery
- Flow control
- Error control
- Multiplexing

Segmentation and Reassembly

A protocol is concerned with exchanging streams of data between two entities. Usually, the transfer can be characterized as consisting of a sequence of blocks of data of some bounded size. At the application level, we refer to a logical transfer of a *message*. Whether the application entity sends data in messages or in a continuous stream, lower level protocols may need to break up the data into blocks of some smaller bounded size. This process is called *segmentation*. For convenience, we shall refer to a block of data exchanged between two entities via a protocol as a PDU.

There are a number of motivations for segmentation, depending on the context. These are among the typical reasons for segmentation:

- The communications network may only accept blocks of data up to a certain size. ARPANET, for example, accepts messages up to 8063 bytes in length.

- Error control may be more efficient with a smaller PDU size. If an error is detected, only a small amount of data may need to be retransmitted.
- More equitable access to shared transmission facilities, with shorter delay, can be provided. For example, without a maximum block size, one station could monopolize a shared medium.
- A smaller PDU size may mean that receiving entities can allocate smaller buffers.
- An entity may require that data transfer comes to some sort of *closure* from time to time, for checkpoint and restart/recovery operations.

There are several disadvantages to segmentation that argue for making blocks as large as possible:

- Each PDU contains a fixed minimum of control information. Hence the smaller the block, the greater the percentage of overhead.
- PDU arrival may generate an interrupt that must be serviced. Smaller blocks result in more interrupts.
- More time is spent processing smaller and more numerous PDUs.

All of these factors must be taken into account by the protocol designer in determining minimum and maximum PDU size.

The counterpart of segmentation is *reassembly*. Eventually, the segmented data must be reassembled into messages appropriate to the application level. If PDUs arrive out of order, this task is complicated. The process of segmentation was illustrated in Fig. 2.2, which showed process data being divided into two segments.

Encapsulation

Each PDU contains not only data but control information. Indeed, some PDUs consist solely of control information and no data. The control information falls into three general categories:

- *Address:* The address of the sender and/or receiver may be indicated.
- *Error detection code:* Some sort of code is often included for error detection.
- *Protocol control:* Additional information is included to implement the protocol functions listed in the remainder of this section.

The addition of control information to data is referred to as *encapsulation*. Data are accepted or generated by an entity and encapsulated into a PDU containing that data plus control information. Encapsulation is also illustrated in Fig. 2.2. Figure 2.3 shows the combined use of segmentation and assembly, and fragmentation. In this figure, a message is segmented into three PDUs before transmission. Upon reception, the PDU headers are stripped off and the segmented data are recombined for delivery to the user.

Connection Control

An entity may transmit data to another entity in an unplanned fashion and without prior coordination. This is known as *connectionless data transfer.* Although this mode can be useful, it is less common than *connection-oriented transfer.*

Connection-oriented data transfer is to be preferred (even required) if stations anticipate a lengthy exchange of data and/or certain details of their protocol must be worked out dynamically. A logical association, or *connection,* is established between the entities. Three phases occur (Fig. 2.4):

- Connection establishment
- Data transfer
- Connection termination

With more sophisticated protocols, there may also be connection interrupt and recovery phases to cope with errors and other sorts of interruptions.

During the connection establishment phase, two entities agree to exchange data. Typically, one station will issue a connection request (in connectionless fashion!) to the other. A central authority may or may not be involved. In simpler protocols, the receiving entity either accepts or rejects the request and, in the former case, away they go. In more complex proposals, this phase includes a negotiation concerning the syntax, semantics, and timing of the protocol. Both entities must, of course, be using the same protocol. But the protocol may allow certain optional features and these must be agreed upon by means of negotiation. For example, the protocol may specify a PDU size of *up to* 8000 bytes; one station may wish to restrict this to 1000 bytes.

After connection establishment, the data transfer phase is entered. During this phase both data and control information (e.g., flow control, error control) is exchanged. Finally, one side or the other wishes to terminate the connection and does so by sending a termination request. Alternatively, a central authority might forcibly terminate a connection.

The key characteristic of connection-oriented data transfer is that sequencing is used. Each side sequentially numbers the PDUs that it sends to the other side. Because each side *remembers* that it is engaged in a logical connection, it can keep track of both outgoing numbers, which

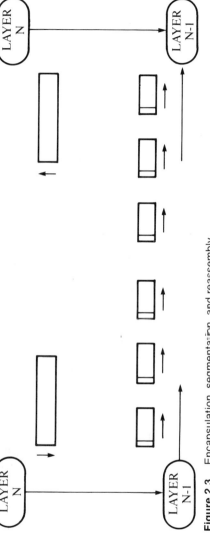

Figure 2.3. Encapsulation, segmentation, and reassembly.

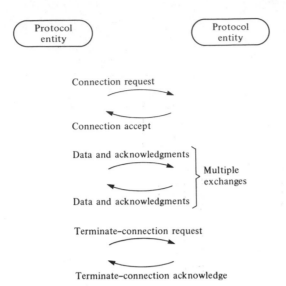

Figure 2.4.   The phases of a connection-oriented data transfer.

it generates, and incoming numbers, which are generated by the other side. Indeed, one can essentially define a connection-oriented data transfer as one in which both sides number PDUs and keep track of both incoming and outgoing numbering. Sequencing supports three main functions:

- Ordered delivery
- Flow control
- Error control

Ordered Delivery

When two entities are in different hosts connected by a network, there is a risk that PDUs will not arrive in the order in which they were sent because they may traverse different paths through the network. In connection-oriented protocols, it is generally required that PDU order be maintained. For example, if a file is transferred between two systems, we would like to be assured that the records of the received file are in the same order as those of the transmitted file, and not shuffled. If each PDU is given a unique number, and numbers are assigned sequentially, then it is a logically simple task for the receiving entity to reorder received PDUs on the basis of sequence number.

Flow Control

Flow control is a technique for assuring that a transmitting entity does not overwhelm a receiving entity with data. The receiving entity typically allocates a data buffer with some maximum length. When data are received, the receiver must do a certain amount of processing (i.e., examine the header and strip it from the PDU) before passing the data to a higher-layer user. In the absence of flow control, the receiver's buffer may fill up and overflow while it is processing old data.

In a connection-oriented protocol, the sequence numbers can be used to provide a flow control mechanism. Different approaches are illustrated in this book, but all involve the same fundamental mechanism. At any given time, the sender is allowed to send PDUs whose numbers are in a contiguous range. Once those PDUs are sent, the entity can send no more until it receives permission from the other entity. For example, the transport protocol in host A has permission to send PDUs number 1 through 7. After it sends these, it waits. At some time, it receives a message from the transport protocol in host B, indicating that it is now prepared to receive numbers 8 through 15.

Flow control is a good example of a protocol function that must be implemented in several layers of an architecture. Consider again Fig. 2.1. One of the responsibilities of the network is to prevent congestion. It does this by restricting, as needed, the flow of PDUs from attached hosts into the network. This flow control is exercised via the network access protocol. At the same time, the transport protocol entity in host A may need to restrict the flow of data over a logical connection from the transport protocol entity in host B, using flow control at the transport level.

Error Control

Error control is a technique that allows a protocol to recover from lost or damaged PDUs. As with flow control, it is based on the use of sequence numbers. Three mechanisms come into play:

- Positive acknowledgment
- Retransmit after timeout
- Error detection

In a connection-oriented protocol, each PDU is numbered sequentially. For error control, it is the responsibility of the receiving protocol entity to acknowledge each PDU that it receives; this is done by sending back the sequence number of the received PDU to the other side. If a PDU is lost in transit, then the intended receiver will obviously not acknowledge it. The sending entity will note the time that it sends each PDU. If a PDU remains unacknowledged after a certain amount of time, the sender assumes that the PDU did not get through and retransmits that PDU.

There is another possibility: the PDU gets through but the bits have been altered by errors in transit. To account for this contingency, an error

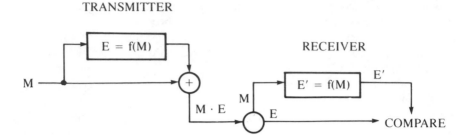

M = Message
E, E′ — Error-detecting code
f = Error-detecting code function

Figure 2.5.   Error detection.

detection technique is needed. This is illustrated in Fig. 2.5. The sending entity performs a calculation on the bits of the PDU and adds the result to the PDU. The receiver performs the same calculation and compares the calculated result to the result stored in the incoming PDU. If there is a discrepancy, the receiver assumes that an error has occurred and discards the PDU. As before the sender fails to receive an acknowledgment and retransmits the PDU.

Multiplexing

Multiplexing is a function that may be exercised when more than one layer of a communications architecture employs a connection-oriented protocol. Consider again Fig. 2.1. The network access protocol may be connection oriented, allowing a host to set up one or more logical connections to other hosts on the network. In packet-switched networks, these network logical connections are referred to as virtual circuits. The transport protocol will set up a logical transport connection for each pair of SAPs that wishes to exchange data. For each transport connection, a separate network connection could be set up (Fig. 2.6). This is a one-to-one relationship, but need not be so. Multiplexing can be used in one of two directions. *Upward multiplexing* occurs when multiple higher-level connections are multiplexed on, or share, a single lower-level connection. This may be done to make efficient use of the lower-level service. For example, public packet-switched networks generally charge for each network logical connection that is set up. Thus, if several transport connections are needed between a pair of hosts, these could all be multiplexed on a single network connection. *Downward multiplexing,* or *splitting,* means that a single higher-level connection is built on top of multiple lower-level connections. This technique may be used to improve reliability, performance, or efficiency.

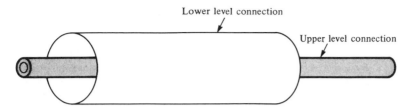

(a) One–to–one

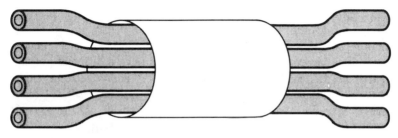

(b) Upward multiplexing

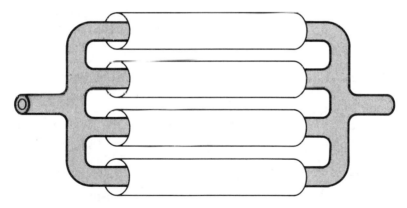

(c) Downward multiplexing

Figure 2.6. Multiplexing of protocol connections.

2.3 OSI ARCHITECTURE

Motivation

When work is done that involves more than one computer, additional elements must be added to the system: the hardware and software to support the communication between or among the systems. Communications hardware is reasonably standard and generally presents few problems. However, when communication is desired among heterogeneous (different vendors, different models of same vendor) machines, the software development effort can be a nightmare. Different vendors use different data formats and data exchange conventions. Even within one vendor's product line, different model computers may communicate in unique ways.

As the use of computer communications and computer networking proliferates, a one-at-a-time special-purpose approach to communications software development is too costly to be acceptable. The only alternative is for computer vendors to adopt and implement a common set of conventions. For this to happen, a set of international or at least national standards must be promulgated by appropriate organizations. Such standards have two effects:

- Vendors feel encouraged to implement the standards because of an expectation that, because of wide usage of the standards, their products would be less marketable without them.
- Customers are in a position to require that the standards be implemented by any vendor wishing to propose equipment to them.

It should become clear from the ensuing discussion that no single standard will suffice. The task of communication in a truly cooperative way between applications on different computers is too complex to be handled as a unit. The problem must be decomposed into manageable parts. Hence, before one can develop standards, there should be a structure or *architecture* that defines the communications tasks.

This line of reasoning led the International Organization for Standardization (ISO) in 1977 to establish a subcommittee to develop such an architecture. The result was the *Open Systems Interconnection* (OSI) reference model, adopted in 1984, that is a framework for defining standards for linking heterogeneous computers. The OSI model provides the basis for connecting *open* systems for distributed applications processing. The term *open* denotes the ability of any two systems conforming to the reference model and the associated standards to connect.

Table 2.1, extracted from the basic OSI document [ISO7498], summarizes the purpose of the model.

Concepts

A widely accepted structuring technique, and the one chosen by ISO, is *layering*. The communications functions are partitioned into a vertical set of layers. Each layer performs a related subset of the functions required to communicate with another system. It relies on the next lower layer to perform more primitive functions and to conceal the details of those functions. It provides services to the next higher layer. Ideally, the layers should be defined so that changes in one layer do not require changes in

Table 2.1.   PURPOSE OF THE OSI MODEL

The purpose of this International Standard Reference Model of Open Systems Interconnection is to provide a common basis for the coordination of standards development for the purpose of systems interconnection, while allowing existing standards to be placed into perspective within the overall Reference Model.

The term Open Systems Interconnection (OSI) qualifies standards for the exchange of information among systems that are "open" to one another for this purpose by virtue of their mutual use of the applicable standards.

The fact that a system is open does not imply any particular systems implementation, technology or means of interconnection, but refers to the mutual recognition and support of the applicable standards.

It is also the purpose of this International Standard to identify areas for developing or improving standards, and to provide a common reference for maintaining consistency of all related standards. It is not the intent of this International Standard either to serve as an implementation specification, or to be a basis for appraising the conformance of actual implementations, or to provide a sufficient level of detail to define precisely the services and protocols of the interconnection architecture. Rather, this International Standard provides a conceptual and functional framework which allows international teams of experts to work productively and independently on the development of standards for each layer of the Reference Model of OSI.

the other layers. Thus we have decomposed one problem into a number of more manageable subproblems.

The task of the ISO subcommittee was to define a set of layers and the services performed by each layer. The partitioning should group functions logically, should have enough layers to make each layer manageably small, but should not have so many layers that the processing overhead imposed by the collection of layers is burdensome. The principles by which ISO went about its task are summarized in Table 2.2. The resulting OSI reference model has seven layers, which are listed with a brief definition in Table 1.1. Table 2.3 provides ISO's justification for the selection of these layers.

Table 1.1 defines, in general terms, the functions that must be performed in a system for it to communicate. Of course, it takes two to communicate, so the same set of layered functions must exist in two systems. Communication is achieved by having corresponding (*peer*) entities in the same layer in two different systems communicate via a protocol.

Figure 2.7 illustrates the OSI model. Each system contains the seven layers. Communication is between applications in the systems, labeled AP X and AP Y in the figure. If AP X wishes to send a message to AP Y, it invokes the application layer (layer 7). Layer 7 establishes a peer relationship with layer 7 of the target machine, using a layer 7 protocol. This protocol requires services from layer 6, so the two layer 6 entities use a protocol of their own, and so on down to the physical layer, which actually passes the bits through a transmission medium.

Table 2.2.   PRINCIPLES USED IN DEFINING THE OSI LAYERS

1. Do not create so many layers as to make the system engineering task of describing and integrating the layers more difficult than necessary.
2. Create a boundary at a point where the description of services can be small and the number of interactions across the boundary are minimized.
3. Create separate layers to handle functions that are manifestly different in the process performed or the technology involved.
4. Collect similar functions into the same layer.
5. Select boundaries at a point which past experience has demonstrated to be successful.
6. Create a layer of easily localized functions so that the layer could be totally redesigned and its protocols changed in a major way to take advantage of new advances in architectural, hardware or software technology without changing the services expected from and provided to the adjacent layers.
7. Create a boundary where it may be useful at some point in time to have the corresponding interface standardized.
8. Create a layer where there is a need for a different level of abstraction in the handling of data (e.g., morphology, syntax, semantics).
9. Allow changes of functions or protocols to be made within a layer without affecting other layers.
10. Create for each layer boundaries with its upper and lower layer only.

Similar principles have been applied to sublayering:

11. Create further subgrouping and organization or functions to form sublayers within a layer in cases where distinct communication services need it.
12. Create, where needed, two or more sublayers with a common, and therefore, minimal functionality to allow interface operation with adjacent layers.
13. Allow bypassing of sublayers.

Note that there is no direct communication between peer layers except at the physical layer. That is, above the physical layer, each protocol entity sends data *down* to the next lower layer to get the data *across* to its peer entity. Even at the physical layer, the OSI model does not stipulate that two systems be directly connected. For example, a packet-switched or circuit-switched network may be used to provide the communications link. This point should become clearer later, when we discuss the network layer.

The attractiveness of the OSI approach is that it promises to solve the heterogeneous computer communications problem. Two systems, no matter how different, can communicate effectively if they have the following in common:

- They implement the same set of communications functions.
- These functions are organized into the same set of layers. Peer layers must provide the same functions, but note that it is not necessary that they provide them in the same way.
- Peer layers must share a common protocol.

Table 2.3.   JUSTIFICATION OF THE OSI LAYERS

a. It is essential that the architecture permit usage of a realistic variety of physical media for interconnection with different control procedures (e.g., V.24, V.25, X.21, etc.). Application of principles 3, 5, and 8 [see Table 2.2] leads to identification of a *Physical Layer* as the lowest layer in the architecture.

b. Some physical communication media (e.g., telephone line) require specific techniques to be used to transmit data between systems despite a relatively high error rate (i.e., an error rate not acceptable for the great majority of applications). These specific techniques are used in data-link control procedures, which have been studied and standardized for a number of years. It must also be recognized that new physical communication media (e.g., fibre optics) will require different data-link control procedures. Application of principles 3, 5, and 8 leads to identification of a *Data Link Layer* on top of the Physical Layer in the architecture.

c. In the open systems architecture, some systems will act as the final destination of data. Some systems may act only as intermediate nodes (forwarding data to other systems). Application of principles 3, 5, and 7 leads to identification of a *Network Layer* on top of the Data Link Layer. Network oriented protocols, such as routing, for example, will be grouped in this layer. Thus, the Network Layer will provide a connection path (network-connection) between a pair of transport-entities, including the case where intermediate nodes are involved.

d. Control of data transportation from source end-system to destination end-system (which is not performed in intermediate nodes) is the last function to be performed to provide the totality of the transport-service. Thus, the upper layer in the transport-service part of the architecture is the *Transport Layer,* on top of the Network Layer. This Transport Layer relieves higher layer entities from any concern with the transportation of data between them.

e. There is a need to organize and synchronize dialogue, and to manage the exchange of data. Application of principles 3 and 4 leads to the identification of a *Session Layer* on top of the Transport Layer.

f. The remaining set of general interest functions are those related to representation and manipulation of structured data for the benefit of application programs. Application of principles 3 and 4 leads to identification of a *Presentation Layer* on top of the Session Layer.

g. Finally, there are applications consisting of application processes that perform information processing. An aspect of these applications processes and the protocols by which they communicate comprise the *Application Layer* as the highest layer of the architecture.

To assure the above, standards are needed. Standards must define the functions and services to be provided by a layer (but not how it is to be done—that may differ from system to system). Standards must also define the protocols between peer layers (each protocol must be identical for the two peer layers). The OSI model, by defining a seven-layer architecture, provides a framework for defining these standards.

Some useful OSI terminology is illustrated in Fig. 2.8. For simplicity, any layer is referred to as the *(N) layer,* and names of constructs

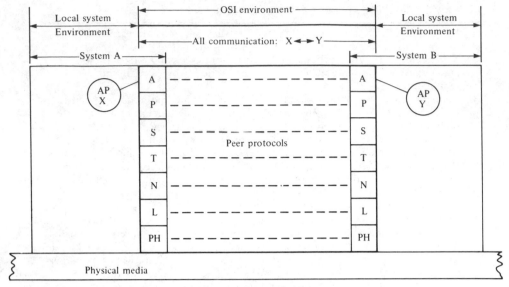

Figure 2.7. The OSI environment. Source: [FOLT81]

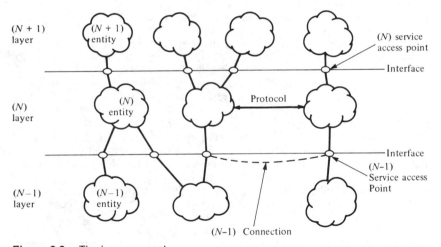

Figure 2.8. The layer concept.

associated with that layer are also preceded by (N). Within a system, there are one or more active entities in each layer. An *(N) entity* implements functions of the (N) layer and also the protocol for communicating with (N) entities in other systems. An example of an entity is a process in a multiprocessing system. Or it could simply be a subroutine. There might be multiple identical (N) entities, if this is convenient or efficient for a given system. There might also be differing (N) entities, corresponding to different protocol standards at that level.

Each entity communicates with entities in the layers above and below it across an *interface*. The interface is realized as one or more *service access points* (SAPs). The (N-1) entity provides *services* to an (N) entity via the invocation of *primitives*. A primitive specifies the function to be performed and is used to pass data and control information. The actual form of a primitive is implementation dependent. An example is a subroutine call.

Four types of primitives are used to define the interaction between adjacent layers in the architecture. These are defined in Table 2.4. The layout of Fig. 2.9 suggests a typical time ordering of these events. For example, consider the transfer of data from an (N) entity to a peer (N) entity in another system. The following steps could occur:

1. The source (N) entity invokes its (N-1) entity with a Data.request primitive. Associated with the primitive are the parameters needed, such as the data to be transmitted and the destination address.
2. The source (N-1) entity prepares an (N-1) PDU to be sent to its peer (N-1) entity.
3. The destination (N-1) entity delivers the data to the appropriate destination (N) entity via a Data.indication, which includes the data and a source address as parameters.
4. If an acknowledgment is called for, the destination (N) entity issues a Data.response primitive to its (N-1) entity.
5. The (N-1) conveys this acknowledgment in an (N-1) PDU.
6. The acknowledgment is delivered to the (N) entity via a Data.indication.

Table 2.4.   PRIMITIVE TYPES (X.210)

Request
A primitive issued by a service user to invoke some service and to pass the parameters needed to fully specify the requested service

Indication
A primitive issued by a service provider either:
(1) to indicate that a procedure has been invoked by the peer service user on the connection and to provide the associated parameters, or
(2) to notify the service user of a provider-initiated action

Response
A primitive issued by a service user to acknowledge or complete some procedure previously invoked by an indication to that user

Confirm
A primitive issued by a service provider to acknowledge or complete some procedure previously invoked by a request by the service user.

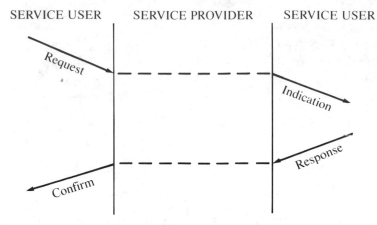

Figure 2.9. Interaction primitives.

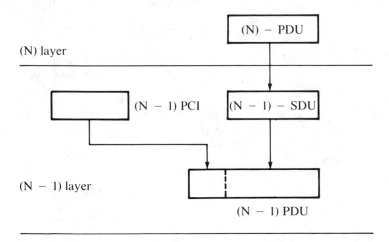

PCI = protocol control information
PDU = protocol data unit
SDU = service data unit

Figure 2.10. Logical relationship between data units in adjacent layers.

This sequence of events is referred to as a *confirmed* type of dialogue, as the initiator receives confirmation that the requested service has had the desired effect at the other end. If only request and indication primitives are involved (steps 1 through 3), then the dialogue is *unconfirmed*.

The data that passes between entities is in the form of a collection of bits known as a data unit. Figure 2.10 illustrates the relationship between types of data units. We are already familiar with the *protocol data unit* (PDU). The PDU is passed as a unit between peer entities. Of course,

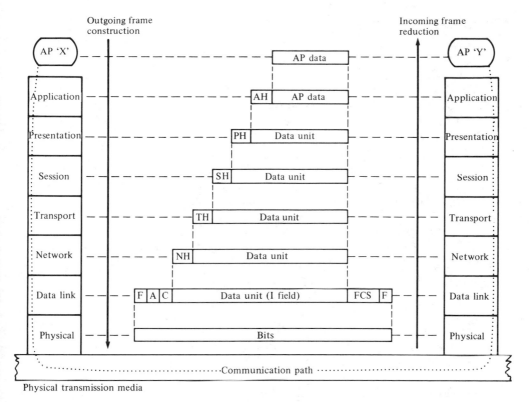

Figure 2.11. OSI operation. Source: [FOLT83]

an entity in the (N) layer cannot directly pass data to a peer entity at the (N) layer. Rather, it must pass its (N) PDUs down to the (N-1) layer. The (N-1) views data coming from the (N) layer as an (N-1) *service data unit* (SDU). The (N-1) entity may map an SDU arriving from above into a single PDU (as indicated in Fig. 2.10). Alternatively, the (N-1) entity may segment the (N-1) SDU into multiple PDUs. In any case the identity of the SDU as a unit is preserved from one end of the connection to the other; if the SDU is segmented by the sending (N-1) entity, it must be reassembled by the receiving (N-1) entity before delivery to the receiving (N) entity. The OSI model was conceived as connection oriented. Two (N) entities communicate, using a protocol, by means of an (N-1) connection. This logical connection is provided by (N-1) entities between (N-1) SAPs. ISO has produced an addendum to the standard that provides a connectionless mode of transfer; see Sec. 2.4.

　　Figure 2.11 illustrates the OSI principles in operation. First, consider the most common way in which protocols are realized. When application *X* has a message to send to application *Y,* it transfers the data to an application entity in the application layer. A *header* is appended to the data that contains the required information for the peer layer 7 protocol (encapsulation). The original data, plus the header, is now passed as a unit to layer 6. The presentation entity treats the whole unit as data, and appends its own header (a second encapsulation). This process continues down through layer 2, which generally adds both a header and a trailer. This layer 2 unit, called a *frame,* is then passed by the physical layer onto the transmission medium. When the frame is received by the target system, the reverse process occurs. As the data ascends, each layer strips off the outermost header, acts on the protocol information contained therein, and passes the remainder up to the next layer.

At each stage of the process, a layer may segment the data unit it receives from the next higher layer into several parts, to accommodate its own requirements. These data units must then be reassembled by the corresponding peer layer before being passed up.

When two peer entities wish to exchange data, this may be done with or without a prior connection. A connection can exist at any layer of the hierarchy. In the abstract, a connection is established between two (N) entities by identifying an (N-1) SAP for each (N) entity.

Layers

In this section we discuss briefly each of the layers and, where appropriate, give examples of standards for protocols at those layers.

Physical Layer.   The *physical layer* covers the physical interface between devices and the rules by which bits are passed from one to another. The physical layer has four important characteristics [BERT80, MCCL83]:

- Mechanical
- Electrical
- Functional
- Procedural

Examples of standards at this layer are RS-232-C, RS-449/422/423, and portions of X.21.

Data Link Layer.   Although the physical layer provides only a raw bit stream service, the *data link layer* attempts to make the physical link reliable and provides the means to activate, maintain, and deactivate the link. The principal service provided by the link layer to the higher layers is that of error detection and control. Thus, with a fully functional data link layer protocol, the next higher layer may assume virtually error-free transmission over the link. However, if communication is between two systems that are not directly connected, the connection will comprise a number of data links in tandem, each functioning independently. Thus the higher layers are not relieved of an error control responsibility. Examples of standards at this layer are HDLC, LAP-B, LLC, and LAP-D.

Network Layer.   The basic service of the *network layer* is to provide for the transparent transfer of data between transport entities. It relieves the transport layer of the need to know anything about the underlying data transmission and switching technologies used to connect systems. The network service is responsible for establishing, maintaining, and terminating connections across the intervening communications facility.

It is at this layer that the concept of a protocol becomes a little fuzzy. This is best illustrated with reference to Figure 2.12, which shows two stations that are communicating, not via direct link, but via a packet-switched network. The stations have direct links to the network nodes. The layer 1 and 2 protocols are station-node protocols (local). Layers 4 through 7 are clearly protocols between (N) entities in the two stations. Layer 3 is a little bit of both.

The principal dialogue is between the station and its node; the station sends addressed packets to the node for delivery across the network. It requests a virtual circuit connection, uses the connection to transmit data, and terminates the connection. All of this is done by means of a station-node protocol. However, because packets are exchanged and virtual circuits are set up between two stations, there are aspects of a station–station protocol as well.

There is a spectrum of possibilities for intervening communications facilities to be managed by the network layer. At one extreme, the simplest, there is a direct link between stations. In this case, there may be little or no need for a network layer, because the data link layer can per-

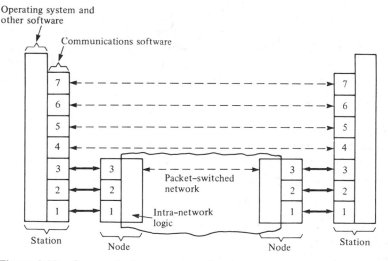

Figure 2.12.   Communication across a network.

form the necessary functions of managing the link. Between extremes, the most common use of layer 3 is to handle the details of using a communication network. In this case, the network entity in the station must provide the network with sufficient information to switch and route data to another station. At the other extreme, two stations might wish to communicate but are not even connected to the same network. Rather, they are connected to networks that, directly or indirectly, are connected to each other. This situation is explored in some detail in Chap. 6. For now it suffices to say that one approach to providing for data transfer in such a case is to use an Internet Protocol (IP) that sits on top of a network protocol and is used by a transport protocol. IP is responsible for internetwork routing and delivery, and relies on a layer 3 at each network for intranetwork services. IP is sometimes referred to as *layer 3.5.*

The best known example of layer 3 is the X.25 layer 3 standard, which is examined in some detail in Chap. 5. The X.25 standard refers to itself as an interface between a station and a node (using our terminology). In the context of the OSI model, it is actually a station-node protocol.

Transport Layer. The purpose of layer 4 is to provide a reliable mechanism for the exchange of data between processes in different systems [STAL85]. The *transport layer* ensures that data units are delivered errorfree, in sequence, with no losses or duplications. The transport layer may also be concerned with optimizing the use of network services and providing a requested quality of service to session entities. For example, the session entity might specify acceptable error rates, maximum delay, priority, and security. In effect, the transport layer serves as the user's liaison with the communications facility.

The size and complexity of a transport protocol depends on the type of service it can get from layer 3. For a reliable layer 3 with a virtual circuit capability, a minimal layer 4 is required. If layer 3 is unreliable, the layer 4 protocol should include extensive error detection and recovery. Accordingly, ISO has defined five classes of transport protocol, each oriented toward a different underlying service [STAL84].

Session Layer. The *session layer* provides the mechanism for controlling the dialogue between applications. At a minimum, the session layer provides a means for two application processes to establish and use a connection, called a *session.* In addition it may provide the following services:

- *Dialogue type:* This can be two-way simultaneous, two-way alternate, or one-way.
- *Recovery:* The session layer can provide a checkpointing mechanism, so that if a failure of some sort occurs between checkpoints, the session entity can retransmit all data since the last checkpoint.

Presentation Layer. The *presentation layer* is concerned with the syntax of the data exchanged between application entities. Its purpose is to resolve differences in format and data representation. The presentation layer defines the syntax used between application entities and provides for the selection and subsequent modification of the representation to be used.

Examples of presentation protocols are encryption and virtual terminal protocol. A virtual terminal protocol converts between specific terminal characteristics and a generic or virtual model used by application programs.

Application Layer. The *application layer* provides a means for application processes to access the OSI environment. This layer contains management functions and generally useful mechanisms to support distributed applications. Examples of protocols at this level are file transfer and electronic mail.

Figure 2.13 provides two useful perspectives on the OSI architecture. The annotation along the right side suggests viewing the 7 layers in three parts, corresponding to the simple 3-layer architecture introduced at the beginning of this chapter. The lower 3 layers contain the logic for a host to interact with a network. The host physically is attached to the network, uses a data link protocol to communicate reliably with the network, and uses a network protocol to request data exchange with another device on the network and to request network services (e.g., priority). Both the X.25 standard for packet-switched networks and the X.21 standard for circuit-switched networks actually encompass all three layers. Continuing from this perspective, the transport layer provides a reliable end-to-end connection regardless of the intervening network facility. Finally, the upper three layers, taken together, are involved in the exchange of data between end users, making use of a transport connection for reliable data transfer.

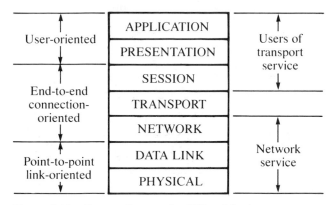

Figure 2.13. Perspectives on the OSI architecture.

Another perspective is suggested by the annotation on the left. Again, consider host systems attached to a common network. The lower two layers deal with the link between the host system and the network. The next three layers are all involved in transferring data from one host to another. The network layer makes use of the communication network facilities to transfer data from one host to another; the transport layer assures that the transfer is reliable; and the session layer manages the flow of data over the logical connection. Finally, the upper two layers are oriented to the user's concerns, including considerations of the application to be performed and any formatting issues.

ISO and CCITT Standards

As was mentioned, the OSI model provides a framework within which standards can be developed for protocols at each layer. This framework has, of course, been used by ISO. It is also the framework used by CCITT, which has adopted the OSI model as a CCITT recommendation (X.200).

Figure 2.14 illustrates some of the most important standards developed by the two organizations. ISO has recently concentrated on layers 3 through 7. They have issued a standard for an internetworking protocol, a transport protocol, and a session protocol. ISO has developed general-

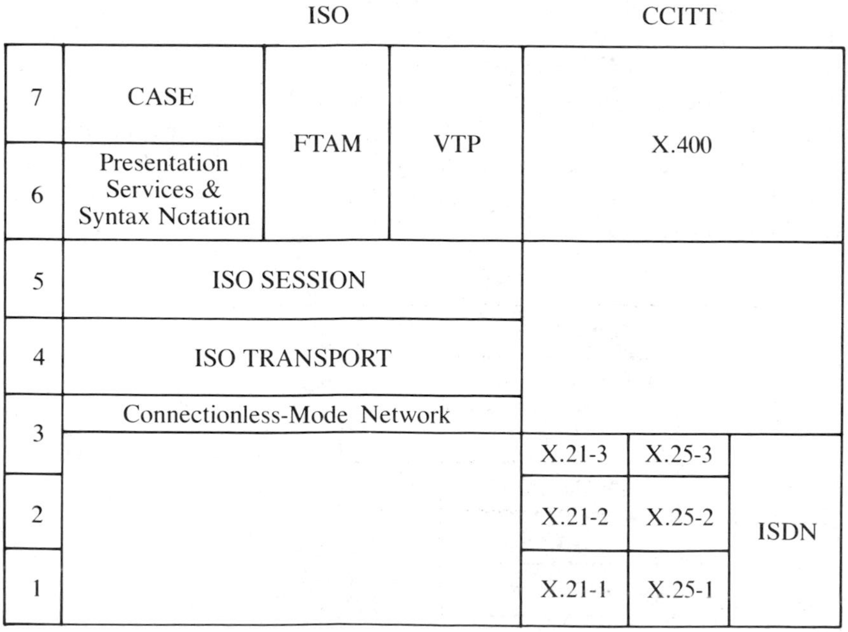

		ISO		CCITT			
7	CASE	FTAM	VTP	X.400			
6	Presentation Services & Syntax Notation						
5	ISO SESSION						
4	ISO TRANSPORT						
3	Connectionless-Mode Network			X.21-3	X.25-3		
2				X.21-2	X.25-2	ISDN	
1				X.21-1	X.25-1		

Figure 2.14.   Some important standards.

purpose standards for the presentation and application layers. They are also working on standards for various applications. Two important examples are *File Transfer, Access, and Management* (FTAM) and *Virtual Terminal Protocol* (VTP); both of these encompass functionality of layers 6 and 7.

CCITT has traditionally been concerned with communication networks. They have developed standards for circuit-switched (X.21) and packet-switched (X.25) networks. In addition, they are developing a family of standards for ISDN. Another important set of standards from CCITT is the X.400 series, which provides message handling and electronic mail services.

Summary

In a few short years, the OSI model has achieved nearly universal acceptance. It provides not only a framework for developing standards but the terms of reference for discussing communications system design. In the latter capacity, we refer to OSI concepts repeatedly in the remainder of the book.

A question that arises naturally concerns the complexity of the model. Is it efficient to require every communication to undergo seven layers of processing, both to enter the communications process and then to leave it? In one sense, this question is no longer open to debate. Virtually all standards activities for communications are proceeding within the OSI model. Government customers and most private customers will demand OSI compatibility. The industry must conform

This does not necessarily foreordain inefficiency. Implementers are free to use virtually null layers where appropriate, or at least very streamlined ones. We have mentioned one example: where direct connection is possible, layer 3 is not needed. When a reliable layer 3 exists, layer 4 can be minimal. And so on.

Another point: Much of the communications processing (e.g., layers 1 through 4) can be offloaded from a host computer to a front-end processor. This is an attractive choice, given the increasing speed and declining cost of small computers.

2.4 CONNECTIONLESS OPERATION

Characteristics of Connection-Oriented and Connectionless Operation

At any layer of the OSI architecture, two basic forms of operation are possible: connection-oriented and connectionless. With *connection-oriented operation*, a logical connection is set up between peer entities prior to the exchange of data. In *connectionless operation*, each data unit that is transmitted is independent of previous or subsequent data units, and no connection is set up.

Table 2.5 contrasts the characteristics of connection-oriented and connectionless data transmission. First consider connection-oriented data transfer. A connection-oriented data transfer has a clearly distinguishable lifetime, consisting of the three phases of establishment, data transfer, and termination (see Fig. 2.4). For data to be exchanged, there must be a prior agreement among the two (N + 1) entities that wish to communicate and the (N) service that provides them with the ability to do so. As long as the connection persists, all three parties agree on the acceptance of each transferred data unit. Any of the three parties may terminate the connection. As was mentioned earlier, the process of connection establishment includes the negotiation of parameters and options that will govern the data transfer. When a connection is requested by one party, it may be rejected by one of the other parties if it cannot provide the resources required to support the requested options and parameters. The negotiation process also allows a variety of access-control, security, accounting, and identity-verification procedures to be carried out, to establish the willingness of the three parties involved to undertake this instance of communication under these conditions. Use of a logical connection allows the use of a connection identifier, which is generally much shorter than a full address. This avoids the overhead of address resolution and transmission on data transfer. Finally, a logical connection allows the use of sequence numbering, which in turn supports ordered delivery, flow control, and error control.

With connectionless data transfer, there is an a priori agreement between (N + 1) entities that is unknown to the (N) service and that is sufficient for them to exchange data. A single service access is required to initiate the transmission of a data unit; this access contains all the information required to deliver the data unit to the other side. Because each data unit is handled with a single service access, no negotiation occurs; the parameters and options to be used must be prearranged. From the point of view of the service provider, previous and subsequent data units are unrelated to the current data unit; thus ordered delivery, flow control,

**Table 2.5. CHARACTERISTICS OF CONNECTOIN-ORIENTED
AND CONNECTIONLESS DATA TRANSMISSiON**

Connection-oriented	Connectionless
Clearly distinguishable lifetime	Two-party agreement
Three-party agreement	Single-access service
Negotiation and renegotiation	No negotiation
Connection identifiers	Data unit independence
Data unit relationship	Self-contained data units

and error control cannot be provided. Finally, because each data unit is treated independently, it must be self-contained. That is, each data unit must contain all the information necessary for its transmission and delivery, including destination address and any services required (e.g., priority).

Comparison of the Two Modes

The strengths of the connection-oriented mode of data transmission are easily described. It allows connection-oriented features such as ordered delivery, flow control, and error control. With connection-oriented transfer, the two entities can agree on their mutual requirements, such as maximum PDU size and priority, and reserve resources needed for the exchange. At the network layer, if a connection is set up across packet-switched network, then the network can design a route to be used for all PDUs, and avoid having to make the routing decision each time. These characteristics are well suited to applications that involve lengthy exchanges of data, such as file transfer, and remote access from a terminal to a time-sharing system.

Connectionless service, however, is more appropriate in some contexts. At the network layer, connectionless service is more robust: since each PDU is handled independently, each can follow a different route from source to destination, avoiding changing conditions of congestion and failure. Furthermore, even at transport and above there is justification for a connectionless service. There are instances in which the overhead of connection establishment and maintenance is unjustified or even counterproductive. Some examples, listed in [CHAP82], include:

- *Inward data collection:* Involves the periodic active or passive sampling of data sources, such as sensors, and automatic self-test reports from security equipment or network components. In a real-time monitoring situation, the loss of an occasional data unit would not cause distress, since the next report should arrive shortly.
- *Outward data dissemination:* Includes broadcast messages to network users, the announcement of a new node or the change of address of a service, and the distribution of real-time clock values.
- *Request-response:* Applications in which a transaction service is provided by a common server to a number of distributed users, and for which a single request–response sequence is typical. Use of the service is regulated at the application level, and lower level connections are often unnecessary and cumbersome.
- *Real-time applications:* Such as voice and telemetry, involving a degree of redundancy and/or a real-time transmission requirement. These must not have connection-oriented functions such as retransmission.

Thus, there is a place at the various levels for both a connection-oriented and a connectionless type of service.

The OSI Connectionless Specification

The original OSI standard, ISO 7498, is connection oriented. The standard states:

> For information to be exchanged between two or morc (N + 1) entities, an association shall be established between them in the (N) layer using an (N) protocol. The association is called an (N) connection.

Thus, at every level, a connection must be set up before data from the next higher level can be exchanged. As we have seen, this orientation may not always be appropriate. ISO acknowledged the need for connectionless service by issuing an addendum to the OSI document (ISO 7498/DAD1). The justification given in the addendum:

> The assumption that a connection is a fundamental prerequisite for communication in the OSI environment permeates the Reference Model and is one of the most useful and important unifying concepts of the architecture which it describes. However, since the International Standard was produced it has been realized that this deeply rooted connection orientation unnecessarily limits the power and scope of the Reference Model, since it excludes important classes of applications and important classes of communication network technology which have a fundamentally connectionless nature.

The addendum focuses on services rather than protocols. It allows connectionless-mode service to be offered by any layer. With connectionless-mode service, an (N + 1) entity provides no information to its (N) entity about the relationship between (N) SDUs apart from the source and destination SAPs. Thus, each SDU is treated independently by the service provider.

One additional issue remains to be addressed by the standard, and that is the relationship between the service provided by adjacent layers. In its simplest form, the architecture would function as follows. A connection-oriented application would be supported by a connection-oriented service at each layer. Thus, an application connection is set up; this is mapped onto a presentation connection; and so on. Similarly, a connectionless application would be supported by a connectionless service at each layer. The architecture, however, need not be so restricted. In principle, the services offered by adjacent layers can be:

- Both connection mode
- Both connectionless mode

- A connection mode service at the (N) layer on top of a connectionless mode service at the (N − 1) layer
- A connectionless mode service at the (N) layer on top of a connection mode service at the (N − 1) layer

The first two cases are clear. For the third case, the (N) protocol will need to be sufficiently rich to provide the connection-oriented features in spite of a connectionless service from the (N − 1) layer. We examine this in detail when we discuss the transport layer. For the fourth case, the (N) protocol makes restricted use of the services available from the (N − 1) layer. This is discussed in an example of internetworking in the network layer.

Although the *conversions* defined in the third and fourth cases above could theoretically be performed at any layer, the OSI standard imposes some restrictions, and these are illustrated in Fig. 2.15. First, the physical layer is not classified as either connection-oriented or connectionless because it depends in a complex way on the characteristics of the underlying medium. Thus the data link protocol must convert between the services offered at the physical layer and the type of data link service needed. At the network layer, conversion may be provided to support a network service of a given mode over a data link service of the other mode. Also, we shall see that the network layer may need to deal with

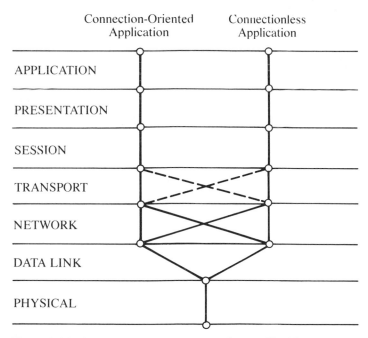

Figure 2.15. Layer service combinations. Source: [CHAP83]

one or more *subnetworks*; if so, the network layer may convert from the subnetwork service to the opposite mode. Support of these conversions is required in the OSI standard, as indicated by the use of solid lines. Conversions may also be made at the transport layer, although support for this service is not required by the standard. Consistent with the definition of the OSI layers, conversion is not permitted above the transport layer. Entities at and above the session layer depend on the lowest four layers to provide the reliability mechanisms required by the application.

chapter 3

Physical Layer

This chapter begins our examination of standards at each of the seven layers of the OSI model. For each layer in the model, the OSI document provides a brief description of the functions and services of that layer. Hence, we begin our discussion of the physical layer (and all subsequent layers) with a summary of the OSI specification for that layer. Next, we introduce the concept of interfacing at the physical layer. Then, several examples of physical-layer standards are examined. An appendix to this chapter introduces the concepts of asynchronous and synchronous transmission.

3.1 OSI DEFINITION

The physical layer provides the mechanical, electrical, functional, and procedural means to activate, maintain, and deactivate the physical link between systems. All of these terms are best explained in terms of concrete examples, and we examine them in that context later in the chapter. For now, we give the following brief definitions:

- *Mechanical:* Related to the physical properties of the interface to a transmission medium (size, configuration)

- *Electrical:* Related to the representation of bits (voltage levels) and the data transmission rate of bits
- *Functional:* Specifies the functions performed by individual elements of the physical interface between a system and the transmission medium
- *Procedural:* Specifies the protocol by which bit streams are exchanged across the physical medium
- *Activate:* Cause the transmission medium to be prepared to pass bit streams in both directions
- *Maintain:* The transmission of bits
- *Deactivate:* Perform termination functions at the end of a transmission

Table 3.1 lists the services and functions of the physical layer. Most of these require little explanation. The physical SDU consists of a single bit. In this respect, the physical layer differs from the other layers; there is no header containing control information. Rather, the physical layer deals only with streams of bits received from or passed to the data link layer. The physical connection endpoint is used to identify a unique physical point of attachment to a transmission medium. This allows both point-to-point configurations, in which there are only two devices at-

Table 3.1. SERVICES AND FUNCTIONS OF THE PHYSICAL LAYER

Services	
Physical connections	Connection of systems via transmission medium
Physical SDUs	SDU consists of a single bit
Physical connection endpoints	Used to identify a unique physical point of attachment to a transmission medium
Data circuit identification	Identifier of physical communication path for reference by higher layers
Sequencing	Bits are delivered in the order in which they are submitted
Fault condition notification	Data-link entities are notified of fault conditions
Quality of service parameters	Characterization of quality of transmission path
Functions	
Physical connection activation and deactivation	Control of the physical link
Physical SDU transmission	Synchronous or asynchronous transmission of bits
Physical layer management	Management activities related to physical layer

tached to a medium, and multipoint configurations, such as a local network or a multidrop configuration of terminals attached to a host computer. The quality of service parameters are derived from the data circuits forming the physical connection; they include error rate, service availability, transmission rate, and transit delay.

There are only three functions associated with the physical layer. The OSI document specifies that transmission may be either asynchronous or synchronous; these concepts are examined in the appendix to this chapter.

The physical layer is quite different from the other layers [MCCL83]. Whereas each of the other layers can rely on a lower layer to transmit its PDUs, the physical layer must make use of transmission media whose characteristics are not part of the OSI model. There is no physical layer PDU structure as such; no header is used, and bits are transmitted as a stream. Thus the protocol at this layer is not apparent in the sense that it is at the other layers.

Consider Fig. 3.1. The upper part shows an example of a real physical connection. System A might be a remote terminal and system B a computer. The connection is made through the concatenation of a coaxial cable link and an optical fiber link. Across the coaxial cable link, a modem is used to convert the digital bits generated by system A into a form suitable for transmission across the medium. The signal is converted back to digital form at modem D and then passed through a transducer, which converts from electrical pulses to light pulses. Finally, the signal is converted back to electrical and presented to system B. Figure 3.1b shows the interpretation of this real environment in terms of the OSI model. A physical layer entity is a logical construct that interfaces to a physical medium. Such entities exist at systems A and B, of course, but there is also a physical layer entity at the interface between D and E. This intermediate entity is a relay operating at the physical layer that interfaces to the two different transmission media.

A physical layer protocol takes place between physical layer entities. The protocol would include such things as whether transmission is synchronous or asynchronous and the data transmission rate. It is desirable that the protocol be as independent as possible of the transmission medium, so that a given system can interface to a variety of media. Thus, standards in this area must include not only entity-to-entity protocol elements but also a specification of the medium interface. Such standards are examined in the next section.

3.2   PHYSICAL INTERFACE STANDARDS

Most digital data processing devices possess limited data transmission capability. Typically, they generate a simple form of digital signal known as NRZ [STAL88], in which a binary 1 is represented by a voltage pulse

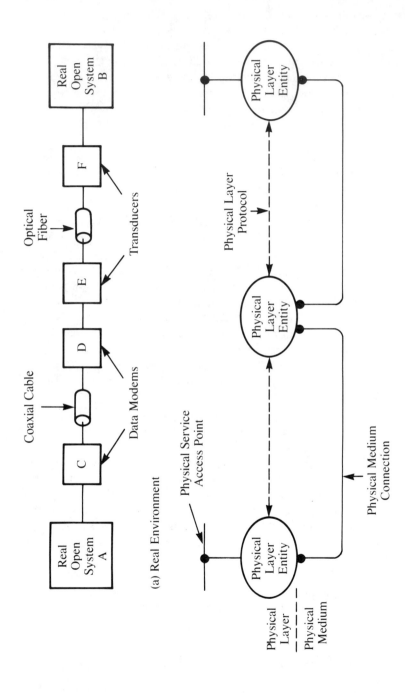

(a) Real Environment

(b) Logical Environment

Figure 3.1. Relationship of the physical layer to the real environment.

48

of a constant amplitude, and binary 0 is represented by a voltage pulse of another amplitude. Such signals can be transmitted only over certain types of transmission media and over very limited distances. Consequently, it is rare for devices such as terminals or computers to attach directly to a transmission medium. The more common situation is illustrated in Fig. 3.2, in which the end system interfaces to a modem or transducer, which in turn interfaces to the transmission medium. The end systems we are discussing, which include terminals and computers, are generically referred to as *data terminal equipment* (DTE). A DTE makes use of the transmission medium through the mediation of *data circuit-terminating equipment* (DCE), of which modems and transducers are examples (a good description of a variety of DCEs can be found in [HELD86]).

On one side, the DCE is responsible for transmitting and receiving streams of bits over a transmission medium. On transmission, the DCE converts the signals obtained from its DTE to a form suitable for transmission. On reception, the DCE performs the opposite conversion. On the other side, the DCE must interact with the DTE. In general, this requires both data and control information to be exchanged. This is done over a set of wires referred to as interchange circuits. For this scheme to work, a high degree of cooperation is required. The two DCEs must understand each other. That is, the receiver of each must use the same signal encoding scheme as the transmitter of the other. In addition, each DTE–DCE pair must be designed to have complementary interfaces and must be able to interact effectively. To ease the burden on data processing equipment manufacturers and users, standards have been developed that specify the exact nature of the interface between the DTE and the DCE.

The interface has four important characteristics [BERT80]:

- Mechanical
- Electrical
- Functional
- Procedural

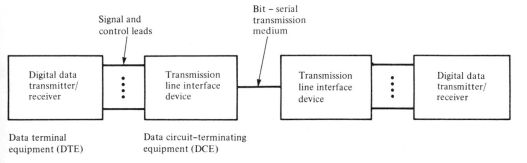

Figure 3.2. Generic interface to transmission medium.

The *mechanical* characteristics pertain to the actual physical connection of the DTE and DCE. Typically, the signal and control leads are bundled into a cable with a terminator plug, male or female, at each end. The DTE and the DCE must each present a plug of opposite gender at one end of the cable, effecting the physical connection. This is analogous to the situation for residential electrical power. Power is provided via a socket or wall outlet, and the device to be attached must have the appropriate plug (two-pronged, two-pronged polarized, three-pronged).

The *electrical* characteristics have to do with the voltage levels and timing of voltage changes. Both DTE and DCE must use the same code (e.g., NRZ), must use the same voltage levels to mean the same thing, and must use the same duration of signal elements. These characteristics determine the data rates and distances that can be achieved.

Functional characteristics specify the functions that are performed, by assigning meaning to the various interchange circuits. Functions can be classified into the broad categories of data, control, timing, and ground.

Procedural characteristics specify the sequence of events for transmitting data, based on the functional characteristics of the interface. Examples below should clarify this point.

A variety of standards for interfacing exist. This section presents three of the most important:

- RS-232-C
- RS-449/422-A/423-A
- X.21

RS-232-C

By far the most common interface standard is RS-232-C. It is used to connect DTE devices to voice-grade modems for use on the public telecommunications system. It is also widely used for many other interconnection functions.

The *mechanical* specification for RS-232-C is illustrated in Fig. 3.3. It calls for a 25-pin connector with a specific arrangement of leads. Thus in theory, a 25-wire cable could be used to connect the DTE to the DCE. In practice, far fewer interchange circuits are used.

The *electrical* characteristics specify the signaling between DTE and DCE. Digital signaling is used on all interchange circuits. The convention specified is that, with respect to a common ground, a voltage more negative than -3 V is interpreted as binary 1 and a voltage more positive than $+3$ V is interpreted as binary 0. The interface is rated at a signal rate of < 20 kbps and a distance of <15 m. Greater distance and data rates are possible with good design, but it is reasonable to assume that these limits apply in practice as well as in theory.

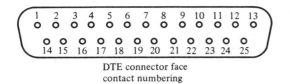

DTE connector face
contact numbering

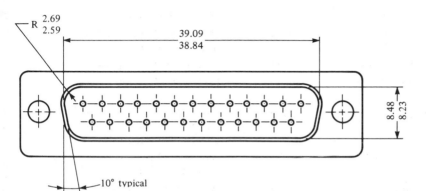

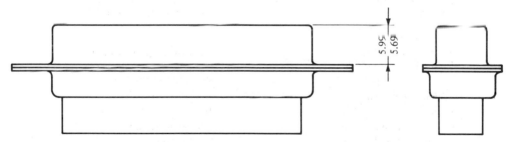

Figure 3.3. RS-232-C connector (dimensions in mm).

Table 3.2 summarizes the *functional* specification of the most important circuits. There is one data circuit in each direction, so full-duplex operation is possible. One ground lead is for protective isolation; the other serves as the return circuit for both data leads. Hence transmission is *unbalanced,* with only one active wire. The timing signals provide clock pulses for synchronous transmission. When the DCE is sending data over circuit BB, it also sends 1-0 and 0-1 transitions on DD, with transitions timed to the middle of each BB signal element. When the DTE is sending data, either the DTE or DCE can provide timing pulses, depending on the

Table 3.2.   RS-232-C CIRCUIT DEFINITIONS

Name	Direction to:	Function
Data signals		
Transmitted Data (BA)	DCE	Data generated by DTE
Received Data (BB)	DTE	Data received by DTE
Control signals		
Request to Send (CA)	DCE	DTE wishes to transmit
Clear to Send (CB)	DTE	DCE is ready to transmit; response to request to send
Data Set Ready (CC)	DTE	DCE is ready to operate
Data Terminal Ready (CD)	DCE	DTE is ready to operate
Ring Indicator (CE)	DTE	Indicates that DCE is receiving a ringing signal on the communication channel
Carrier Detect (CF)	DTE	Indicates that DCE is receiving a carrier signal
Signal Quality Detector (CG)	DTE	Asserted when there is reason to believe there is an error in the received data
Data Signal Rate Selector (CH)	DCE	Asserted to select the higher of two possible data rates
Data Signal Rate Selector (CI)	DTE	Asserted to select the higher of two possible data rates
Timing signals		
Transmitter Signal Element Timing (DA)	DCE	Clocking signal, transitions to ON and OFF occur at center of each signal element
Transmitter Signal Element Timing (DB)	DTE	Clocking signal, as above; both leads relate to signals on BA
Receiver Signal Element Timing (DD)	DTE	Clocking signal, as above, for circuit BB
Ground		
Protective Ground (AA)	NA	Attached to machine frame and possibly external grounds
Signal Ground (AB)	NA	Establishes common ground reference for all circuits.

circumstances. The control signals are explained by *procedural* specifications, and a few examples are given below.

The first example is for an asynchronous private line modem, also known as a limited distance modem, used to connect two devices with a point-to-point link. The modem, as a DCE, requires only the following circuits:

- Signal ground (AB)
- Transmitted data (BA)
- Received data (BB)
- Request to send (CA)
- Clear to send (CB)
- Data set ready (CC)
- Carrier detect (CF)

The first three circuits have been reasonably well explained. When the DTE is ready to send data, it asserts Request to Send. The modem responds, when ready, with Clear to Send, thereby indicating that data may be transmitted over circuit BA. If the arrangement is half-duplex, then Request to Send also inhibits the receive mode. The Data Set Ready circuit is asserted when the modem is ready to operate. This lead should be asserted before the DTE attempts Request to Send. Finally, Carrier Detect indicates that the remote modem is transmitting. Note that it is not necessary to use timing circuits, because this is asynchronous transmission.

Figure 3.4 shows a state diagram of this operation. EIA divides the six major control circuits into two groups. Group A (CC, CD, CE) relates to the alerting and readiness of the equipment to operate, and group B (CA, CB, CF) relates to preparing the communications equipment to transmit and receive data. The ON and OFF states of these two groups are coded in octal as indicated. The coding also includes DTE power on for this operation.

The circuits described so far are sufficient for private line modems used point-to-point, but additional circuits are required when the telephone network is to be used. Now, the initiator of a connection must call the destination station. Two additional leads are required.

- Data terminal ready (CD)
- Ring indicator (CE)

With the addition of these two leads, the DTE-modem system can effectively use the telephone lines in a way analogous to voice telephone usage. Table 3.3 lists the steps involved in dial-up operation. When a call is made, either manually or automatically, the telephone system sends a ringing signal. A telephone set would respond by ringing its bell; a modem

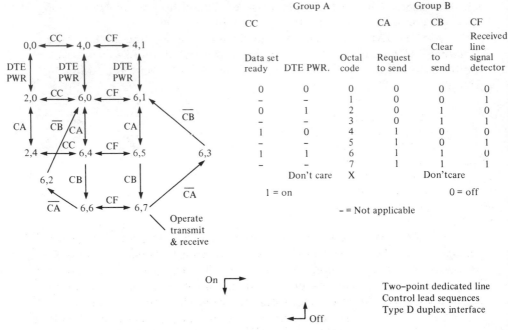

Figure 3.4. RS-232-C state diagram.

responds by asserting Ring Indicator. A human being answers the call by lifting the handset; a DTE answers by asserting Data Terminal Ready. The person will then listen for another's voice and, if nothing is heard, hang up; the DTE will listen for Carrier Detect, which will be raised by the modem when a carrier is present, and if this circuit is not asserted, drop Data Terminal Ready. You might wonder how this last contingency could arise. One common way is if a person accidentally dials the number of a modem. This activates the DTE, but when no carrier tone comes through, the problem is resolved.

As an aside, it is instructive to consider situations in which the distances between devices are so close as to allow two DTEs to directly signal each other. In this case, the RS-232-C leads can still be used, but now no DCE equipment is provided. For the scheme to work, a *null modem* is needed, which interconnects leads in such a way as to fool both DTEs into thinking that they are connected to modems. The reasons for the particular connections in Fig. 3.5 should be apparent if the reader has grasped the preceding discussion.

RS-449/422-A/423-A

The most notable shortcoming of RS-232-C is its limited distance/speed characteristics. Also, in the case of its use with a modem, it provides very

Table 3.3.   RS-232-C DIAL-UP OPERATION

Establish Connection

1. TA sets Data Terminal Ready ON, to indicate to the modem that it is ready to make a call.
2. MA opens the phone circuit and dials number. Number may be already stored in modem, or it is conveyed to the modem from TA via Transmitted Data pin.
3. MB detects ring on phone line and set Ring Indicator ON, to inform TB that a call has arrived.
4. TB sets Data Terminal Ready ON, to accept the call.
5. MB *answers* the call by transmitting a carrier signal to MA over the phone line. It also sets Data Set Ready ON, to indicate to TB that it is ready to communicate.
6. MA sets both Data Set Ready and Carrier Detect ON, to indicate to TA that a circuit has been established and that it is ready to communicate.
7. For full-duplex operation, MA also transmits a carrier signal to MB. MB then sets Carrier Detect ON.

Send Data

8. When TA wants to send data, it sets Request to Send ON.
9. MA responds by setting Clear to Send ON.
10. TA transmits data one bit at a time to MA over the Transmitted Data pin. MA modulates its carrier signal (e.g., ASK) to transmit the data to MB.
11. MB receives the modulated signal from MA, demodulates to recover the data, and sends the data to TB over the Received Data pin.

Break Connection

12. When TA is finished, it sets Request to Send OFF.
13. MA sets Clear to Send OFF and drops the carrier (hangs up).

TA = DTE A; MA = Modem A; TB = DTE B; MB = Modem B.

little DTE control of the modem. To make improvements in these areas, the Electronic Industries Association (EIA) issued a set of standards to replace the older standard: RS-449, RS-422-A, and RS-423-A [FOLT80]. Although RS-232-C remains the most popular DTE–DCE interface, these new standards are finding increasingly widespread use. RS-449 defines the mechanical, functional, and procedural characteristics of the new interface; RS-422-A and RS-423-A define electrical characteristics. We turn first to RS-449.

RS-449 is similar to RS-232-C and is intended to exhibit a degree of interoperability with the older interface. Functionally, RS-449 retains all of the interchange circuits of RS-232-C, with the exception of protective ground, and adds 10 new circuits (Table 3.4). The most important of these are:

- *Terminal In Service (IS):* Indicates to the DCE that the DTE is operational. This allows an attached device to signal whether it is available to answer calls.

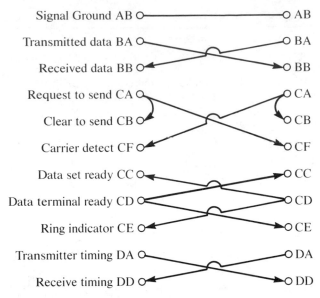

Signal Ground AB ⊙────────────────⊙ AB

Transmitted data BA ⊙────────⊙ BA

Received data BB ⊙────────⊙ BB

Request to send CA ⊙────────⊙ CA

Clear to send CB ⊙────────⊙ CB

Carrier detect CF ⊙────────⊙ CF

Data set ready CC ⊙────────⊙ CC

Data terminal ready CD ⊙────────⊙ CD

Ring indicator CE ⊙────────⊙ CE

Transmitter timing DA ⊙────────⊙ DA

Receive timing DD ⊙────────⊙ DD

Figure 3.5.   The null modem.

- *New Signal (NS):* Tells the DCE to prepare to acquire a new line signal. This improves overall response time on a polling line.
- *Select Frequency (SF):* When two modems communicate, the transmit frequency of one must be the receive frequency of the other (see Fig. 3.10). This circuit allows selection of the frequency mode of the DCE in a multipoint configuration.
- *Local Loopback (LL):* Requests that the DCE loop signals from the local DTE (on SD) back to the same DTE (on RD). This checks the functioning of the local interface and DCE.
- *Remote Loopback (RL):* Requests that signals from the local DTE loop to the remote DCE and back. This tests the operation of the transmission channel and the remote DCE (Fig. 3.6).
- *Test Mode (TM):* Indicates that local DCE is in a test condition. The ON condition is in response to a local LL, local or remote RL, or activation of a test condition by some other means.

Procedurally, RS-449, is similar to RS-232-C. Each circuit has a single function and communication is based on action–reaction pairs. For example, if the DTE turns on Request to Send, it then waits for the DCE to respond with Clear to Send. Mechanically, the RS-449 standard specifies a 37-pin connector for the basic interface and a separate 9-pin connector if a secondary channel is used. As with RS-232-C, in most cases only a few of these pins are used.

Thus RS-449 improves over RS-232-C by providing greater DTE control over the modem, if used. However, the major improvement is in the electrical characteristics of the new standard, and these are specified by RS-422-A and RS-423-A. Whereas RS-232-C was designed in the era

Table 3.4. **RS-449 AND RS-232-C INTERCHANGE CIRCUITS**

RS-449		RS-232C	
		AA	Protective Ground
SG	Signal Ground	AB	Signal Ground
SC	Send Common		
RC	Receive Common		
IS	Terminal in Service		
IC	Incoming Call	CE	Ring Indicator
TR*	Terminal Ready	CD	Data Terminal Ready
DM*	Data Mode	CC	Data Set Ready
SD*	Send Data	BA	Transmitted Data
RD*	Receive Data	BB	Received Data
TT*	Terminal Timing	DA	Transmitter Signal Element Timing (DTE source)
ST*	Send Timing	DB	Transmitter Signal Element Timing (DCE Source)
RT*	Receive Timing	DD	Receiver Signal Element Timing
RS*	Request to Send	CA	Request to Send
CS*	Clear to Send	CB	Clear to Send
RR*	Receiver Ready	CF	Received Line Signal Detector
SQ	Signal Quality	CG	Signal Quality Detector
NS	New Signal		
SF	Select Frequency		
SR	Signaling Rate Selector	CH	Data Signal Rate Selector (DTE source)
SI	Signaling Rate Indicator	CI	Data Signal Rate Selector (DCE source)
SSD	Secondary Send Data	SBA	Secondary Transmitted Data
SRD	Secondary Receive Data	SBB	Secondary Received Data
SRS	Secondary Request to Send	SCA	Secondary Request to Send
SCS	Secondary Clear to Send	SCB	Secondary Clear to Send
SRR	Secondary Receiver Ready	SCF	Secondary Received Line Signal Detector
LL	Local Loopback		
RL	Remote Loopback		
TM	Test Mode		
SS	Select Standby		
SB	Standby Indicator		

*Category 1 circuits.

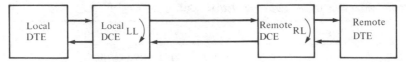

Figure 3.6. Local and remote loopback.

of discrete electronic components, the new standards take advantage of the superior performance possibilities of integrated circuit technology. To understand these standards we need to define several modes of transmission.

In a conventional telephone system and indeed in most uses of twisted pair, signals are carried on a *balanced transmission* line consisting of two conductors. Signals are transmitted as a current that travels down one conductor and returns on the other; the two conductors form a complete circuit. For digital signals this technique is known as *differential signaling,* since the binary value depends on the direction of the voltage difference between the two conductors. *Unbalanced transmission* uses a single conductor to carry the signal, with ground providing the return path. There is also a third mode, known as current-mode transmission, in which two conductors are used and current is sent in one direction down either of the two conductors, depending on the binary value.

The balanced mode tolerates more, and produces less, noise than the unbalanced. Ideally, interference on a balanced line will act equally on both conductors and not affect the voltage difference. For this reason, unbalanced transmission is generally limited to coaxial cable or very short distances, such as used in RS-232-C.

RS-423-A specifies unbalanced transmission and achieves the following rated performance: 3 kbps at 1000 m to 300 kbps at 10 m. This is a significant improvement over RS-232-C, which is a constant limit of 20 kbps up to 15 m. RS-422-A specifies balanced transmission and achieves even better performance: 100 kbps at 1200 m to 10 Mbps at 12 m; a graph of the rated performances are shown in Fig. 3.7.

For lower performance and presumably lower cost, RS-423-A can be used on all RS-449 interchange circuits. Even for higher performance, most of the circuits carry low-speed control signals and do not need better electrical characteristics. Accordingly, 10 circuits have been designated as category I and it is only these circuits that require RS-422-A for higher performance:

- Send data (SD)
- Receive data (RD)
- Terminal timing (TT)
- Send timing (ST)
- Receive timing (RT)
- Request to send (RS)

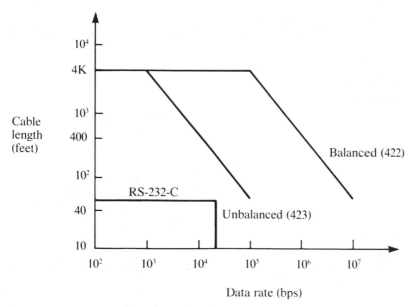

Figure 3.7. Cable length versus data rate.

- Clear to send (CS)
- Receiver ready (RR)
- Terminal ready (TR)
- Data mode (DM)

Each of these circuits requires two wires for RS-422-A; twisted pair is used. Both the balanced and unbalanced leads are usually housed in the same cable sheath.

X.21

The benefits to be derived from RS-449 are achieved at the expense of extra circuits and connections. This is a rather expensive way to achieve results. An alternative would be to provide fewer circuits but to add more logic at the DTE and DCE interfaces. With the dropping costs of logic circuitry this is an attractive approach and the one taken for the X.21 standard [YANO81].

X.21 specifies a 15-pin connector but at present makes use of fewer leads than that. Table 3.5 summarizes the defined interface circuits. As with RS-232-C and RS-449, there is a transmit circuit in both directions (T and R). Now, however, these circuits may provide both user data and control information. In addition, there are two other circuits (C and I), one in each direction, for control and status information. These two circuits do not carry digital data streams, but may be either in an ON or an

Table 3.5. X.21 CIRCUIT DEFINITIONS

Name	Direction to:	Function
Signal Ground (G)	NA	
DTE Common Return (Ga)	DCE	
Transmit (T)	DCE	Used to convey both user data and network control information, depending on state of C and I
Receive (R)	DTE	Same as T in opposite direction
Control (C)	DCE	Provides control information to DCE (e.g., ON/OFF hook)
Indication (1)	DTE	Provides indicators to DTE (e.g., start of transparent data phase)
Signal Element Timing (S)	DTE	Provides bit timing
Byte Timing (B)	DTE	Provides byte (8-bit) timing

OFF state. X.21 is defined only for synchronous operation, for which a bit timing circuit is provided. These five circuits are sufficient for many applications. A little-used byte timing signal is optional for synchronizing control characters.

Balanced and unbalanced modes, similar to RS-422-A and RS-423-A, are provided in the standard. Thus, the same speed/distance levels can be achieved. In most cases, only the balanced mode is used on all circuits.

Most of the procedures defined for X.21 circuits have to do with operation over a circuit-switched communications network. Thus they are not properly part of a physical layer protocol. Procedures associated with the readiness status of the DTE and DCE do, however, have a physical layer flavor and are presented here. Two states are defined for the DCE and the three for the DTE:

- *DTE ready:* Indicates readiness to operate. This is signaled by a steady 1 on T and a control OFF (binary 1) on C.
- *DTE uncontrolled not ready:* Indicates that DTE is unable to enter operational phases because of an abnormal condition. The signals are T = 0, C = OFF.
- *DTE controlled not ready:* The DTE is operational but unable to accept calls. Signals are T = 010101 . . . and C = OFF.
- *DCE ready:* The DCE is ready to operate. Signals are R = 1 and I = OFF.
- *DCE not ready:* No service is available. Signals are R = 0 and I = OFF.

The various allowable combined states, called quiescent states, and possible transitions are shown in Fig. 3.8. To ensure proper detection,

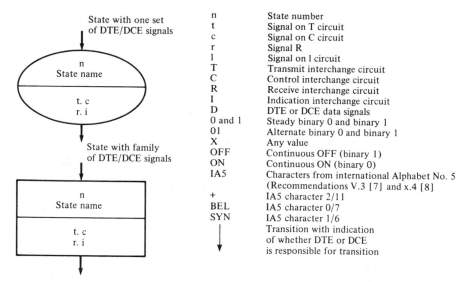

n	State number
t	Signal on T circuit
c	Signal on C circuit
r	Signal R
l	Signal on l circuit
T	Transmit interchange circuit
C	Control interchange circuit
R	Receive interchange circuit
I	Indication interchange circuit
D	DTE or DCE data signals
0 and 1	Steady binary 0 and binary 1
01	Alternate binary 0 and binary 1
X	Any value
OFF	Continuous OFF (binary 1)
ON	Continuous ON (binary 0)
IA5	Characters from international Alphabet No. 5 (Recommendations V.3 [7] and x.4 [8]
+	IA5 character 2/11
BEL	IA5 character 0/7
SYN	IA5 character 1/6
↓	Transition with indication of whether DTE or DCE is responsible for transition

(a) Symbols used in the state diagram

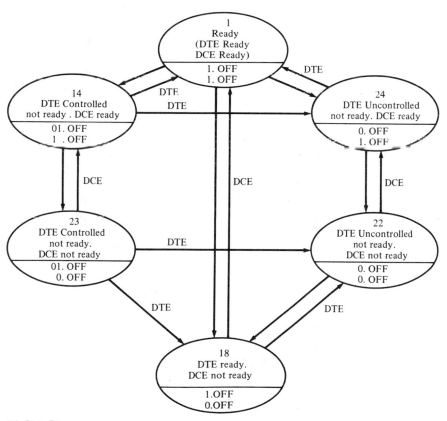

(b) State Diagram

Figure 3.8. X.21 quiescent state diagram.

61

X.21 requires that the DTE and DCE be prepared to send these signals for at least 24 bit intervals. Detection of the signals for 16 contiguous bit intervals is required.

X.21 represents a major improvement over RS-232-C and RS-449. It is more flexible and should cost less. The use of streams of control characters gives an unlimited set of options to meet future needs.

X.21 is a good example of the basic dilemma or paradox inherent in standards, a theme that will be echoed again in this book. Standards are needed to permit equipment built by various vendors and owned by various users to work together (referred to by DOD as *interoperability*). Standards also encourage the cost saving realized by efficient mass production techniques. Unfortunately, standards tend to freeze technology and become obsolete almost as soon as they are issued. In the case of physical interface standards, the following is a brief history. RS-449, RS-422-A, and RS-423-A were specifically developed as interim standards to improve performance over RS-232-C while awaiting a new and far more efficient standard, namely X.21. X.21 was expected to have a long lifetime and become *the* universal interface. Alas, time and events have overcome X.21 and it is now also considered interim. A newer, more efficient standard, using even fewer interchange circuits, is on the drawing boards. This new standard will be part of a more ambitious effort known as ISDN. In the meantime, users and manufacturers are faced with the prospect of relying on relatively inefficient interfaces, such as RS-232-C or RS-449/422-A/423-A, or making a capital investment in an interface (X.21) that will soon be replaced.

APPENDIX 3A.   DATA TRANSMISSION TOPICS

In this chapter, reference was made to two particular aspects of data transmission: the encoding of binary data for signaling and the use of synchronous and asynchronous transmission. These topics are briefly explored in this chapter. For more detail, see [STAL88].

3A.1   Encoding of Binary Data

As was mentioned, the digital signals produced by terminals and computers to represent binary 1 and 0 are not suitable for transmission over appreciable distance. For that purpose, the binary data is typically encoded as either a digital or analog signal whose characteristics are more appropriate for the transmission medium to be used. Both approaches are briefly examined.

Digital Data, Analog Signals.   The basis for analog signaling is a continuous constant-frequency signal known as the *carrier signal*. Digital data are encoded by modulating one of the three characteristics of the carrier:

amplitude, frequency, or phase, or some combination of these. Figure 3.9 illustrates the three basic forms of modulation of analog signals for digital data:

- *Amplitude-shift keying* (ASK)
- *Frequency-shift keying* (FSK)
- *Phase-shift keying* (PSK)

In all these cases, the resulting signal contains a range of frequencies on both sides of the carrier frequency. That range is referred to as the *bandwidth* of the signal.

In ASK, the two binary values are represented by two different amplitudes of the carrier frequency. In some cases, one of the amplitudes is zero; that is, one binary digit is represented by the presence, at constant amplitude, of the carrier, the other by the absence of the carrier. ASK is susceptible to sudden gain changes and is a rather inefficient modulation technique. On voice-grade lines, it is typically used only up to 1200 bps.

In FSK, the two binary values are represented by two different fre-

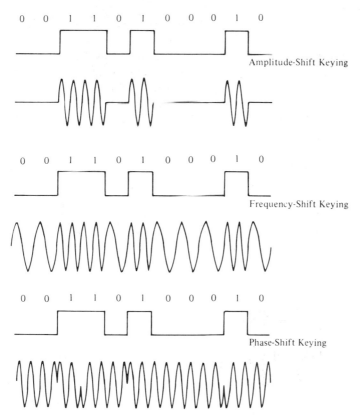

Figure 3.9. Modulation of analog signals for digital data.

quencies near the carrier frequency. This scheme is less susceptible to error than ASK. On voice grade lines, it is typically used up to 1200 bps. It is also commonly used for high frequency (3 to 30 MHz) radio transmission. It can also be used at even higher frequencies on local networks that use coaxial cable.

Figure 3.10 shows an example of the use of FSK for full-duplex operation over a voice-grade line. *Full duplex* means that data can be transmitted in both directions at the same time. To accomplish this, one bandwidth is used for sending, another for receiving. The figure is a specification for the Bell System 108 series modems. In one direction (transmit or receive), the modem passes frequencies in the range 300 to 1700 Hz. The two frequencies used to represent 1 and 0 are centered on 1170 Hz, with a shift of 100 Hz on either side. Similarly, for the other direction (receive or transmit) the modem passes 1700 to 3000 Hz and uses a center frequency of 2125 Hz. The shaded area around each pair of frequencies indicates the actual bandwidth of each signal. Note that there is little overlap and thus little interference.

In PSK, the phase of the carrier signal is shifted to represent data. In this system, a 0 is represented by sending a signal burst of the same phase as the previous signal burst sent. A 1 is represented by sending a signal burst of opposite phase to the previous one. PSK can use more than two phase shifts. A four-phase system would encode two bits with each signal burst. The PSK technique is more noise resistant and efficient than FSK; on a voice-grade line, rates up to 9600 bps are achieved.

Finally, the techniques discussed above may be combined. A common combination is PSK and ASK, where some or all of the phase shifts may occur at one of two amplitudes.

Digital Data, Digital Signals.   The most common and easiest way to transmit digital signals is to use two different voltage levels for the two binary digits. For example, the absence of voltage (which is also the absence of current) is often used to represent 0, whereas a constant positive voltage is used to represent 1. It is also common to use a negative voltage (low)

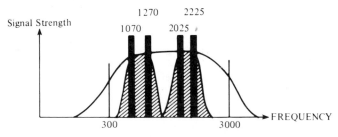

Figure 3.10.   Full-duplex FSK transmission on a voice-grade line.

for 0 and a positive voltage (high) for 1. The latter technique, shown in Fig. 3.11a, is known as *Non-Return to Zero* (NRZ).

There are several disadvantages to NRZ transmission. It is difficult to determine where one bit ends and another begins. There needs to be some means of keeping the transmitter and receiver *clocked* or synchronized. [*Note:* this is true for both synchronous and asynchronous transmission (see discussion below).] Also, there is a direct-current (dc) component during each bit time that will accumulate if 1's or 0's predominate. Thus alternating-current (ac) coupling, which uses a transformer and provides excellent electrical isolation between data communicating devices and their environment, is not possible. Furthermore, the dc component can cause plating or other deterioration at attachment contacts.

There is a set of alternative coding techniques, grouped under the term *biphase,* that overcomes these disadvantages. All of the biphase schemes require at least one transition per bit time and may have as many as two transitions. Thus the maximum modulation rate is twice that for NRZ; this means that the bandwidth or transmission capacity consumed

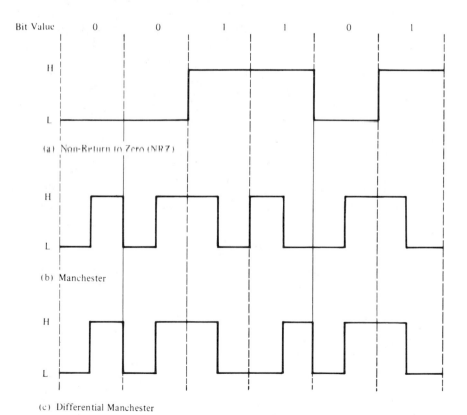

(a) Non-Return to Zero (NRZ)

(b) Manchester

(c) Differential Manchester

Figure 3.11. Digital signal encoding.

is correspondingly greater. To compensate for this, the biphase schemes have several advantages:

- *Synchronization:* Because there is a predictable transition during each bit time, the receiver can synchronize on that transition. For this reason, the biphase codes are known as self-clocking codes.
- *No dc component:* Because of the transition in each bit time, biphase codes have no dc component, yielding the benefits described earlier.
- *Error detection:* The absence of an expected transition can be used to detect errors. Noise on the line would have to invert both the signal before and after the expected transition to cause an undetected error.

In the *Manchester code* (Fig. 3.11B), there is a transition at the middle of each bit period. The mid-bit transition serves as a clock and also as data: a high-to-low transition represents a 1, and a low-to-high transition represents a 0. In *Differential Manchester* (Fig. 3.11C), the mid-bit transition is used only to provide clocking. The encoding of a 0 (1) is represented by the presence (absence) of a transition at the beginning of the bit period.

Differential Manchester exhibits a further advantage, in addition to those listed above, in that it uses differential encoding. In *differential encoding,* the signal is decoded by comparing the polarity of adjacent signal elements rather than the absolute value of a signal element. One benefit of this scheme is that it may be more reliable to detect a transition in the presence of noise than to compare a value to a threshold. Another benefit is that with a complex transmission layout, it is easy to lose the sense of polarity of the signal. For example, on a multidrop twisted-pair line, if the leads from an attached device to the twisted pair are accidentally inverted, all 1's and 0's will be inverted unless differential encoding is used.

3A.2   Asynchronous and Synchronous Transmission

A fundamental requirement of digital data communication (analog or digital signal) is that the receiver knows the starting time and duration of each bit that it receives.

The earliest and simplest scheme for meeting this requirement is asynchronous transmission. In this scheme, data are transmitted one character (of 5 to 8 bits) at a time. Each character is preceded by a start code and followed by a stop code (Fig. 3.12). The *start code* has the encoding for 0 and a duration of one bit time; in other words, the start code is one bit with a value of zero. The *stop code* has a value of 1, and a minimum duration, depending on the system, of from one to two bit times. When there are no data to send, the transmitter sends a continuous

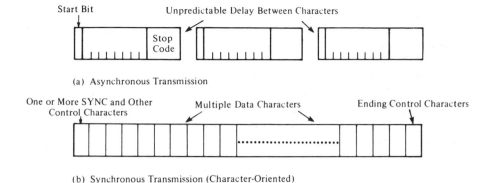

(a) Asynchronous Transmission

(b) Synchronous Transmission (Character-Oriented)

Figure 3.12. Asynchronous and synchronous transmission.

stop code. The receiver identifies the beginning of a new character by the transition from 1 to 0. The receiver must have a fairly accurate idea of the duration of each bit to recover all the bits of the character. However, a small amount of drift (e.g., 1 percent per bit) will not matter because the receiver resynchronizes with each stop code. This means of communication is simple and cheap, but requires an overhead of 2 to 3 bits per character. This technique is referred to as *asynchronous* because characters are sent independently from each other. Thus characters may be sent at a nonuniform rate.

A more efficient means of communication is synchronous transmission. In this mode, blocks of characters or bits are transmitted without start and stop codes, and the exact departure or arrival time of each bit is predictable. To prevent timing drift between transmitter and receiver, their clocks must somehow be synchronized. One possibility is to provide a separate clock line between transmitter and receiver. Otherwise, the clocking information must be embedded in the data signal. For digital signals, this can be achieved with biphase encoding. For analog signals, a number of techniques can be used; the carrier frequency itself can be used to synchronize the receiver based on the phase of the carrier.

With synchronous transmission, there is another level of synchronization required, to allow the receiver to determine the beginning and end of a block of data. To achieve this, each block begins with a *preamble* bit pattern and ends with *postamble* bit pattern. The data plus preamble and postamble is called a *frame*. The nature of the preamble and postamble depends on whether the block of data is character-oriented or bit-oriented.

With *character-oriented* schemes, each block is preceded by one or more *synchronization characters* (see Fig. 3.12b). The synchronization character, usually called *SYNC*, is chosen such that its bit pattern is significantly different from any of the regular characters being transmitted.

The postamble is another unique character. The receiver thus is alerted to an incoming block of data by the SYNC characters and accepts data until the postamble character is seen. The receiver can then look for the next SYNC pattern.

   With *bit-oriented* transmission, the block of data is treated as a sequence of bits. Neither data nor control information needs to be interpreted in units of 8-bit characters. As with character-oriented schemes, a special bit pattern signals the beginning of a block. The most common bit-oriented standard, HDLC, is examined in the next chapter.

chapter 4

Data Link Layer

The data link layer must deal with both the requirements of the communications medium and the requirements of the user [CONA83]. The primary purpose of this layer is to provide a reliable means to transmit data across a physical link. The protocol mechanisms required to do this repay close examination because many of these same mechanisms will be seen again at higher layers. Accordingly, we will devote considerable space to an explanation of data link protocol mechanisms.

As usual, the chapter begins with a summary of the OSI specification for this layer. Then, the types of line configurations that must be managed are described. The next section deals with the key mechanisms of flow control and error control. We are then in a position to examine a specific protocol standard, HDLC, which is the best known standard. Other link control standards are briefly mentioned. Finally, the ISO data link service standard is examined. An appendix looks at an error detection algorithm commonly used in data link control protocols, the cyclic redundancy check (CRC).

4.1 OSI DEFINITION

The OSI document characterizes the data link layer as providing the functional and procedural means to establish, maintain, and release data-link connections on behalf of network entities.

Table 4.1 lists the services and functions of the data link layer. Most of the services are self-explanatory. The last item on the list (quality of service parameters) refers to parameters that may be requested by a network entity. These include—

- Mean time between detected but unrecoverable errors.
- Undetected error rate.
- Service availability.
- Transit delay.
- Throughput.

Table 4.1. SERVICES AND FUNCTIONS OF THE DATA LINK LAYER

Services	
Data-link connection	Connection of network entities
Data-link SDUs	Exchange of SDUs
Data-link connection endpoint identifiers	Identifies connection at SAP
Sequencing	Ordered delivery
Error notification	Notification of unrecoverable error
Flow control	Control of SDU rate
Quality of service parameters	Optionally selectable

Functions	
Data-link connection establishment and release	
Data-link SDU mapping	One-to-one, SDU to PDU
Data-link connection splitting	One data link connection onto several physical connections
Delimiting and synchronization	Framing of bits
Sequence control	Ordered delivery
Error detection	Transmission, format, and operational errors
Error recovery	Retransmission of PDUs
Flow control	Between data link entities
Identification and parameter exchange	Control information between entities
Control of data-circuit interconnection	Provides for network layer control
Data link layer management	Management activities related to data link layer

The data link entity attempts to satisfy these requests and, if it cannot, notify the network entity of refusal. For example, the error performance characteristics of the data link service depend on the error-detection algorithm used and the size of the error-detecting code in data link PDUs (see Appendix 4A). To enhance throughput or minimize delay, the data link layer may split a data-link connection onto several physical connections; that is, the data to be transmitted will be split up and transmitted across several physical links between two devices.

The functions of the data link layer are best explained by examining a specific protocol, which we do later in this chapter.

4.2 LINE CONFIGURATIONS

The three characteristics that distinguish various data link configurations are topology, duplexity, and line discipline.

Topology and Duplexity

The *topology* of a data link refers to the physical arrangement of stations on a link. If there are only two stations, the link is *point-to-point*. If there are more than two stations, then it is a *multipoint* topology. Traditionally, a multipoint link has been used in the case of a computer (primary station) and a set of terminals (secondary stations). More recently, more complex versions of the multipoint topology are found in local networks.

Traditional multipoint lines are made possible when the terminals are only transmitting a fraction of the time. Figure 4.1 illustrates the advantages of the multipoint configuration. If each terminal has a point to

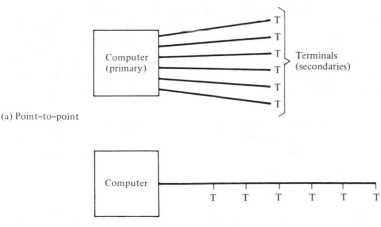

(a) Point–to–point

(b) Multipoint

Figure 4.1.   Traditional computer/terminal configurations.

point link to its computer, then the computer must have one I/O port for each terminal. Also, there is a separate transmission line from the computer to each terminal. In a multipoint configuration, the computer needs only a single I/O port, saving hardware costs. Only a single transmission line is needed, which also saves costs.

The *duplexity* of a link refers to the direction and timing of signal flow. In *simplex* transmission, the signal flow is always in one direction. For example, an input device, such as a card reader or remote sensor, could be attached to a host so that the device could only transmit, and never receive. An output device, such as a printer or an actuator, could be configured to only receive. Simplex is not in general use since it is not possible to send error or control signals back down the link to the data source. Simplex is similar to a one-lane, one-way bridge.

A *half-duplex* link can transmit and receive, but not simultaneously. This mode is also referred to as *two-way alternate,* suggestive of the fact that two stations on a half-duplex link must alternate in transmitting. This is similar to a one-lane, two-way bridge. On a *full-duplex* link, two stations can simultaneously send and receive data from each other. Thus this mode is known as *two-way simultaneous* and may be compared to a two-lane, two-way bridge.

With digital signaling, which requires a transmission line, full-duplex usually requires two separate transmission paths (e.g., two twisted pair), whereas half-duplex requires only one. For analog signaling, duplexity depends on frequency, whether an antenna or a transmission line is used. If a station transmits and receives on the same frequency, it must operate in half-duplex mode (exception: line transmission using two separate, isolated conductors; this is rarely done). If a station transmits on one frequency and receives on another, it may operate in full-duplex mode (see Fig. 3.10).

A number of combinations of topology and duplicity are possible. Figure 4.2 depicts the most common configurations. The figure always shows a single primary station (P) and one or more secondary (S) stations (this point is explored when we discuss line discipline). For point-to-point links, the two possibilities are self explanatory. For multipoint links, three configurations are possible:

- Primary full-duplex, secondaries half-duplex (multi-multipoint)
- Both primary and secondaries half-duplex (multipoint half-duplex)
- Both primary and secondaries full-duplex (multipoint duplex)

Line Discipline

Some discipline is needed in the use of a transmission link. On a half-duplex line, only one station at a time should transmit. On either a half- or full-duplex line, a station should only transmit if it knows that the intended receiver is prepared to receive.

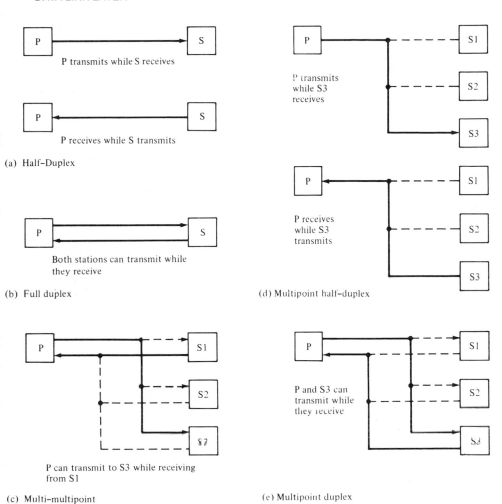

Figure 4.2. Data link configurations.

Point-to-Point Links.   Line discipline is simple with a point-to-point link. Let us consider first a half-duplex link in which either station may initiate an exchange. An example exchange is depicted in Fig. 4.3. If either station wishes to send data to the other, it first performs an enquiry (depicted as ENQ) of the other station to see if it is prepared to receive. The second station responds with a positive acknowledgment (ACK) to indicate that it is ready. The first station then sends some data, which the figure depicts as a frame. In asynchronous communication, the data would be sent as an asynchronous stream of characters. In any case, after some quantum of data is sent, the first station pauses to await results. The second station acknowledges successful receipt of the data (ACK). The first station then sends an end of transmission message (EOT), which terminates the exchange and returns the system to its initial state.

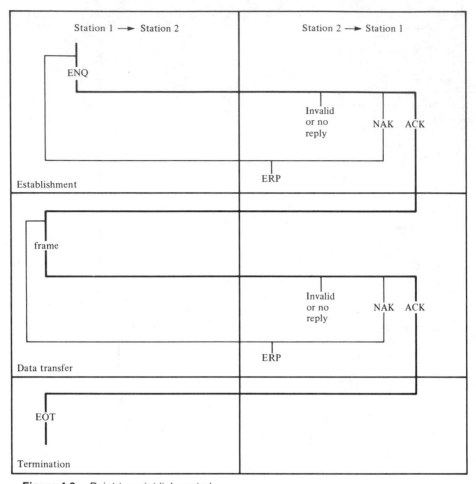

Figure 4.3. Point-to-point link control.

Several additional features are added to Fig. 4.3 to provide for coping with errors. A negative acknowledgment (NAK) is used to indicate that a station is not ready to receive, or that data were received in error. A station may fail to respond or respond with an invalid message. The result of these conditions is indicated by light lines in the figure; the heavy line is the normal sequence of communication events. If an unexpected event occurs, such as a NAK or invalid reply, a station may retry its last action or may institute some error recovery procedure (ERP).

There are three distinct phases in this communication control procedure:

- *Establishment:* This determines which station is to transmit and which to receive, and that the receiver is prepared to receive.

- *Data Transfer:* The data are transferred in one or more acknowledged blocks.
- *Termination:* This terminates the logical connection (transmitter–
  receiver relationship).

These three phases, in some form, are a part of all line disciplines for both
point-to-point and multipoint links.

Several refinements can be added to our discussion. The relationship described above was peer; that is, either station could initiate transmission. A common situation is to have one of the stations designated
primary and the other *secondary*. The primary has the responsibility of
initiating the exchange. This is a common situation when one station is a
computer (primary) and the other is a terminal (secondary). Figure 4.3
depicts a sequence in which the primary has data to send to the secondary. If the secondary has data to send, it must wait for the primary to
request the data, and only then enter a data transfer phase.

If the link is full-duplex, data and control messages can be transmitted in both directions simultaneously. We shall see the advantages of this
when we discuss flow and error control.

Multipoint Links.   The choice of line discipline for multipoint links depends primarily on whether there is a designated primary station or not.
When there is a primary station, data are exchanged only between the
primary and a secondary, not between two secondaries. The most common disciplines used in this situation are all variants of a scheme known
as *poll and select*:

- *Poll:* The primary requests data from a secondary.
- *Select:* The primary has data to send and informs a secondary that
  data are coming.

Figure 4.4 illustrates these concepts. In Fig. 4.4a, the primary polls
a secondary by sending a brief polling message. In this case, the secondary has nothing to send and responds with some sort of NAK message.
Figure 4.4b depicts the case of a successful poll. The select function is
shown in Fig. 4.4c. Note that four separate transmissions are required to
transfer data from the primary to the secondary. An alternative technique
is *fast select*. In this case, the selection message includes the data to be
transferred (Fig. 4.4d). The first reply from the secondary is an acknowledgment that indicates that the station was prepared to receive and did
receive the data successfully. Fast selection is particularly well suited for
applications where short messages are frequently transmitted and the
transfer time for the message is not appreciably longer than the reply
time.

Another form of line discipline is *contention*. In this mode, there is typically no primary but rather a collection of peer stations. A station can transmit if the line is free; otherwise, it must wait. This technique has found widespread use in local networks and satellite systems. A characteristic of all multipoint line disciplines is the need for addressing. In the case of roll-call polling, transmissions from the primary must indicate the intended secondary; transmissions from a secondary must identify the secondary. In a peer situation, both transmitter and receiver must be identified. Thus there are three cases:

- *Point-to-point:* No address needed
- *Primary-secondary multipoint:* One address needed, to identify secondary
- *Peer multipoint:* Two addresses needed, to identify transmitter and receiver

In practice, the first case is subsumed into the second, so that most data link control protocols require one address even for point-to-point transmission. This simplifies the demands on the station by allowing a single protocol to be used in both circumstances. The peer multipoint case is seen in local networks.

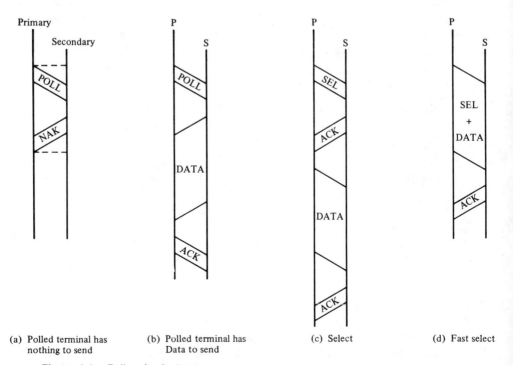

(a) Polled terminal has nothing to send

(b) Polled terminal has Data to send

(c) Select

(d) Fast select

Figure 4.4. Poll and select sequences.

4.3 FLOW CONTROL

Flow control is a technique for assuring that a transmitting station does not overwhelm a receiving station with data. The receiver will typically allocate a data buffer with some maximum length. When data are received, it must do a certain amount of processing before it can clear the buffer and be prepared to receive more data.

The simplest form of flow control, known as *stop and wait,* works as follows. The receiver indicates its willingness to accept data by sending a poll or responding to a select. The sender then transmits its data. Following reception, the receiver must again indicate its willingness to accept data before more are sent. This procedure works fine, and indeed can hardly be improved on, when a message is sent as one contiguous block or frame of data. However, it is often the case that a transmitter will break a large block of data up into smaller blocks and send these one at a time. This is done for one or more of the following reasons:

- The longer the transmission, the more likely that there will be an error, necessitating retransmission of the entire block. With smaller blocks, errors are less likely per block, and fewer data need be transmitted.
- On a multipoint line, it is usually desirable not to permit one station to occupy the line for very long, thus causing long delays at the other stations.
- The buffer size of the receiver may be limited.

With the use of multiple frames for a single message, the stop-and-wait procedure may be inadequate. The essence of the problem is that only one frame at a time can be in transit. In situations where the bit length of the link is greater than the frame length, serious inefficiencies result. The obvious solution is to allow multiple frames to be in transit at one time.

Let us examine how this might work for two stations, *A* and *B*, connected via full-duplex link. Station *B* allocates seven buffers for reception instead of the one discussed above. Thus *B* can accept seven frames, and *A* is allowed to send seven frames without waiting for an acknowledgment. To keep track of which frames have been acknowledged, each is labeled with a sequence number in the range 0 to 7 (modulo 8). *B* acknowledges a frame by sending an acknowledgment that includes the sequence number of the next frame expected. Thus, if *B* returns the sequence number 5, this acknowledges receipt of frame number 4, and says that *B* is now expecting frame number 5. This scheme can be used to acknowledge multiple frames. For example, *B* could receive frames 2, 3, and 4, but withhold acknowledgment until frame 4 arrives. By then returning sequence number 5, *B* acknowledges frames 2, 3, and 4 at one time. *A* maintains a list of sequence numbers that it is allowed to send and *B* maintains a list of sequence numbers that it is prepared to receive. Each of these lists can be thought of as a *window* of frames.

An example of this *sliding window* operation is shown in Fig. 4.5. Initially, *A* and *B* have seven-frame windows. After transmitting three frames with no acknowledgment, *A* has shrunk its window to four frames. When frame 2 is acknowledged, *A* is back up to seven frames. Later, *B* decides to restrict flow to three frames. This is easily accomplished by withholding acknowledgment of some frames.

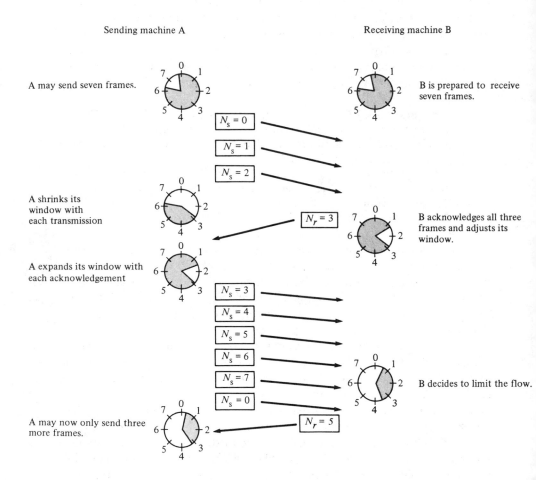

N_s = sequence number of frame sent
N_r = sequence number of next frame expected
Shaded part designates window

Figure 4.5.   Example of a sliding-window protocol.

4.4 ERROR CONTROL

The most common techniques for error control are based on two functions:

- *Error detection:* As discussed in Chap. 2 (see Fig. 2.5).
- *Automatic repeat request (ARQ):* When an error is detected, the receiver requests that the frame be retransmitted.

This is a straightforward approach that results in the conversion of an unreliable data link into a reliable one. Three versions of ARQ are in popular use:

- Stop-and-wait ARQ
- Go-back-N continuous ARQ
- Selective-repeat continuous ARQ

Stop-and-wait ARQ uses the simple stop-and-wait acknowledgment scheme described in Sec. 4.3 and is depicted in Fig. 4.6a. The sending station transmits a single frame and then must await an acknowledgment. No other data frames can be sent until the receiving station's reply arrives at the transmitting station. The receiver sends a positive acknowledgment (ACK) if the frame is correct and a negative acknowledgment (NAK) otherwise.

The algorithm so far described does not cover all contingencies. The transmitted frame could be so corrupted by noise as not to be received,

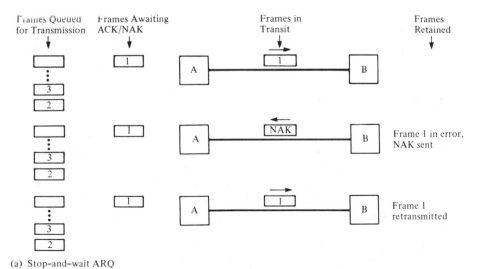

(a) Stop–and–wait ARQ

Figure 4.6. Automatic repeat request (ARQ) techniques.

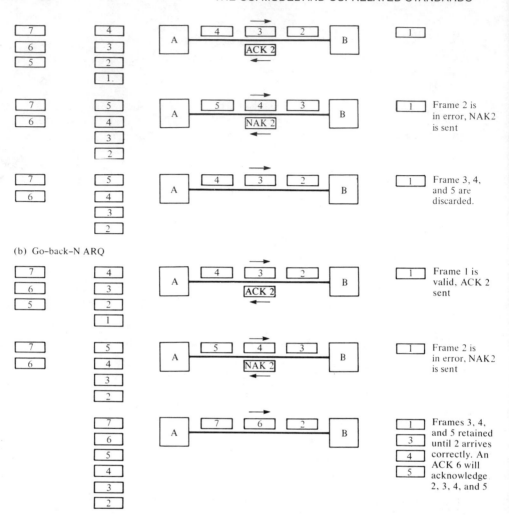

(b) Go–back–N ARQ

(c) Selective–report ARQ

Figure 4.6 (continued)

in which case the receiver will not acknowledge. To account for this possibility, the sender is equipped with a timer. After a frame is transmitted, the sender waits for an acknowledgment (ACK or NAK). If no recognizable acknowledgment is received by the time that the timer expires, then the same frame is sent again. Note that this system requires that the transmitter maintain a copy of a transmitted frame until an ACK is received for that frame.

One more refinement is needed. Consider the following situation. Station *A* sends a frame. The frame is received correctly by station *B*, which responds with an ACK. The ACK is damaged in transit and is not recognizable by *A*, which must resend the same frame. This duplicate frame arrives and is accepted by *B*. To avoid this problem, frames are alternately labeled with 0 or 1 and positive acknowledgments are of the form ACK0 or ACK1.

The principal advantage of stop-and-wait ARQ is its simplicity. Its principal disadvantage, as discussed in Sec. 4.3, is that this is an inefficient protocol. The sliding-window technique introduced before can be adapted to provide more efficient line use. In this context, it is referred to as *continuous ARQ*.

One variant of continuous ARQ is known as *go-back-N ARQ*. In this technique, a station may send a series of frames determined by window size. If the receiving station detects an error on a frame, it sends a NAK for that frame. The receiving station will discard all future incoming frames until the frame in error is correctly received. Thus the transmitting station, when it receives a NAK, must retransmit the frame in error plus all succeeding frames.

Figure 4.6B shows the frame flow for go-back-N ARQ on a full-duplex line. While frames 2, 3, and 4 are being transmitted, from station *A* to station *B*, an ACK of the previously received frame 1 is going from *B* to *A*. Some time later, frame 2 is received in error. Frames 3, 4, and 5 are in transit. *B* sends a NAK2 to *A*, which is received after frame 5 has been sent but before *A* has a chance to send frame 6. *A* must now retransmit frames 2, 3, 4, and 5, even though only frame 2 was in error. Again, note that station *A* must maintain a copy of each unacknowledged frame.

With go-back-N ARQ, it is not required that each individual frame be acknowledged. For example, station *A* sends frames 0, 1, 2, and 3. Station *B* responds with ACK1 after frame 0, but then does not respond to frames 1 and 2. After frame 3 is received, *B* issues ACK4, indicating that frame 3 and all previous frames are accepted.

A sequence space of 2^n can support a window size of only $2^n - 1$, because of the interaction of error control and acknowledgment. In most schemes, for efficiency, a station will send an ACK with each transmitted data frame; this is known as *piggybacking*. This means that a station will send an ACK with a frame even if the ACK has already been sent. This is because a fixed-length acknowledgment field of n bits is incorporated into the frame and some number must be put into the frame. Now consider that a station transmits frame 0 and gets an ACK1, and then transmits frame 1, 2, 3, 4, 5, 6, 7, 0 and gets another ACK1. This could mean that all eight frames were received correctly, or that all eight frames were lost in transit, and the receiving station is repeating its previous ACK1.

Selective repeat ARQ provides a more refined approach than go-back-N. The only frames retransmitted are those that receive a NAK. In Fig. 4.6c, only frame 2 need be retransmitted. This would appear to be more efficient than the go-back-N approach. On the other hand, the receiver must contain storage to save post-NAK frames until the error frame is retransmitted, and the logic for reinserting the frame in the proper sequence. The transmitter, too, will require more complex logic to be able to send frames out of sequence. Because of such complications, the go-back-N algorithm is more commonly used.

The window-size requirement is more restrictive for selective-repeat than for go-back-N. We have seen that for 2^n sequence numbers, a window of $2^n - 1$ can be used for go-back-N. Now, consider the case of a three-bit field (sequence space is eight), and consider the following scenario:

1. Station A sends frames 0 through 6 to station B.
2. Station B receives and acknowledges all seven frames.
3. Because of a long noise burst, all seven acknowledgments are lost.
4. Station A times out and retransmits frame 0.
5. Station B has already advanced its window to accept frames 7, 0, 1, 2, 3, 4, 5. Thus it assumes that this is a new frame 0 and accepts it.

The problem with the foregoing scenario, for selective-repeat ARQ, is that there is an overlap between the sending and receiving windows. To overcome the problem, the maximum window size should be no more than half the range of sequence numbers. In the scenario above, if only four unacknowledged frames may be outstanding, no confusion can result.

Figure 4.7 compares the two approaches. In Fig. 4.7a, the go-back-N technique is used and the window size is seven. The third frame (frame 2) is transmitted in error. Because of propagation delays, the effect of the error is that three good frames are sent and discarded. Using selective repeat, these frames are stored and acknowledged by the receiver.

4.5 HDLC

Data link control protocols are designed to deal with a variety of physical link characteristics and modes of operation including:

• Point-to-point and multipoint links
• Long- and short-distance connections
• Half-duplex (two-way alternate) and full-duplex (two-way simultaneous) operation
• Primary-secondary (e.g., host-terminal) and peer (e.g., computer-computer) interaction

In addition, these protocols are intended to satisfy the following objectives:

• *Code independence:* The user should be able to use any character codes or bit patterns in the data to be transmitted.

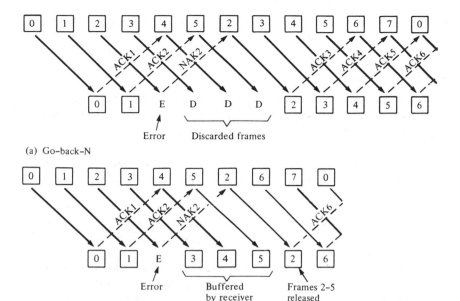

Figure 4.7. Examples of continuous ARQ.

- *High efficiency:* The format should minimize overhead bits and permit efficient error and flow control.
- *High reliability:* The protocol should have a powerful set of error detection and recovery procedures.

These requirements can best be met by a bit-oriented synchronous data link protocol. A number of very similar bit-oriented protocols have achieved widespread use:

- *High-level data link control (HDLC):* Developed by the International Organization for Standardization [ISO4335].
- *Advanced data communication control procedures (ADCCP):* Developed by the American National Standards Institute (ANSI X3.66). With very minor exceptions, ADCCP has been adopted by the U.S. National Bureau of Standards (FIPS PUB 71-1) for use on federal government procurements, and by the Federal Telecommunications Standards Committee (FED-STD- 1003A) as the standard for the national-defense-related National Communications System.
- *Link access procedure, balanced (LAP-B):* Adopted by the International Telegraph and Telephone Consultative Committee (CCITT) as part of its X.25 packet-switched network standard.
- *Synchronous data link control (SDLC):* Used by IBM. This is not a standard, but is in widespread use.

There are virtually no differences between HDLC and ADCCP. LAP-B is a subset of HDLC. SDLC is also a subset of HDLC, but also includes several minor additional features [BROD83]. The following discussion is based on HDLC.

Basic Characteristics

To satisfy the variety of requirements listed above, HDLC defines three types of stations, two link configurations, and three data transfer modes of operation [ISO 7809]. The three stations types are:

- *Primary station:* Has the responsibility for controlling the operation of the link. Frames issued by the primary are called *commands*.
- *Secondary station:* Operates under the control of the primary station. Frames issued by the secondary station(s) are called *responses*. The primary maintains a separate logical link with each secondary station on the line.
- *Combined station:* Combines the features of primary and secondary stations. A combined station may issue both commands and responses.

The two link configurations are (Fig.4.8):

- *Unbalanced configuration:* Used in point-to-point and multipoint operation. This configuration consists of one primary and one or more secondary stations and supports both full-duplex and half-duplex transmission.
- *Balanced configuration:* Used only in point-to-point operation. This configuration consists of two combined stations and supports both full-duplex and half-duplex transmission.

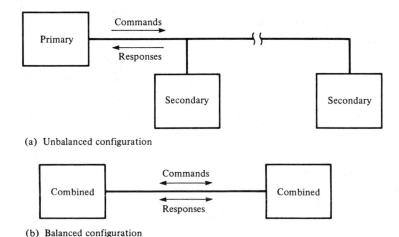

(a) Unbalanced configuration

(b) Balanced configuration

Figure 4.8. HDLC link configurations.

The three data transfer modes of operation are:

- *Normal response mode (NRM):* This is an unbalanced configuration. The primary may initiate data transfer to a secondary, but a secondary may only transmit data in response to a poll from the primary.
- *Asynchronous balanced mode (ABM):* This is a balanced configuration. Either combined station may initiate transmission without receiving permission from the other combined station.
- *Asynchronous response mode (ARM):* This is an unbalanced configuration. In this mode, the secondary may initiate transmission without explicit permission of the primary (i.e., send a response without waiting for a command). The primary still retains responsibility for the line, including initialization, error recovery, and logical disconnection.

The normal response mode is used on multidrop lines, in which a number of terminals are connected to a computer. The computer polls each terminal for input. NRM is also often used on point-to-point links, particularly if the link connects a terminal or other peripheral to a computer. The asynchronous balanced mode makes more efficient use of a full-duplex point-to-point link because there is no polling overhead. The asynchronous response mode is rarely used; it is applicable to hub polling and other special situations in which a secondary may need to initiate transmission.

Frame Structure

HDLC uses synchronous transmission. All transmissions are in frames, and a single frame format suffices for all types of data and control exchanges.

Figure 4.9 depicts the structure of the HDLC frame [ISO 3309]. The frame has the following fields:

- *Flag:* 8 bits
- *Address:* One or more octets
- *Control:* 8 or 16 bits
- *Data:* variable
- *Frame check sequence (FCS):* 16 or 32 bits
- *Flag:* 8 bits

The flag, address, and control fields that precede the data field are known as a *header.* The FCS and flag fields following the data field are referred to as a *trailer.*

Flag Fields.   Flag fields delimits the frame at both ends with the unique pattern 01111110. A single flag may be used as the closing flag for one

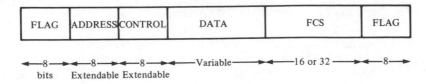

| FLAG | ADDRESS | CONTROL | DATA | FCS | FLAG |

◄—8—►◄—8—►◄—8—►◄—Variable—►◄—16 or 32—►◄—8—►
bits   Extendable Extendable

(a) Frame format

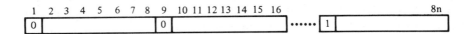

	1	2	3	4	5	6	7	8
I: Information	O		N(S)		P/F		N (R)	
S: Supervisory	1	O	S		P/F		N (R)	
U: Unnumbered	1	1	M		P/F		M	

N (S) = Send sequence number
N (R) = Receive sequence number
S = Supervisory function bits
M = Unnumbered function bits
P/F = Poll/final bit

(b) Control field format

1 2 3 4 5 6 7 8 9 10 11 12 13 14 15 16   8n
| 0 | | | | | | | | 0 | | | | | | | | •••••• | 1 | | |

(c) Extended address field

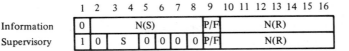

	1	2	3	4	5	6	7	8	9	10 11 12 13 14 15 16
Information	0			N(S)					P/F	N(R)
Supervisory	1	0	S	0	0	0	0		P/F	N(R)

(d) Extended control fields

Figure 4.9. HDLC frame structure.

frame and the opening flag for the next. All active stations attached to the
link are continuously hunting for the flag sequence to synchronize on the
start of a frame. While receiving a frame, a station continues to hunt for
that sequence to determine the end of the frame. Since the HDLC frame
allows arbitrary bit patterns, however, there is no assurance that the pattern 01111110 will not appear somewhere inside the frame, thus destroy-
ing frame-level synchronization. To avoid this problem, a procedure
known as *bit stuffing* is used. The transmitter will always insert an extra
0 bit after each occurrence of five 1's in the frame (with the exception of
the flag fields). After detecting a starting flag, the receiver monitors the
bit stream. When a pattern of five 1's appears, the sixth bit is examined.

If this bit is 0, it is deleted. If the sixth bit is a 1 and the seventh bit is a 0, the combination is accepted as a flag. If the sixth and seventh bits are both 1, the sending station is signaling an abort condition.

   With the use of bit stuffing, arbitrary bit patterns can be inserted into the data field of the frame. This property is known as *data transparency*.

   Figure 4.10 shows an example of bit stuffing. Note that in the first two cases, the extra 0 is not strictly necessary for avoiding a flag pattern, but is necessary for the operation of the algorithm. The pitfalls of bit stuffing are also illustrated in this figure. When a flag is used as both an ending and starting flag, a 1-bit error merges two frames into one. Conversely, a 1-bit error inside the frame could split it in two.

Address Field.   The address field is used to identify the secondary station that transmitted or is to receive the frame. This field is not needed for point-to-point links, but is always included for the sake of uniformity. An

Original pattern

   1 1 1 1 1 1 1 1 1 1 1 1 0 1 1 1 1 1 0 1 1 1 1 1 0

After bit–stuffing

   1 1 1 1 1 0 1 1 1 1 1 0 1 1 0 1 1 1 1 1 0 1 0 1 1 1 1 1 0 1 0

(a) Example

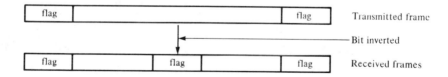

(b) An inverted bit splits a frame in two.

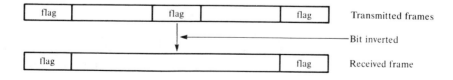

(c) An inverted bit merges two frames.

Figure 4.10.   Bit stuffing.

address is normally eight bits long, but, by prior agreement, an extended format may be used in which the address length is a multiple of seven bits. The least significant bit in each octet is 1 or 0 according as it is or is not the last octet of the address field; the remaining seven bits form part of the address. The single address of 11111111 is interpreted as the all-stations address in both basic and extended formats. It is used to allow the primary to broadcast a frame for reception by all secondaries.

Control Field.   HDLC defines three types of frames, each with a different control field format. *Information frames* (I-frames) carry the data to be transmitted for the station, known as *user data*. Additionally, flow and error control data using the ARQ mechanism, may be piggybacked on an information frame. *Supervisory frames* (S-frames) provide the ARQ mechanism when piggybacking is not used, and *unnumbered frames* (U-frames) provide supplemental link control functions. The first one or two bits of the control field serves to identify the frame type. The remaining bit positions are organized into subfields as indicated in Fig. 4.10b and 4.10d. Their use is explained in the discussion of HDLC operation, below.

Note that the basic control field for S- and I- frames uses 3-bit sequence numbers. With the appropriate set-mode command, an extended control field that employs 7-bit sequence numbers can be used for S- and I-frames.

Data Field.   The data field is present only in I-frames and some unnumbered frames. The field can contain any sequence of bits. Its length is undefined in the standard, but is generally limited by each implementation to a specified maximum. Frequently, the length must be a multiple of eight bits.

Frame Check Sequence Field.   The frame check sequence is applied to the remaining bits of the frame, exclusive of flags. The normal FCS is the 16-bit CRC-CCITT. An optional 32-bit FCS, using CRC-32, may be employed if the frame length or line reliability dictates this choice. These codes are defined in the appendix to this chapter.

Operation

The operation of HDLC consists of the exchange of I-frames, S-frames, and U-frames between a primary and a secondary or between two primaries. The various commands and responses defined for these frame types are listed in Table 4.2. To describe HDLC operation, we will first discuss these three types of frames, and then give some examples.

Information Frames.   The basic operation of HDLC involves the exchange of information frames (I-frames) containing user data. Each I-

Table 4.2. HDLC COMMANDS AND RESPONSES

Name	Function	Description
Information (I)	C/R	Exchange user data
Supervisory (S)		
Receive Ready (RR)	C/R	Positive acknowledgment; ready to receive I-frame
Receive Not Ready (RNR)	C/R	Positive acknowledgment; not ready to receive
Reject (REJ)	C/R	Negative acknowledgment; go back N
Selective Reject (SREJ)	C/R	Negative acknowledgment; selective repeat
Unnumbered (U)		
Set Normal Response/ Extended Mode (SNRM/ SNRME)	C	Set mode; extended = 7-bit sequence numbers
Set Asynchronous Response/Extended Mode (SARM/SARME)	C	Set mode; extended = 7-bit sequence numbers
Set Asynchronous Balanced/Extended Mode (SABM/SABME)	C	Set mode; extended = 7-bit sequence numbers
Set Initialization Mode (SIM)	C	Initialize link control functions in addressed station
Disconnect (DISC)	C	Terminate logical link connection
Unnumbered Acknowledgment (UA)	R	Acknowledges acceptance of one of the above set-mode commands
Disconnected Mode (DM)	R	Secondary is logically disconnected
Request Disconnect (RD)	R	Request for DISC command
Request Initialization Mode (RIM)	R	Initialization needed; request for SIM command
Unnumbered Information (UI)	C/R	Used to exchange control information
Unnumbered Poll (UP)	C	Used to solicit control information
Reset (RSET)	C	Used for recovery; resets N(R), N(S)
Exchange Identification (XID)	C/R	Used to request/report identity and status
Test (TEST)	C/R	Exchange identical information fields for testing
Frame Reject (FRMR)	R	Reports receipt of unacceptable frame

frame contains the sequence number of the transmitted frame as well as a piggybacked positive acknowledgment. The acknowledgment is the sequence number of the *next* frame expected. A maximum window size of 7 or 127 is allowed.

The I-frame also contains a poll/final (P/F) bit. The bit is a poll bit for commands (from primary) and a final bit (from secondary) for responses. In normal response mode (NRM), the primary issues a poll giving permission to send by setting the poll bit to 1, and the secondary sets the final bit to 1 on the last I-frame of its response. In asynchronous response mode (ARM) and asynchronous balanced mode (ABM), the P/F bit is sometimes used to coordinate the exchange of S- and U-frames.

Supervisory Frames.   The supervisory frame (S-frame) is used for flow and error control. Both go-back-N ARQ (REJ) and selective-repeat ARQ (SREJ) are allowed. The latter is rarely implemented because of the buffering requirements. A frame may be positively acknowledged with a receive ready (RR) when an I-frame is not available for piggybacking. In addition, a receive not ready (RNR) is used to accept a frame but request that no more I-frames be sent until a subsequent RR is used.

The P/F bit on a supervisory frame may be employed as follows. The primary may set the P bit in an RR frame to poll the secondary. This is done when the primary has no I-frame upon which to piggyback the poll. The secondary responds with an I-frame if it has one; otherwise, it sends an RR with the F bit set to indicate that it has no data to send. The primary (combined station) may set the P bit in the RNR command to solicit the receive status of a secondary/combined station. The response will be an RR with the F bit set if the station can receive I-frames, and an RNR with the F bit set if the station is busy.

Unnumbered Frames.   Unnumbered frames are used for a variety of control functions. As the name indicates, these frames do not carry sequence numbers and do not alter the sequencing or flow of numbered I-frames. We can group these frames into the following categories:

- Mode-setting commands and responses
- Information transfer commands and responses
- Recovery commands and responses
- Miscellaneous commands and responses

Mode-setting commands are transmitted by the primary/combined station to initialize or change the mode of the secondary/combined station. The secondary/combined station acknowledges acceptance by responding with an unnumbered acknowledgment (UA) frame; the UA has the F bit set to the same value as the received P bit. Once established, a mode remains in effect at a secondary station until the next mode-setting command is accepted, and at a combined station until the next mode-setting command is either accepted or transmitted and acknowledged.

The commands SNRM, SNRME, SARM, SARME, SABM, and SABME are self-explanatory. Upon acceptance of the command, the I-frame sequence numbers in both directions are set to 0. The set initialization mode (SIM) command is used to cause the addressed secondary/combined station to initiate a station specified procedure to initialize its data link control functions (e.g., accept a new program or update operational parameters). While in initialization mode, the required information is sent using unnumbered information (UI) frames. The disconnect command (DISC) is used to inform the addressed station that the transmitting station is suspending operation.

In addition to UA, there are several other responses related to mode setting. The disconnected mode (DM) response is sent in response to all commands to indicate that the responding station is logically disconnected. When sent in response to a mode-setting command, DM is a refusal to set the requested mode. The request initialization mode (RIM) response is used in response to a mode-setting command when the station is not ready and wishes to initialize. The request disconnect (RD) response is used to request a disconnect of the logical link.

Information transfer commands and responses are used to exchange information between stations. This is done primarily through the unnumbered information (UI) command/response. Examples of UI frame information are higher-level status, operational interruption, time of day, and link initialization parameters. The unnumbered poll (UP) command is used to solicit an unnumbered response, as a way of establishing the status of the addressed station.

Recovery commands and responses are used when the normal ARQ mechanism does not apply or will not work. The frame reject (FRMR) response is used to report an error in a received frame, such as:

- Invalid control field
- Data field too long
- Data field not allowed with received frame type
- Invalid receive count (i.e., a frame is acknowledged that has not yet been sent)

The reset (RSET) command is used to clear the FRMR condition. RSET announces that the sending station is resetting its send sequence number, and the addressed station should reset its receive sequence number.

Finally, there are two *miscellaneous* command/responses that fit into no neat category. The exchange identification (XID) command/response is used for two stations to exchange station identification and the characteristics of the two stations. The actual information exchanged is implementation dependent. A recently added frame type is the test

(TEST) command/response. A test command must be echoed with a test response at the earliest opportunity. This is a simple means of testing that the link and the addressed station are still functioning.

Examples.   Figure 4.11 contains a number of examples of HDLC operation for both point-to-point and multipoint links. The reader is urged to study this figure carefully.

4.6   OTHER DATA LINK STANDARDS

In addition to HDLC, there are many other data link protocols. Three are worth brief mention:

- *Multilink procedures*
- *LLC*
- *LAP-D*

Multilink Procedures

HDLC, and most other link control protocols, are designed to operate over a single physical circuit between two systems. In some cases, multiple parallel physical circuits exist between a single pair of systems. ISO has defined a multilink procedure (MLP) to operate over multiple lines to achieve greater throughput and reliability [DIS 7478]. Over each line, a single link procedure (SLP), such as HDLC, is used. The MLP operates above the SLP, and might be thought of as an upper sublayer of the data link layer.

When a layer 3 protocol data unit (PDU) is presented to the MLP for transmission, any available link may be chosen. Indeed, the MLP may assign one PDU to several links to satisfy throughput or availability constraints. To keep track of the transmitted PDUs, an MLP frame is defined, which consists of the layer 3 PDU encapsulated with a 16-bit multilink control (MLC) field (Fig. 4.12a). The MLC contains a 12-bit sequence number that is unique (modulo 2^{12}) across all links. Once an MLP frame is constructed, it is assigned to a particular link, and further encapsulated in an SLP frame. The SLP frame, such as an HDLC frame, includes a sequence number specific to that link.

There are two principal reasons for needing an MLP sequence number. First, frames sent out over different links may arrive in a different order from that in which they were first constructed by the sending MLP. The destination MLP will buffer incoming frames and reorder them according to MLP sequence number. Second, if repeated attempts to transmit a frame over one link fails, the sending MLP will send the frame over one or more other links. The MLP sequence number is needed for duplicate detection in this case.

These examples present some HDLC exchanges of control and information. (These examples are not necessarily restricted to the configuration in which they are shown.) The symbolic format for the transmission shown, following. is:

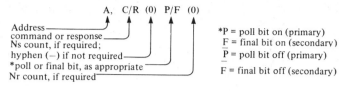

A, C/R (0) P/F (0)

Address ⎯⎯⎯⎯⎯⎯
command or response ⎯⎯⎯
Ns count, if required;
hyphen (−) if not required ⎯⎯⎯
*poll or final bit, as appropriate
Nr count, if required

*P = poll bit on (primary)
F = final bit on (secondary)
P̄ = poll bit off (primary)
F̄ = final bit off (secondary)

(a) Point–to point duplex exchange

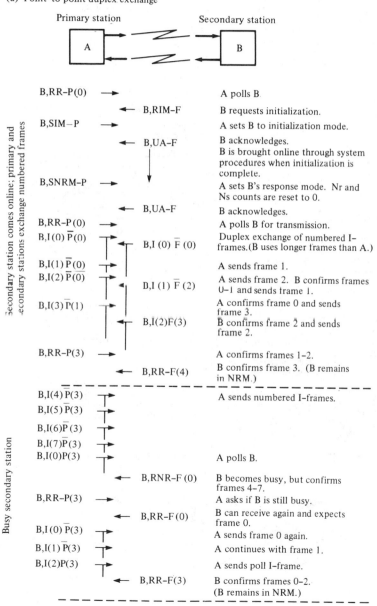

Primary station   Secondary station

A   B

Secondary station comes online; primary and secondary stations exchange numbered frames

B,RR–P(0) →   A polls B.

← B,RIM–F   B requests initialization.

B,SIM−P →   A sets B to initialization mode.

← B,UA–F   B acknowledges.
B is brought online through system procedures when initialization is complete.

B,SNRM–P →   A sets B's response mode. Nr and Ns counts are reset to 0.

← B,UA–F   B acknowledges.

B,RR–P(0) →   A polls B for transmission.

B,I(0) P̄(0)   Duplex exchange of numbered I-
← B,I (0) F̄ (0)   frames.(B uses longer frames than A.)

B,I(1) P̄(0)   A sends frame 1.

B,I(2) P̄(0)   A sends frame 2. B confirms frames
← B,I (1) F̄ (2)   0–1 and sends frame 1.

B,I(3) P̄(1)   A confirms frame 0 and sends frame 3.

← B,I(2)F(3)   B confirms frame 2 and sends frame 2.

B,RR–P(3) →   A confirms frames 1–2.

← B,RR–F(4)   B confirms frame 3. (B remains in NRM.)

Busy secondary station

B,I(4) P̄(3)   A sends numbered I-frames.

B,I(5) P̄(3)

B,I(6)P̄ (3)

B,I(7)P̄(3)

B,I(0)P(3)   A polls B.

← B,RNR–F (0)   B becomes busy, but confirms frames 4–7.

B,RR–P(3) →   A asks if B is still busy.

← B,RR–F(0)   B can receive again and expects frame 0.

B,I (0) P̄(3)   A sends frame 0 again.

B,I(1) P̄(3)   A continues with frame 1.

B,I(2)P(3)   A sends poll I-frame.

← B,RR–F(3)   B confirms frames 0–2. (B remains in NRM.)

Figure 4.11. Examples of HDLC operation.

93

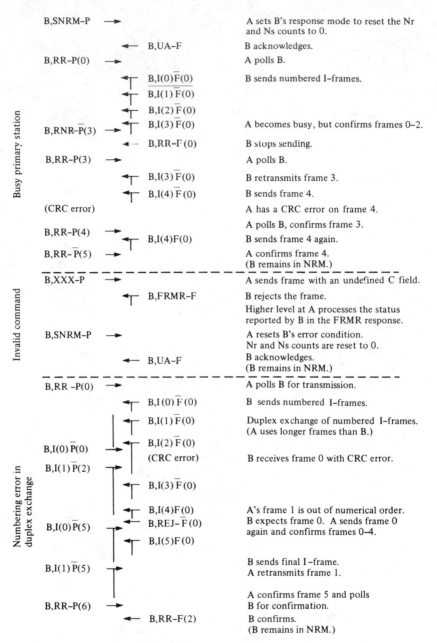

Busy primary station

B,SNRM-P →		A sets B's response mode to reset the Nr and Ns counts to 0.
	← B,UA-F	B acknowledges.
B,RR-P(0) →		A polls B.
	← B,I(0)F̄(0)	B sends numbered I-frames.
	← B,I(1) F̄(0)	
	← B,I(2) F̄(0)	
B,RNR-P̄(3) →	← B,I(3) F̄(0)	A becomes busy, but confirms frames 0–2.
	← B,RR-Γ(0)	B stops sending.
B,RR-P(3) →		A polls B.
	← B,I(3) F̄(0)	B retransmits frame 3.
	← B,I(4) F̄(0)	B sends frame 4.
(CRC error)		A has a CRC error on frame 4.
B,RR-P(4) →		A polls B, confirms frame 3.
	← B,I(4)F(0)	B sends frame 4 again.
B,RR- P̄(5) →		A confirms frame 4. (B remains in NRM.)

Invalid command

B,XXX-P →		A sends frame with an undefined C field.
	← B,FRMR-F	B rejects the frame.
		Higher level at A processes the status reported by B in the FRMR response.
B,SNRM-P →		A resets B's error condition. Nr and Ns counts are reset to 0.
	← B,UA-F	B acknowledges. (B remains in NRM.)

Numbering error in duplex exchange

B,RR -P(0) →		A polls B for transmission.
	← B,I(0) F̄(0)	B sends numbered I-frames.
	← B,I(1) F̄(0)	Duplex exchange of numbered I-frames. (A uses longer frames than B.)
B,I(0) P̄(0) →	← B,I(2) F̄(0)	
	(CRC error)	B receives frame 0 with CRC error.
B,I(1) P̄(2) →		
	← B,I(3) F̄(0)	
	← B,I(4)F(0)	A's frame 1 is out of numerical order.
B,I(0)P̄(5) →	← B,REJ- F̄(0)	B expects frame 0. A sends frame 0 again and confirms frames 0–4.
	← B,I(5)F(0)	
B,I(1) P̄(5) →		B sends final I-frame. A retransmits frame 1.
B,RR-P(6) →		A confirms frame 5 and polls B for confirmation.
	← B,RR-F(2)	B confirms. (B remains in NRM.)

Figure 4.11   (continued)

(b) Multipoint duplex exchanges

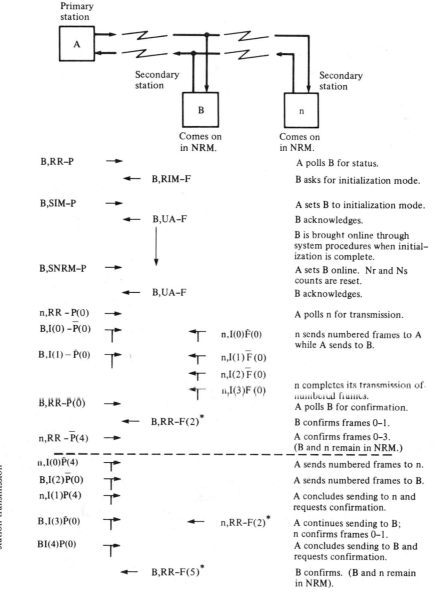

*If a secondary station has information to send, this confirmation may be in the I format.

Figure 4.11   (continued)

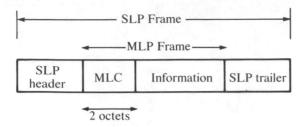

(a) SLP and MLP Frames

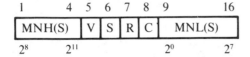

MNH(S) = bits 9 to 12 of 12-bit multilink send sequence number
MNL(S) = bits 1 to 8 of 12-bit multilink send sequence number
V = void sequencing bit
S = sequence check option bit
R = MLP reset request bit
C = MLP reset confirmation bit

(b) Multilink Control Field (MLC)

Figure 4.12. Multilink procedure formats.

Figure 4.12b shows the format of the MLC. The 12-bit sequence number is split into two parts, and the figure indicates the proper interpretation of the sequence number bits. The V bit is set at 1 to indicate that resequencing is not required prior to release of the data unit to the network layer; the receiving MLP may release data units in the order in which they arrive. This feature is appropriate to support a connectionless network service. The S bit has significance only if $V = 1$ (sequencing not required). If $S = 0$, the transmitting MLP has assigned sequence numbers; although the receiving MLP need not release data units to the network layer in sequence number order, it should avoid delivering duplicates. The R bit is set to 1 to request that the sequencing scheme be reset; the next frame to be transmitted by the MLP will have a sequence number of 0. The C bit is set by the other MLP on the next available frame to acknowledge the reset.

Note that there is no explicit acknowledgment of data units in MLP. It is assumed that the SLP is reliable and that, therefore, acknowledgment at the MLP level is unnecessary. If the SLP associated with a particular link fails to successfully transmit a frame after repeated attempts, it reports this to the MLP, which then attempts transmission over another link.

Logical Link Control

Logical link control (LLC) is the data link standard [DIS 8802/2] defined for local networks as part of the IEEE 802 family of standards. The key difference between LLC and traditional standards, such as HDLC, is that LLC is designed to operate over a peer multipoint link. In this case, there are multiple devices attached to a transmission medium, all of which are capable of initiating transmission; there is no unique primary on the link. To account for this, each transmitted data unit includes both the sending and receiving address, rather than just the address of a secondary.

The LLC standard specifies three types of services that may be offered to the network layer: *unacknowledged connectionless service, connection-oriented service,* and *acknowledged connectionless service.* The first two services we are familiar with from our previous discussion. The final service, though connectionless, provides for the acknowledgment of individual frames. This service may be useful in some real-time environments such as factory LANs. For example, certain alarm or control signals may be very important and time-critical. Because of their importance, an acknowledgment is needed so that the sender can be assured that the signal has got through. Because of the urgency of the signal, the user might not want to take the time to first establish a logical connection and then send the data.

A detailed discussion of LLC is contained in the second volume of this series, which deals with local network standards.

LAP-D

LAP-D is a data link standard developed as part of the ISDN standardization effort [I.440, I.441]. It specifies a link access protocol to be used over a logical channel, known as the D channel, that is part of a time-multiplexed link between a network subscriber and the ISDN central office. LAP-D is based on LAP-B, which is, in turn, a variant of HDLC.

LAP-D has to deal with two levels of multiplexing. First, at a subscriber site, there may be multiple user devices sharing the same physical interface. Second, within each user device, there may be multiple types of traffic, specifically packet-switched data and control signalling. To accommodate these levels of multiplexing, LAP-D employs a two-part address, consisting of a *terminal endpoint identifier* (TEI) and a *service access point identifier* (SAPI). Typically, each user device is given a unique TEI. It is also possible for a single device to be assigned more than one TEI. This might be the case for a terminal concentrator. The SAPI identifies traffic type.

A detailed discussion of LAP-D will be included in the volume of this series dealing with ISDN standards.

4.7   ISO DATA LINK SERVICE DEFINITION

The standards discussed above (HDLC, MLP, LLC, and LAP-D) are specifications for data link protocols. With the exception of LAP-D, which is new, all are well established and widely implemented. In keeping with the OSI model, a service definition as well as a protocol specification is needed. Accordingly, ISO has developed a data link service definition [DIS 8886]. This service definition is intended to be independent of any particular data link protocol, and to be usable with any of the protocols described above.

Two types of data link service are defined. The connection-mode service provides for the establishment of a logical connection, the negotiation of quality of service, the reliable transfer of data, and an expedited data service. The connectionless-mode service provides for the transfer of a data unit without the establishment of a logical connection. In general, the connectionless-mode service may perform any of the following actions:

- Discard data units
- Duplicate data units
- Deliver data units in a different order than they were presented by the user

The standard specifies that the above actions may be disallowed by prior agreement between the data link service user and the data link service. In this latter case, the service is substantially that of the acknowledged connectionless service of LLC.

The data link services are specified in terms of primitives, which can be viewed as commands or procedure calls with parameters. Table 4.3 lists these primitives.

The connection-mode service consists of six primitive types and a total of 15 different primitives. The first two primitive types are concerned with connection management. The DL-CONNECT primitives are used to establish a connection. The expedited data selection parameter indicates the use/availability of the expedited data service. The quality of service parameter set includes throughput and transit delay; these are negotiated as follows:

1. The calling data link service user specifies a desired and least-acceptable value in a request primitive.
2. If the data link service cannot provide service in the acceptable range, it rejects the connection request with a DL-DISCON-NECT.indication to the calling user. Otherwise, the service issues a DL-CONNECT.indication primitive to the called user with a parameter value that the service is willing to provide and

Table 4.3.   ISO DATA LINK SERVICE PRIMITIVES

Connection-Mode Primitives

DL-CONNECT.request (Called Address, Calling Address, Expedited Data Selection, Quality of Service Parameter Set)

DL-CONNECT.indication (Called Address, Calling Address, Expedited Data Selection, Quality of Service Parameter Set)

DL-CONNECT.response (Responding Address, Expedited Data Selection, Quality of Service Parameter Set)

DL-CONNECT.confirm (Responding Address, Expedited Data Selection, Quality of Service Parameter Set)

DL-DISCONNECT.request (Originator, Reason)
DL-DISCONNECT.indication (Originator, Reason)

DL-DATA.request (User-Data)
DL-DATA.indication (User-Data)

DL-EXPEDITED-DATA.request (User-Data)
DL-EXPEDITED-DATA.indication (User-Data)

DL-RESET.request (Originator, Reason)
DL-RESET.indication (Originator, Reason)
DL-RESET.response
DL-RESET.confirm

DL-ERROR-REPORT.indication (Reason)

Connectionless-Mode Primitives

DL-UNITDATA.request (Source Address, Destination Address, Quality of Service, User Data)
DL-UNITDATA.indication (Source Address, Destination Address, Quality of Service, User Data)

---

a least-acceptable value that is identical to that specified in the request primitive.

3. If the called user rejects the offered range of parameter values, it issues a DL-DISCONNECT.request. Otherwise, it issues a DL-CONNECT.response with a selected value that is in the allowable range.

4. The data link service issues a confirm primitive to the calling user and supplies the selected value.

DL-DISCONNECT provides for an abrupt connection termination; there is no guarantee that all outstanding data units have been delivered. Termination can be initiated by either side or by one of the data link protocol entities. The primitive is also used to reject a connection request.

The next two primitive types are concerned with data transfer over a data-link connection. In the case of expedited data, the data link service attempts to deliver the data as quickly as possible, and need not obey normal flow control constraints. The reset primitives are used to clear a connection, discarding any outstanding data units; this will unblock the flow in the case of congestion. Finally, the error report primitive is used to notify the user of the occurrence of an error situation that could cause a loss of data being transferred.

The connectionless-mode service consists of a single primitive type. Each data unit is handled independently.

APPENDIX 4A.   CYCLIC REDUNDANCY CHECK

The error control mechanism used in HDLC and many other data link protocols is based on the use of an error-detecting code and procedure (see Fig. 2.5). By far, the most widespread code used for data link protocols is the CRC. The use of this code can be explained as follows. Given a k-bit frame or message, the transmitter generates an n-bit sequence, known as a *frame check sequence* (FCS) so that the resulting frame, consisting of $k + n$ bits is exactly divisible by some predetermined number. The receiver then divides the incoming frame by the same number and, if there is no remainder, assumes that there was no error.

To clarify the above, we present the procedure in several ways:

- Modulo 2 arithmetic
- Polynomials
- Shift registers and exclusive-or gates

First, we work with binary numbers and modulo 2 arithmetic. Modulo 2 arithmetic uses binary addition with no carries, which is just the exclusive-or operation.

Examples:

$$
\begin{array}{r}
1111 \\
+\,1010 \\
\hline
0101
\end{array}
\qquad
\begin{array}{r}
11001 \\
\times\quad 11 \\
\hline
11001 \\
11001 \\
\hline
101011
\end{array}
$$

Now define:

$T = (k + n)$-bit frame to be transmitted, with $n < k$

$M = k$-bit message, the first k bits of T

F = n-bit FCS, the last n bits of T
P = pattern of $n + 1$ bits; this is the predetermined divisor mentioned above

We would like T/P to have no remainder. It should be clear that

$$T = 2^n M + F$$

That is, by multiplying M by 2^n, we have in effect shifted it to the left by n bits and padded out the result with 0's. Adding F gives us the concatenation of M and F, which is T. Now we want T to be exactly divisible by P. Suppose that we divided $2^n M$ by P:

$$\frac{2^n M}{P} = Q + \frac{R}{P} \tag{4.1}$$

There is a quotient and a remainder. Since division is binary, the remainder is always one bit less than the divisor. We will use this remainder as our FCS. Then

$$T = 2^n M + R$$

Question: Does this R satisfy our condition? To see that it does, consider

$$\frac{T}{P} = \frac{2^n M + R}{P}$$

substituting eq. 4.1, we have

$$\frac{T}{P} = Q + \frac{R}{P} + \frac{R}{P}$$

However, any binary number added to itself modulo 2 yields zero. Thus

$$\frac{T}{P} = Q + \frac{R + R}{P} = Q$$

There is no remainder, and therefore, T is exactly divisible by P. Thus, the FCS is easily generated. Simply divide $2^n M$ by P and use the remainder as the FCS. On reception, the receiver will divide T by P and will get no remainder if there have been no errors.

A simple example of the procedure is now presented:

1. Given

$$\text{Message } M = 110011 \text{ (6 bits)}$$
$$\text{Pattern } P = 11001 \text{ (5 bits)}$$
$$\text{FCS } R = \text{ to be calculated (4 bits)}$$

2. The message is multiplied by 2^4, yielding 1100110000.

3. This product is divided by P:

$$
\begin{array}{r}
100001 \leftarrow Q \\
P \rightarrow 11001 \overline{\smash{)}\ 1100110000 \leftarrow 2^n M} \\
\underline{11001} \\
10000 \\
\underline{11001} \\
1001 \leftarrow R
\end{array}
$$

4. The remainder is added to $2^n M$ to give $T = 1100111001$, which is transmitted.
5. If there are no errors, the receiver receives T intact. The received frame is divided by P:

$$
\begin{array}{r}
100001 \\
11001 \overline{\smash{)}\ 1100111001} \\
\underline{11001} \\
11001 \\
\underline{11001} \\
00000
\end{array}
$$

Since there is no remainder, it is assumed that there have been no errors.

The pattern P is chosen to be one bit longer than the desired FCS, and the exact bit pattern chosen depends on the type of errors expected. At minimum, both the high- and low-order bits of P must be 1.

The occurrence of an error is easily expressed. An error results in the reversal of a bit. Mathematically, this is equivalent to taking the exclusive-or of the bit and 1: $0 + 1 = 1$; $1 + 1 = 0$. Thus the errors in an $(n + k)$-bit frame can be represented by an $(n + k)$-bit field with 1's in each error position. The resulting frame T_r can be expressed as

$$
T_r = T + E
$$

where T = transmitted frame
        E = error pattern with 1's in positions where errors occur
        T_r = received frame

The receiver will fail to detect an error if and only if T_r is divisible by P, that is, if and only if E is divisible by P. Intuitively, this seems an unlikely occurrence.

A second way of viewing the CRC process is to express all values as polynomials in a dummy variable X with binary coefficients. The coefficients correspond to the bits in the binary number. Thus for $M = 110011$, we have $M(X) = X^5 + X^4 + X + 1$, and for $P = 11001$, we have $P(X) = X^4 + X^3 + 1$. Arithmetic operations are again modulo 2. The CRC process can now be described as:

1. $\dfrac{X^n M(X)}{P(X)} = Q(X) + \dfrac{R(X)}{P(X)}$

2. $T(X) = X^n M(X) + R(X)$

An error $E(X)$ will only be undetectable if it is divisible by $P(X)$. It can be shown [PETE61] that all of the following are not divisible by $P(X)$ and hence are detectable:

1. All single-bit errors
2. All double-bit errors, as long as $P(X)$ has a factor with at least three terms
3. Any odd number of errors, as long as $P(X)$ contains a factor $(X + 1)$
4. Any burst error for which the length of the burst is less than the length of the FCS
5. Most larger burst errors

The first assertion is clear. A single-bit error can be represented by $E(X) = X^i$ for some i. We have said that for $P(X)$ both the first and last terms must be nonzero. Thus $P(X)$ has at least two terms and cannot divide the one-term $E(X)$. Similarly, a two-bit error can be represented by $E(X) = X^i + X^j = X^i(1 + X^{j-i})$ for some i and j with $i > j$. Thus $P(X)$ must divide either X^i or $(1 + X^{j-i})$. We have shown that it does not divide X^i, and it can be shown [PETE61] that it does not divide $(1 + X^{j-i})$ except for very large values of $j - i$, beyond the practical frame length. To see the third assertion, assume that $E(X)$ has an odd number of terms and is divisible by $(X + 1)$. Then we can express $E(X)$ as $E(X) = (X + 1)F(X)$. Then $E(1) = (1 + 1)F(1) = 0$ since $1 + 1 = 0$. But $E(1)$ will be 0 if and only if $E(X)$ contains an even number of terms. For the fourth assertion, we define a burst of length j as a string of bits beginning and ending with 1 and containing intervening 1's and 0's. This can be represented as $E(X) = X^i(X^{j-1} + \ldots + 1)$ where i expresses how far the burst is shifted from the right-hand end. We know that $P(X)$ does not divide X^i. For $j < n$, where n is the length of the FCS, $P(X)$ will not divide the second factor, since $P(X)$ is of higher order.

Finally, it can be shown that if all error patterns are considered equally likely, then for a burst of length $r + 1$, the probability that $E(X)$ is divisible by $P(X)$ is $1/2^{r-1}$, and for a longer burst, the probability is $1/2^r$ [PETE61].

Four versions of $P(X)$ are widely used:

$$\text{CRC-12} = X^{12} + X^{11} + X^3 + X^2 + X + 1$$
$$\text{CRC-16} = X^{16} + X^{15} + X^2 + 1$$
$$\text{CRC-CCITT} = X^{16} + X^{12} + X^5 + 1$$

$$CRC\text{-}32 = X^{32} + X^{26} + X^{23} + X^{22} + X^{16} + X^{12} +$$
$$X^{11} + X^{10} + X^8 + X^7 + X^5 + X^4 + X^2 + X + 1$$

The CRC-12 system is used for transmission of streams of 6-bit characters and generates a 12-bit FCS. Both CRC-16 and CRC-CCITT are popular for 8-bit characters, in the United States and Europe, respectively, and both result in a 16-bit FCS. This would seem adequate for most applications, although CRC-32 is specified as an option in some point-to-point synchronous transmission standards. CRC-CCITT and CRC-32 are the two versions used in HDLC.

As a final representation, Fig. 4.13 shows that the CRC process can be easily implemented with shift registers and exclusive-or gates. In a

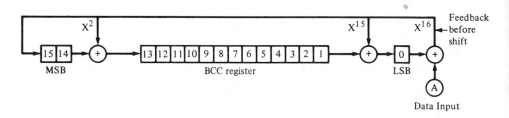

Shift no.			13	12	11	10	9	8	7	6	5	4	3	2	1				
Start	0	0	0	0	0	0	0	0	0	0	0	0	0	0	0	0	–		1
1	1	0	1	0	0	0	0	0	0	0	0	0	0	0	0	1	1 LSB		1	Arrows indicate
2	1	1	1	1	0	0	0	0	0	0	0	0	0	0	0	1	0		1	exclusive–or of
3	1	1	0	1	1	0	0	0	0	0	0	0	0	0	0	1	0		1	data bit and LSB
4	1	1	0	0	1	1	0	0	0	0	0	0	0	0	0	1	0		1	of BCC register
5	1	1	0	0	0	1	1	0	0	0	0	0	0	0	0	1	0		1	prior to shift
6	1	1	0	0	0	0	1	1	0	0	0	0	0	0	0	1	0		1	
7	1	1	0	0	0	0	0	1	1	0	0	0	0	0	0	1	0		1	
8	1	1	0	0	0	0	0	0	1	1	0	0	0	0	0	1	0		1	
9	1	1	0	0	0	0	0	0	0	1	1	0	0	0	0	1	0		1	
10	1	1	0	0	0	0	0	0	0	0	1	1	0	0	0	1	0		1	
11	1	1	0	0	0	0	0	0	0	0	0	1	1	0	0	1	0		1	
12	1	1	0	0	0	0	0	0	0	0	0	0	1	1	0	1	0		1	
13	1	1	0	0	0	0	0	0	0	0	0	0	0	1	1	1	0		1	
14	1	1	0	0	0	0	0	0	0	0	0	0	0	0	1	0	0		0	
15	0	1	1	0	0	0	0	0	0	0	0	0	0	0	0	1	0		1	
16	1	0	0	1	0	0	0	0	0	0	0	0	0	0	0	1	0 MSB		1	

Block check character (bcc) — 16 bit data word

NOTES:

▫ = BCC register stage

⊕ = Exclusive–or

CRC–16 Polynomial = $X^{16} + X^{15} + X^2 + 1$

LSB = Least significant bit of register (sent first)

MSB = Most significant bit of register (sent last)

Figure 4.13.   CRC-16 implemented with shift registers and exclusive-or gates.

transmitter, the shift registers are initialized to all 0's. As each bit of M is transmitted, it is also applied to the point marked A in the figure, and a shifting pulse is applied to the register. The figure shows the state of the system after 16 bits have been transmitted. After the last bit of M is transmitted, the shift register contains the FCS, or R, which can then be transmitted.

At the receiver, the same logic is used. As each bit of M arrives it is inserted into the shift register at A. If there have been no errors, the shift register should contain the bit pattern for R at the conclusion of M. The transmitted bits of R now begin to arrive, and the effect is to zero out the register so that, at the conclusion of reception, the register contains all 0's.

The shift register implementation makes clear the power of the CRC algorithm. Due to the feedback arrangement, the state of the shift register depends, in a complex way, on the past history of bits presented. Thus it will take an extremely rare combination of errors to fool the system. Further, it is evident that the CRC algorithm is easy to implement in hardware.

chapter 5

Network Layer: Subnetwork Interface

The structure of the network layer is perhaps the most complex in the OSI model [WARE83]. The network layer provides a means of transmitting data units across any sort of network or even a *network of networks*. Thus, the network layer needs to deal with a variety of network types and with the various services that may be offered by different networks. To avoid confusion, the communication networks that are used to interconnect open systems are called *subnetworks*. Unlike the other OSI layers, a network layer entity is dependent not only on the services provided by the next lower layer (in this case, the data link layer), but also on the services of the intervening subnetwork or subnetworks.

Protocols and services for the network layer have evolved in a manner that reflects this complexity. Initial efforts at standardization have focused on the case in which a single subnetwork intervenes between open systems. Usually, the services offered in this case are connection oriented. More recent efforts have considered the case of multiple independent subnetworks interconnected with each other and supporting a number of open systems. Both connection-oriented and connectionless approaches have been standardized for this latter case.

In this chapter, we concentrate on the case of a single subnet-

work. We begin, as usual, with a summary of the OSI layer specification, in this case for layer 3. Then we show that the layer 3 protocol for use over a single subnetwork depends on the key issue of
how to interface to the subnetwork. Next, a very common layer 3
protocol is examined: X.25. Finally, the ISO connection-oriented
network service is examined. An appendix provides a brief tutorial
on packet-switched networks, for which the X.25 protocol is
intended.

5.1 OSI DEFINITION

The OSI document characterizes the network layer as providing the
means to establish, maintain, and terminate network connections and to
exchange network service data units (NSDUs) between transport entities.
It provides the transport entities with independence from the details of
the intervening subnetwork or subnetworks, including consideration of
the routing and relaying functions required to transmit data units across
subnetworks.

Table 5.1 lists the services and functions of the network layer. Several services warrant elaboration. A *network address* is needed for the
transport entity to uniquely identify other end open systems with which
it wishes to communicate. This is a deceptively complex topic and is explored in Chap. 6. The *expedited data service* provides a means for ex-
pediting the delivery of occasional urgent data. Some data submitted by
the transport entity may supersede data submitted previously. Examples
are an interrupt, an alarm, or an abrupt connection termination. The network service will endeavor to have the expedited data transmitted across
the intervening subnetwork or subnetworks as rapidly as possible, perhaps overtaking some previously transmitted ordinary data. The *reset service* allows the transport entity to abort the current activity without losing
the network connection to the other end. Some data units in transit may
be lost, and both sides may begin again to transmit data units over the
connection.

The functions of the network layer are those required to support the
services offered to the transport layer. Some of the listed functions illus-
trate the complexities and issues that exist at this layer. In transmitting
data across a network, *routing and relaying functions,* which operate at
layer 3, are needed. The discussion on packet-switched networks in the
Appendix to this chapter demonstrates this. A packet-switched network
consists of a set of packet-switched nodes interconnected by data links.
Data transmitted from one open system to another across the network
must be routed through a series of nodes. Each node receives a data unit
on an incoming link and relays it to an outgoing link heading toward the
destination. Logic is needed at each of these intermediate nodes to per-

Table 5.1.   SERVICES AND FUNCTIONS OF THE NETWORK LAYER

	Services
Network addresses	Used to uniquely identify transport entities
Network connections	Connection of transport entities
Network connection endpoint identifiers	Identifies connection at SAP
Network SDU transfer	Exchange of SDUs
Quality of service parameters	Optionally selectable
Error Notification	Unrecoverable errors are reported
Sequencing	Ordered delivery
Flow Control	Control of SDU rate
Expedited NSDU transfer	Expedited handling of SDUs; normal flow control mechanisms are bypassed
Reset	NSDUs in transit are discarded and the logical connection is reinitialized
Release	Network connection is released and the transport entity at the other end is notified
	Functions
Routing and relaying	Intermediate open systems may provide relaying; a route through these is determined
Network connections	Using data-link connection or tandem subnetwork connections
Network connection multiplexing	Multiple network connections onto a data-link connection or subnetwork connection
Segmenting and blocking	NSDUs may be segmented or blocked to facilitate transfer
Error detection	Uses data link error notification and additional mechanisms
Error recovery	Recovery from detected errors
Sequencing	Ordered delivery
Flow control	Between network entities
Expedited data transfer	Supports expedited data service
Reset	Supports the reset service
Service selection	Ensures that the service is the same at each end of a network connection that spans several dissimilar networks
Network layer management	Management activities related to the network layer

form the routing and relaying functions. These functions are clearly above the data link layer and, to provide a transparent service to the transport layer, must be below the transport layer. Hence, each intermediate node performs layer 3 functions (see Fig. 2.12). Thus, whereas operations at other layers generally involve only two entities in two end systems, at layer 3 there may be a number of network entities that act as a sort of bucket brigade to pass data from source to destination. We will also see these concepts in Chap. 6.

To provide for a *network connection* between transport entities, the network layer may make use of a logical connection across a network. An example of this is a virtual circuit across a packet-switched network; this case is examined in this chapter. If several networks in tandem are required to connect source and destination, then tandem subnetwork connections may be used. This latter case raises several issues. If the subnetworks involved employ the same subnetwork protocols and offer the same quality of service, then it is a simple matter to concatenate subnetwork connections to form an end-to-end (transport entity to transport entity) connection. This technique is illustrated with X.75, which is examined in Chap. 6. If the subnetworks are of differing qualities, then interconnection may be achieved in one of two ways, as depicted in Fig. 5.1:

- The two subnetworks are interconnected as they stand. The quality of the resulting network connection is no higher than the lower-quality subnetwork service.
- Mechanisms in the network layer are used to enhance the lower quality subnetwork so that the overall service is approximately the same as that of the higher quality subnetwork service.

These considerations apply in the case of a connection-oriented network service. As we shall see in Chap. 6, a more flexible approach is provided by using a connectionless network service and relying on the transport layer to provide enhanced services as needed.

5.2 THE NETWORK INTERFACE

Communication across a subnetwork between two processes in separate systems can be thought of as involving two types of entities: the systems that contain the processes and the systems that manage communications across the network. The former are the *open systems* that are the focus of this text, and contain the seven layers of the OSI model. The latter are part of the communication network (e.g., packet-switching nodes) and require only layers 1 through 3 of the OSI model. CCITT recommendations refer to these two entities as DTEs and DCEs, respectively.

Consider now the nature of the interaction between a DCE and a

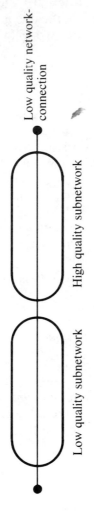

(a) Interconnection of a low quality subnetwork and a high quality subnetwork

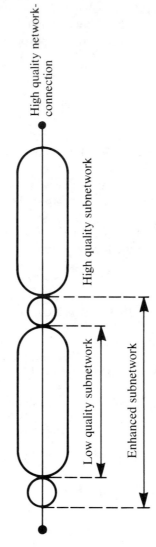

(b) Interconnection of an enhanced low quality subnetwork and a high quality subnetwork

Figure 5.1. OSI network connections.

110

DTE. In OSI terms, the transport layer is *DTE-oriented*, providing an end-to-end service. The network layer is responsible for making use of the subnetwork facilities to route data from source to destination. Thus, this layer is DTE-oriented in the sense that it is concerned with transferring data between source and destination DTEs, and it is DCE-oriented in the sense that it deals with the actions of the DCE to which the DTE is attached. How do these concepts relate to the DCE–DTE interaction?

Figure 2.12 depicts the relationship. Between the DTE and the DCE to which it is attached, a protocol is needed by which the DTE can invoke the services of the subnetwork and by which data units are exchanged. The operation is as follows. The data that originate at the application layer plus all the headers generated by layers 7 through 4 are treated as a unit (network service data unit) by layer 3 in the DTE. Layer 3 has the responsibility of routing this data unit to the destination DTE. It does this by means of a protocol with the local DCE at layer 3. Of course, to transmit a layer 3 data unit from DTE to DCE, a data link (layer 2) over a physical link (layer 1) is needed. Hence, the DTE–DCE interaction consists of protocols at layers 1, 2, and 3. The local DCE uses a different set of protocols to route the data unit through the subnetwork to the destination DCE, which in turn has a layer 1, 2, 3 set of protocols with the destination DTE. In CCITT jargon, this set of protocols between DTE and DCE is known as a DTE–DCE interface.

The nature of the DTE–DCE interface depends, of course, on the nature of the subnetwork and on whether connectionless or connection-oriented service is used. In this chapter, we examine the common case of interfacing to a packet-switched network, for which the X.25 standard is typically used.

5.3   X.25

One of the most important types of subnetworks used in data communications is the packet-switched network. We begin this section with a brief discussion of the requirements for interfacing an open system to a packet-switched network. Then, we examine the most common standard for such an interface: CCITT Recommendation X.25 [DHAS86]. The Appendix to this chapter briefly discusses the internal operation of a packet-switched network.

Requirements

Transmission of data across a packet-switched network involves the use of packets. In OSI terms, a packet is equivalent to a network protocol data unit (NPDU). Packets contain not only user data intended for another DTE on the network, but also control information by means of which the attached DTE and the network communicate.

Consider the requirements that must be met by the protocols between the attached device and the network. Of course there needs to physical and data link control protocols to move data between the attached device and the network. Other functions are needed, and these are at the network layer.

At minimum, the network layer protocol must provide a service for transferring data between DTEs. This service may be either a virtual-circuit service (connection-oriented) or a datagram service (connectionless). Most public networks provide a virtual-circuit service. Additional functions that must be performed by the network-layer protocol include:

- Flow control
- Error control
- Multiplexing

Flow control is needed in both directions. The network must protect itself from congestion, and to do this it may need to limit the flow of packets from the attached DTEs. Similarly, a DTE needs to be able to control the rate at which the network delivers packets to it. The network allocates resources to maintain that data rate. The stations may use flow control end-to-end or at the data link to limit data flow.

Because DTE and DCE are exchanging control information as well as data, some form of *error control* is needed to assure that all of the control information is received properly.

Finally, most packet-switched networks provide a *multiplexing* service. With this service, a station can establish multiple virtual circuits with other stations at the same time.

Figure 5.2 depicts the protocol architecture implied by these requirements. Each node, including intermediate nodes, performs functions up through layer 3. We now turn to a specific example that should help clarify Fig. 5.2.

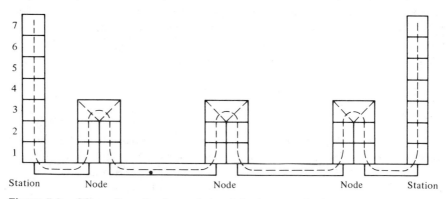

Figure 5.2.   OSI configuration for packet-switched communication.

A Packet-Switched Network Access Standard: X.25

Perhaps the best known and widely used protocol standard is X.25, which was originally approved in 1976 (and has been revised twice since, in 1980 and 1984). This standard specifies a DTE–DCE interface. In the case of X.25, the DCE provides access to a packet-switched network. The standard specifically calls out three levels (Fig. 5.3):

- Physical level
- Link level
- Packet level

For the physical level, the physical level portion of X.21 is specified. Optionally (and at present most commonly), X.21 *bis* may be used; this is similar to RS-232-C. The link level makes use of LAP-B over a single physical link between DTE and DCE. LAP-B is a subset of the asynchronous balanced mode of HDLC. Optionally, there may be multiple physical links between a DTE and its DCE. In that case, LAP-B is used on each individual physical link and the ISO multilink procedures (MLP) is used as the upper sublayer of the link level. This section is devoted to a discussion of the packet level.

The packet level specifies a *virtual-circuit service*. A compatible version of the packet level standard has been issued by ISO [ISO 8208]. A variety of packet types are used (Table 5.2) all using the same basic format, with variations (Fig. 5.4).

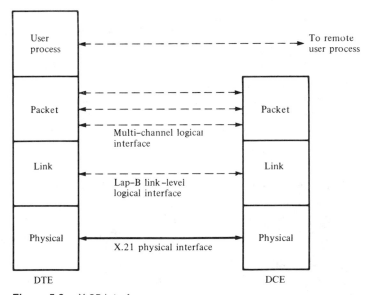

Figure 5.3.   X.25 interface.

Table 5.2. X.25 PACKET TYPES

Packet type		Service	
From DCE to DTE	From DTE to DCE	VC	PVC
Call Setup and Clearing			
Incoming call	Call request	X	
Call connected	Call accepted	X	
Clear indication	Clear request	X	
DCE clear confirmation	DTE clear confirmation	X	
Data and Interrupt			
DCE data	DTE data	X	X
DCE interrupt	DTE interrupt	X	X
DCE interrupt confirmation	DTE interrupt confirmation	X	X
Flow Control and Reset			
DCE RR	DTE RR	X	X
DCE RNR	DTE RNR	X	X
	DTE REJ	X	X
Reset indication	Reset request	X	X
DCE reset confirmation	DTE reset confirmation	X	X
Restart			
Restart indication	Restart request	X	X
DCE restart confirmation	DTE restart confirmation	X	X
Diagnostic			
Diagnostic		X	X
Registration			
Registration confirmation	Registration request	X	X

The virtual circuit service of X.25 provides for two types of virtual circuit: virtual call and permanent virtual call. A *virtual call* is a dynamically established virtual circuit using a call setup and call clearing procedure. A permanent virtual circuit is a permanent, network-assigned virtual circuit. Data transfer occurs as with virtual calls, but no call setup or clearing is required.

The X.25 virtual-circuit service is quite complex. We begin by describing a typical sequence of events for the progress of a virtual call. Then we examine each of the key features of X.25.

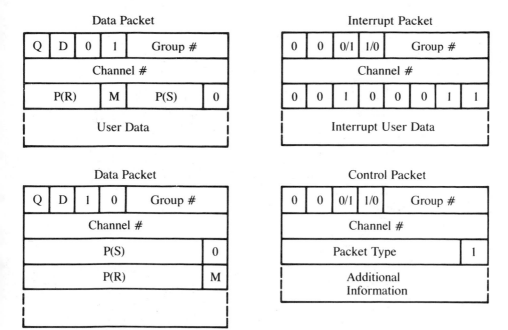

Figure 5.4.   X.25 packet formats.

Virtual Calls.   Figure 5.5 shows a typical sequence of events in a virtual call. The left-hand part of the figure shows the packets exchanged between DTE A and its DCE; the right-hand part shows the packets exchanged between DTE B and its DCE. The routing of packets between the DCEs is the responsibility of the internal logic of the network.

The sequence of events is as follows:

1. *A* requests a virtual circuit to *B* by sending a Call Request packet to its DCE. The packet includes a virtual circuit number (group, channel), as well as source and destination addresses. Future incoming and outgoing data transfers will be identified by the virtual circuit number.
2. The network routes this call request to *B*'s DCE.
3. *B*'s DCE receives the call request and sends an Incoming Call packet to *B*. This packet has the same format as the Call Request packet but a different virtual circuit number, selected by *B*'s DCE from the set of locally unused numbers.
4. *B* indicates acceptance of the call by sending a Call Accepted packet specifying the same virtual circuit number as that of the Call Indication packet.
5. *A* receives a Call Connected packet with the same virtual circuit number as that of the Call Request packet.
6. *A* and *B* send data and control packets using their respective virtual circuit numbers.

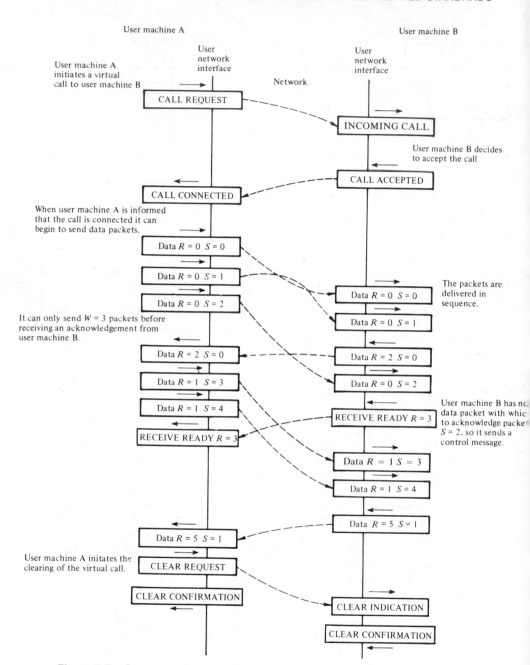

Figure 5.5. Sequence of events—X.25 virtual call.

7. *A* (or *B*) sends a Clear Request packet to terminate the virtual circuit and receives a local Clear Confirmation packet.
8. *B* (or *A*) receives a Clear Indication packet and transmits a Clear Confirmation packet.

We point out that this DTE–DCE interface is asymmetric. That is, only selected layer 3 protocol information is transferred end-to-end between subscriber DTEs. Much of the information, such as flow control and acknowledgment, usually has only local significance; however, see below.

The way in which data are encapsulated is of some interest. The transmitting DTE must break its data up into units of some maximum length. X.25 specifies that network must support a maximum user field length of at least 128 octets (i.e., the user data field may be some number of bits up to the maximum). In addition, the network may allow selection of some other maximum field length in the range 16 to 4096 octets. The length may differ for the two ends of the virtual circuit. The DTE constructs control packets and encapsulates data in data packets. These are then transmitted to the DCE via LAP-B. Thus the packet is encapsulated in a layer 2 frame (one packet per frame). The DCE strips off the layer 2 header and trailer and may encapsulate the packet according to some internal network protocol.

The description above is the essence of the X.25 virtual circuit service. We now turn to the details, in the following categories:

- Packet format
- Multiplexing
- Flow control
- Packet sequences
- Reset and restart
- Interrupt packets
- Call progress signals
- User facilities

Packet Format.   There are two basic types of packet formats: data packets and control packets (see Fig. 5.4). In addition to user data, a data packet includes the virtual circuit number, the send and receive sequence numbers, and the M, D, and Q bits. The M and D bits are described below. The Q bit is not defined in the standard, but allows the user to distinguish two types of data.

Control packets include a virtual circuit number, a packet type identifier, and additional information pertinent to the particular control function. For example, a CALL REQUEST packet includes the following additional fields:

- Calling DTE address length (4 bits): Length of the corresponding address field in semi-octets.

- Called DTE address length (4 bits): Length of the corresponding address field in semi-octets.
- DTE addresses (variable): The calling and called DTE addresses.
- Facility length (16 bits): length of the facilities field in octets.
- Facilities: This field contains a sequence of facility specifications. Each specification consists of an 8-bit facility code and zero or more parameter codes.

Another example of a control packet is the interrupt packet, also shown in Fig. 5.4. Table 5.3 lists the parameters for all of the X.25 control packets.

Table 5.3. X.25 CONTROL PACKET TYPES AND PARAMETERS

Packet Type	Parameters
Call Request	Calling DTE address, Called DTE address, Facilities, Call user data
Incoming Call	Calling DTE address, Called DTE address, Facilities, Call user data
Call Accepted	Calling DTE address, Called DTE address, Facilities, Called user data
Call Connected	Calling DTE address, Called DTE address, Facilities, Called user data
Clear Request	Clearing cause, Diagnostic code, Calling DTE address, Called DTE address, Facilities, Clear user data
Clear Indication	Clearing cause, Diagnostic code, Calling DTE address, Called DTE address, Facilities, Clear user data
Clear Confirmation	Calling DTE address, Called DTE address, Facilities
Interrupt	Interrupt user data
Interrupt Confirmation	—
RR	P(R)
RNR	P(R)
REJ	P(R)
Reset Request	Resetting cause, Diagnostic code
Reset Indication	Resetting cause, Diagnostic code
Reset Confirmation	—
Restart Request	Restarting cause, Diagnostic code
Restart Indication	Restarting cause, Diagnostic code
Restart Confirmation	—
Diagnostic	Diagnostic code, Diagnostic explanation
Registration Request	DTE address, DCE address, Registration
Registration Confirmation	Cause, Diagnostic, DCE address, DTE address, Registration

Multiplexing. Perhaps the most important service provided by X.25 is multiplexing. A DTE is allowed by its DCE to establish up to 4095 simultaneous virtual circuits with other DTEs over a single physical DTE–DCE link. The DTE can internally assign these circuits in any way it pleases. Individual circuits could correspond to applications, processes, or terminals for example. The DTE–DCE link provides full-duplex statistical multiplexing. That is, at any time a packet associated with a given virtual circuit can be transmitted in either direction.

To sort out which packets belong to which virtual circuit, each packet contains a 12-bit virtual circuit number (expressed as a 4-bit logical group number plus an 8-bit logical channel number). The assignment of virtual-circuit numbers follows the convention depicted in Fig. 5.6. Number zero is always reserved for restart and diagnostic packets common to all virtual circuits. If only a single virtual circuit is allowed (no multiplex-

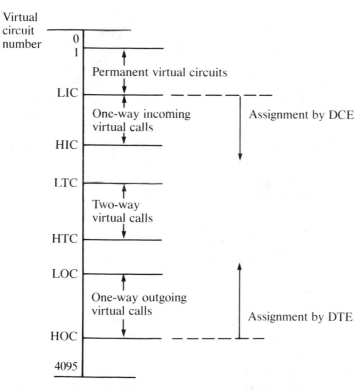

LIC = Lowest incoming channel
HIC = Highest incoming channel
LTC = Lowest two-way channel
HTC = Highest two-way channel
LOC = Lowest outgoing channel
HOC = Highest outgoing channel

Virtual circuit
number = logical group
number + logical channel
number

Figure 5.6. Virtual circuit number assignment.

ing), number 1 is used. Otherwise, contiguous ranges of numbers are allocated for four categories of virtual circuits. Permanent virtual circuits are assigned numbers beginning with 1. The next category is one-way incoming virtual calls. This means that only incoming calls from the network can be assigned these numbers; the circuit, however, is two-way. When a call request comes in, the DCE selects an unused number from this category and places it in the Call Indication packet that it sends to the DTE.

The last category, one-way outgoing virtual calls, is used by the DTE to initiate virtual calls via Call Request packets. Again, the DTE selects an unused number for each new call request. This separation of categories is intended to avoid the simultaneous selection of the same number for two different virtual circuits by the DTE and DCE.

The two-way virtual call category provides an overflow for allocation shared by DTE and DCE. This allows for peak differences in traffic flow.

Flow Control.   Flow control at the X.25 packet level is virtually identical in format and procedure to flow control at the link level. A sliding window protocol is used (see Chap. 4). Normally, each data packet includes a 3-bit packet send sequence number, P(S), and a 3-bit packet receive sequence number, P(R). Optionally, a DTE may request, via the user facility mechanism described below, the use of extended 7-bit sequence numbers. In this case, the extended sequence numbers apply to all virtual circuits of the DTE. P(S) is assigned by the DTE on outgoing packets on a virtual circuit basis. The default window size is 2, but it may be set as high as 7 with the 3-bit field or as high as 127 using a 7-bit field. Incoming data packets on each virtual circuit contain a P(R) that is the number of the next packet expected to be received from the DTE on that virtual circuit. When there are no data packets available for piggybacking, receive ready (RR) and receive not ready (RNR) control packets may be used, with the same meaning as for HDLC. Additionally, X.25 specifies an optional DTE REJ packet.

Acknowledgment (in the form of the P(R) field or RR, RNR packets) and hence flow control may have either local or end-to-end significance, based on the setting of the D bit. When D = 0 (the usual case), acknowledgment is being exercised between the DTE and the network. This is used by the DCE and/or the network to acknowledge receipt of packets and control the flow from the DTE into the network. Note from Fig. 5.7A that the acknowledgment may be from the attached DCE or from the remote DCE. In either case, the acknowledgment is said to have *local* (network) significance. When D = 1, acknowledgments come from the remote DTE.

Packet Sequences.   X.25 provides the capability to identify a contiguous sequence of packets, which is called a *complete packet sequence*. This

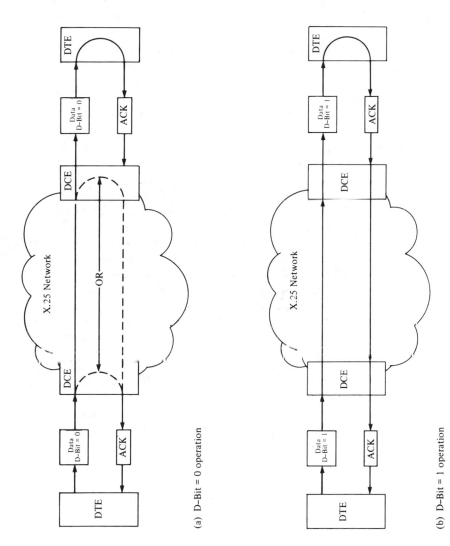

(a) D–Bit = 0 operation

(b) D–Bit = 1 operation

Figure 5.7. Treatment of acknowledgments for data packets.

121

feature has several uses. It can provide a service to higher layers within the DTE. For example, a process may need to segment messages to get down to the allowable packet size, but wishes to keep track of data on a message basis. This technique is also used when the DCE blocks or segments data to conform to network packet size restrictions; this can be useful in internetworking when networks with different packet sizes are connected.

To specify this mechanism, X.25 defines two types of packets: A packets and B packets. An *A packet* is one in which the M bit is set to 1, the D bit is set to 0, and the packet is full (equal to the maximum packet length). A *B packet* is any packet that is not an A packet. Now, a complete packet sequence consists of zero or more A packets followed by a B packet. The network can combine this sequence to make one larger packet. The network may also fragment a B packet into smaller packets to produce a complete packet sequence.

The way in which the B packet is handled depends on the setting of the M and D bits. If D = 1, an end-to-end acknowledgment is sent by the receiving DTE to the sending DTE. This is in effect an acknowledgment of the entire complete packet sequence. M = 1 indicates that there are additional complete packet sequences to follow. This enables the formation of subsequences as part of a larger sequence, so that end-to-end acknowledgment can occur before the end of the larger sequence.

Figure 5.8 shows examples of these concepts. Note that it is the responsibility of the DCEs to reconcile the changes in sequence numbering that segmentation and reassembly cause.

EXAMPLE PACKET SEQUENCES

Original seq.

Pkt type	M	D
A	1	0
A	1	0
A	1	0
A	1	0
A	1	0
B	0	1

Combined seq.

Pkt type	M	D
A	1	0
A	1	0
B	0	1

Segmented seq

	M	D
B	0	0
A	1	0
B	0	0

EXAMPLE PACKET SEQUENCE WITH INTERMEDIATE E-E ACK

Pkt type	M	D	
A	1	0	
A	1	0	*
A	1	0	
B	1	1	
A	1	0	
A	1	0	*
B	1	1	
A	1	0	
A	1	0	*
A	1	0	
B	0	1	

end of sequence

* Groups of packets that can be combined

Figure 5.8. X.25 packet sequences.

Reset and Restart. X.25 provides two facilities for recovering from errors. The reset facility is used to reinitialize a virtual circuit. This means that the sequence numbers on both ends are set to 0. Any data or interrupt packets in transit are lost. It is up to a higher level protocol to recover from the loss of packets.

A reset can be triggered by a number of error conditions, including loss of a packet, sequence number error, congestion, or loss of the network's internal virtual circuit. In this latter case, the two DCEs must rebuild the internal virtual circuit to support the still-existing X.25 DTE–DTE virtual circuit.

Either a DTE or a DCE can initiate a reset, with a *Reset Request* or *Reset Indication*. The recipient responds with a *Reset Confirmation*. Regardless of who indicated the reset, the DCE is responsible for informing the other end.

A more serious error condition calls for a restart. The issuance of a Restart Request packet, which uses virtual circuit 0, is equivalent to sending a Clear Request on *all* active virtual calls and a Reset Request on all active permanent virtual circuits. Again, either DTE or DCE may initiate action. An example of a condition warranting restart is temporary loss of access to the network.

Interrupt Packets. A DTE may send an interrupt packet that bypasses the flow control procedures used for data packets. The packet does not contain send and receive sequence numbers and is not blocked by an RNR or a closed window. The interrupt packet carries up to 32 octets of user data, and is to be delivered to the destination DTE by the network at a higher priority than data packets in transit. An example of the use of this service is to transmit a terminal break character. Confirmation of interrupt packets is end-to-end; that is, the sending DTE receives a confirmation of an interrupt packet only after it has been delivered to the remote DTE. A DTE may not send another interrupt packet on any virtual circuit until the outstanding interrupt packet is confirmed. This prevents flooding the network with packets that are not flow controlled.

Call Progress Signals. X.25 includes provision for call progress signals, and these are defined by X.96 (Table 5.4). The call progress signals fall into two general and overlapping categories. *Clearing call progress signals* are used to indicate the reason why a CALL REQUEST is denied; they are also used to indicate the reason for a CLEAR REQUEST. In both cases, the signal is carried in a CLEAR INDICATION packet.

Resetting call progress signals are used to indicate the reason why a virtual circuit is being reset, or why a restart takes place. The code is contained in a RESET REQUEST, RESET INDICATION, RESTART REQUEST, or RESTART INDICATION packet.

Table 5.4.   PACKET-SWITCHED CALL PROGRESS SIGNALS (X.96)

Signal	VC	PVC	Usage†	Description
	Applicable to:*			
Local Procedure Error	X	X	C, R	Procedure error caused by local DTE
Network Congestion	X	X	C, R	Temporary network congestion or fault
Invalid Facility Request	X		C	Requested user facility not valid
RPOA Out of Order	X		C	Recognized private operating agency unable to forward call
Not Obtainable	X		C	Called DTE address unassigned or unknown
Access Barred	X			Calling DTE not permitted connection to called DTE
Reverse Charging Acceptance Not Subscribed	X		C	Called DTE will not accept charges on collect call
Fast Select Acceptance Not Subscribed	X		C	Called DTE does not support fast select
Incompatible Destination	X		C, R	The remote DTE does not have a function used or a facility requested
Out of Order	X	X	C, R	Remote DTE out of order
Number Busy	X		C	Called DTE is busy
Remote Procedure Error	X	X	C, R	Procedure error caused by remote DTE
Network Operational	X	X	R	Network ready to resume after temporary failure or congestion
Remote DTE Operational		X	R	Remote DTE ready after temporary failure
DTE Originated	X	X	C, R	Remote DTE has refused call or requested reset
Ship absent	X		C	Called ship absent (used with mobile maritime service)
Network Out of Order		X	R	Network temporarily unable to handle data traffic
Registration cancellation confirmed	X	X	R	Facility request confirmed

*VC, virtual call; PVC, permanent virtual circuit.
†C. clearing call progress signal: R, resetting or restarting call progress signal.

User Facilities. X.25 provides for the use of optional user facilities. These are facilities that may be provided by the network and that may, at the user's option, be employed by a particular user. Some facilities are selectable for use for an agreed period of time. Other facilities are requested on a per-virtual-call basis, as part of the Call Request packet; with these facilities, the capability or value applies only to the one virtual call.

The facilities that may be provided are defined in X.2, which contains a rather long list. Some of these are termed *essential*. Essential facilities must be offered by the network, although their use is optional (Table 5.5). The remaining facilities are termed *additional,* and need not be offered by the network.

Finally, a network may provide facilities not specified in X.2 and X.25; these, of course, are beyond the scope of the standard.

Table 5.5. ESSENTIAL OPTIONAL PACKET-SWITCHED USER FACILITIES (X.2)

Assigned for an Agreed Contractual Period	
Flow Control Parameter Negotiation	This facility permits negotiation on a per call basis of the window size and maximum user data field length to be used on that call in each direction
Throughput Class Negotiation	This facility permits negotiation on a per call basis of the throughput of data that can be transferred on a virtual circuit. The range of values is 75 bps to 48 Kbps
Closed User Group	This enables the DTE to belong to one or more closed user groups. A closed user group permits the DTEs belonging to the group to communicate with each other but precludes communication with all other DTEs. Thus members are protected by the network from unauthorized access. A DTE may belong to one or more closed user groups
Fast Select Acceptance	This facility authorizes the DCE to transmit to the DTE incoming Fast Select calls. Without such authorization, the DCE blocks such incoming calls. This is useful to prevent the enlarged Fast Select packets from being delivered to a DTE that has not implemented Fast Select

Table 5.5   (continued)

Incoming Calls Barred	This facility prevents incoming calls from being presented to the DTE
Outgoing Calls Barred	This facility prevents the DCE from accepting outgoing virtual calls
One-way Logical Channel Outgoing	This facility sets the Lowest Outgoing Channel boundary (Figure 5.6). A subscriber reserves a number of logical channels in this fashion to match an expected or desired pattern of calls
Requested on a Per-Virtual Call Basis	
Flow Control Parameter Negotiation	When a DTE has subscribed to this facility, it may, in a CALL REQUEST packet, separately request user data field sizes and window sizes. The DCE indicates its acceptance or modification of these values in the CALL CONNECTED packet. The DCE may modify window size requests in the direction of $W = 2$, and may modify user data field size requests in the direction of 128 octets
Throughput Class Negotiation	Operates in a manner similar to Flow Control Parameter Negotiation. The DCE may revise the proposed values in either direction to values smaller than those requested
Closed User Group Selection	When a DTE has subscribed to this facility, it may, in a CALL REQUEST packet, indicate the closed user group applicable to this call. Similarly, the DCE can indicate the closed user group applicable to an incoming call in a INCOMING CALL packet
Fast Select	The DTE may employ the fast select facility
Transit Delay Selection and Identification	The DTE may request a particular transit delay that the network will attempt to meet

Fast Select Facility. The X.25 standard was initially intended to be purely a virtual-circuit service. In response to demand for connectionless network service, two capabilities were included in the 1980 standard: datagram service and the fast select facility. Because of a complete lack of support for the datagram service, it was subsequently dropped in the 1984 edition of the standard.

The fast select facility is designed to handle transaction-oriented applications in which at least one and sometimes only one inquiry and response take place. The virtual call mechanism is used with the following adjustment. To use fast select, a DTE requests the fast select facility in the facilities field of the Call Request packet. The normal Call Request packet allows only 16 octets of data, but when the fast select facility is employed, 128 octets are allowed. These data are delivered to the destination DTE in a Call Indication packet.

The calling DTE must also specify an unrestricted or restricted response option (Fig. 5.9). If the restricted option is selected, the destination DTE must respond to the Call Indication with a Clear Request packet, which may also contain up to 128 octets of user data. Thus a virtual circuit has been created and destroyed with one exchange, and 128 octets have been transmitted in both directions.

If the response is unrestricted, the destination DTE may respond as above. Alternatively, the destination DTE may respond with a Call Accepted packet, augmented with up to 128 octets of user data. A virtual circuit has now been established and functions as usual.

5.4 ISO CONNECTION-MODE NETWORK SERVICE DEFINITION

ISO has issued a standard for connection-mode network service [DIS 8348]; a compatible (and virtually identical) document has been issued by CCITT [X.213]. Key characteristics of the network service, as listed in the standard, are:

- *Independence of underlying communications facility:* Network users need not be aware of the details of the subnetwork facilities used.
- *End-to-end transfer:* All routing and relaying is performed by the network layer, and is not of concern to the network service user.
- *Transparency:* The network service does not restrict the content, format, or coding of the user data.
- *Quality of service selection:* The network service user has some ability to request a given quality of service.
- *User addressing:* A system of addressing is used that allows network service users to refer unambiguously to one another. Discussion of this topic is deferred until Chap. 6.

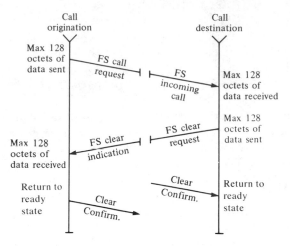

(a) Restricted

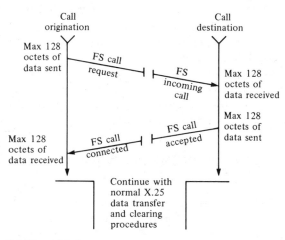

(b) Unrestricted

Figure 5.9. Fast select operation.

The standard specifies a set of parameters that define the quality of service as observed by network service users over a network connection. Most of these deal with the speed or accuracy/reliability characteristics during the three phases of a connection (Table 5.6). The parameters are listed and briefly defined in Table 5.7. Two of these parameters, through-put and transit delay, are negotiated during connection establishment. The remainder are selected or provided by other means not specified in the standard.

For all of these parameters, the network service attempts to provide the expected quality of service within the constraints imposed by the ca-

Table 5.6.   CLASSIFICATION OF QUALITY-OF-SERVICE PARAMETERS

Phase	Performance Criterion	
	Speed	Accuracy/Reliability
NC establishment	NC establishment delay	NC establishment failure probability
Data transfer	Throughput Transit delay	Residual error rate Resilience of the NC Transfer failure probability
NC release	NC release delay	NC release failure probability

Table 5.7.   QUALITY OF SERVICE PARAMETERS FOR THE ISO NETWORK SERVICE

NC Establishment Delay	Maximum acceptable delay between an N-CONNECT.request and the corresponding N-CONNECT. confirm
NC Establishment Failure Probability	Proportion of connection establishment attempts that fail as a result of NS provider behavior, such as misconnection, NC refusal, or excessive delay. Connection failures due to NS user behavior are excluded from the calculation
Throughput	Rate of NSDU transfer that can be sustained by the NS provider. Desired and minimum acceptable values are specified
Transit Delay	Average elapsed time between an N-DATA.request and the corresponding N-DATA.indication, using a nominal NSDU size of 128 octets. Desired and maximum acceptable values are specified
Residual Error Rate	Equal to $(N(e) + N(l) + N(x))/N$, where $N(e)$ = incorrect NSDUs; $N(l)$ = lost NSDUs; $N(x)$ = duplicate NSDUs; and N = Total NSDUs transferred
Transfer Failure Probability	Applies to Throughput, Transit Delay, and Residual Error Rate. For each of these parameters, the transfer failure probability is the observed proportion of time that the NS provider fails to provide the minimum acceptable service

Table 5.7   (continued)

NC Resilience	Two parameters: Probability of an NS-provider-invoked NC release, and the probability of an NS-provider-invoked reset
NC Release Delay	Maximum acceptable delay between an NS user invoked N-DISCONNECT.request and the successful release of the NC at the peer NS user
NC Release Failure Probability	Proportion of release requests that are not satisfied within the maximum acceptable delay
NC Protection	A set of four features that may be provided in any combination: (1) Prevention of unauthorized monitoring; (2) Detection of modification, deletion, replay, or insertion of data; (3) Peer entity authentication to prevent masquerading; and (4) Authentication of NSDU origin
NC Priority	Specifies the relative priority of NCs with respect to (1) the order in which connections have their quality of service downgraded, if necessary, and (2) the order in which NCs are broken to recover resources, if necessary
Maximum Acceptable Cost	Maximum acceptable cost for an NC, composed of communications and end-system resource costs

pabilities and services of the intervening subnetwork or subnetworks. Some parameters can be supported independent of the subnetwork. For example, prevention of unauthorized monitoring can be achieved by encryption. Other parameters, such as throughput and transit delay, are quite dependent on the performance to be expected from the subnetwork. For some subnetwork interface protocols, such as X.25, the attached system can request certain network facilities that may be used to satisfy the network service requirements. Again, throughput and transit delay are examples.

As usual, the service definition is in the form of a set of primitives and their parameters. Table 5.8 lists these for the ISO network service; note the similarity to those for the data link service (see Table 4.3). The first four primitives deal with connection establishment. In addition to specifying the calling and called addresses, the user can request certain

Table 5.8.   ISO CONNECTION-ORIENTED NETWORK SERVICE PRIMITIVES

N-CONNECT.request (Called Address, Calling Address, Receipt Confirmation Selection, Expedited Data Selection, QOS-Parameter Set, NS-User-Data)

N-CONNECT.indication (Called Address, Calling Address, Receipt Confirmation Selection, Expedited Data Selection, QOS-Parameter Set, NS-User-Data)

N-CONNECT.response (Responding Address, Receipt Confirmation Selection, Expedited Data Selection, QOS-Parameter Set, NS-User-Data)

N-CONNECT.confirm (Responding Address, Receipt Confirmation Selection, Expedited Data Selection, QOS-Parameter Set, NS-User-Data)

N-DISCONNECT.request (Reason, NS-User-Data, Responding Address)
N-DISCONNECT.indication (Originator, Reason, NS-User-Data, Responding Address)

N-DATA.request (NS-User-Data, Confirmation Request)
N-DATA.indication (NS-User-Data, Confirmation Request)

N-DATA-ACKNOWLEDGE.request
N-DATA-ACKNOWLEDGE.indication

N-EXPEDITED-DATA.request (NS-User-Data)
N-EXPEDITED-DATA. indication (NS-User-Data)

N-RESET.request (Reason)
N-RESET.indication (Originator, Reason)
N-RESET.response
N-RESET.confirm

services to be provided for the requested connection. Ordinarily, the network service will not confirm that data has been delivered to the other side; it is assumed that the data is delivered. However, the user may request that explicit confirmation be provided. The user may also request that an expedited data service be available. Both of these services are optional and may not be provided by the network service provider. Next, the user may specify two quality-of-service parameters: throughput and transit delay. These parameters are negotiated in the same fashion as was described in Sec. 4.7 for the data link service. Also as with the data link service, the disconnect primitives provide for abrupt connection termination and are also used for connection rejection. If the receipt confirmation service is available, then a user may request receipt confirmation of individual NSDUs. For each NSDU with that parameter set, the receiving user should return an N-DATA-ACKNOWLEDGE.request. The remaining primitives are self-explanatory.

APPENDIX 5A.   PACKET SWITCHING

A packet-switched network is a communication network that transmits data in units known as packets. The network consists of a set of interconnected packet-switched nodes. A device attaches to the network at one of the packet-switched nodes, and presents data for transmission in the form of a stream of packets. Each packet is routed through the network. As each node along the route is encountered, the packet is received, stored briefly, and then transmitted along a link to the next node in the route.

The activity related to a single packet can be explained with reference to Fig. 5.10. Consider data to be sent from system *A* to system *E*. *A* constructs a packet containing the data plus control information, including an indication of *E*'s address, and sends it to node 4. Node 4 stores the packet and determines the next leg of the route (say to 5). Then node 4 queues the packet for transmission over the 4–5 link. When the link is available, the packet is transmitted to node 5, which will forward the packet to node 6, and finally to *E*.

Of course, communication will typically involve a stream of packets exchanged in both directions between end systems. Two approaches are used to manage the transfer and routing of these streams of packets: datagram and virtual circuit.

In the datagram approach, each packet is treated independently. Let

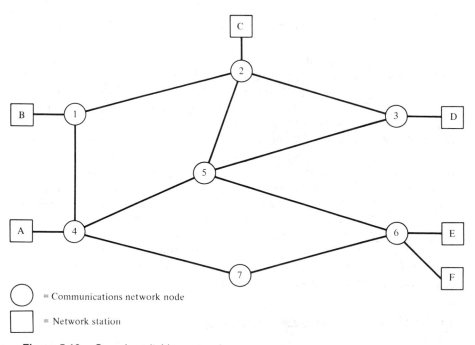

○ = Communications network node

▢ = Network station

Figure 5.10.   Generic switching network.

us consider the implications of this approach. Suppose that station A has a three-packet message to send to E. It pops the packets out, 1-2-3, to node 4. On *each* packet, node 4 must make a routing decision. Packet 1 comes in and node 4 determines that its queue of packets for node 5 is shorter than for node 7, so it queues the packet for node 5. Ditto for packet 2. But for packet 3, node 4 finds that its queue for node 7 is shortest and so queues packet 3 for that node. So the packets, each with the same destination address, do not all follow the same route. Furthermore, it is just possible that packet 3 will beat packet 2 to node 6. Thus it is possible that the packets will be delivered to E in a different sequence from the one in which they were sent. It is up to E to figure out how to reorder them. In this technique each packet, treated independently, is referred to as a datagram.

In the *virtual circuit* approach, a *logical* connection is established before any packets are sent. For example, suppose that A has one or more messages to send to E. It first sends a Call Request packet to 4, requesting a connection to E. Node 4 decides to route the request *and* all subsequent data to 5, which decides to route the request and all subsequent data to 6, which finally delivers the Call Request packet to E. If E is prepared to accept the connection, it sends out a Call Accept packet to 6. This packet is passed back through nodes 5 and 4 to A. Stations A and E may now exchange data over the logical connection or virtual circuit that has been established. Each packet now contains a virtual circuit identifier as well as data. Each node on the preestablished route knows where to direct such packets; no routing decisions are required. Thus every data packet from A traverses nodes 4, 5, and 6; every data packet from E traverses nodes 6, 5, and 4. Eventually, one of the stations terminates the connection with a Clear Request packet. At any time, each station can have more than one virtual circuit to any other station and can have virtual circuits to more than one station. The main characteristic of the virtual-circuit technique is that a route between stations is set up prior to data transfer. A packet is buffered at each node, and queued for output over a line. The difference from the datagram approach is that the node need not make a routing decision for each packet. It is made only once for each connection. Figure 5.11 is a comparison of the two techniques.

If two stations wish to exchange data over an extended period of time, there are certain advantages to virtual circuits. They all have to do with relieving the stations of unnecessary communications processing functions. A virtual circuit facility may provide a number of services, including sequencing, error control, and flow control. We emphasize the word *may* because not all virtual circuit facilities will provide all these services completely reliably. With that proviso, we define terms. *Sequencing* refers to that fact that, since all packets follow the same route, they arrive in the original order. *Error control* is a service that assures not

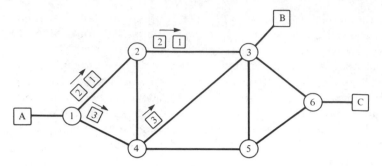

(a) Datagram. Each packet is treated independently by the network. Packets are labeled with a destination address and may arrive at the destination node out of sequence.

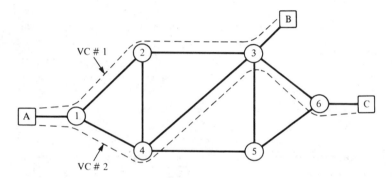

(b) Virtual circuit. A route for packets between two stations is defined and labeled. All packets for that virtual circuit follow the same route and arrive in sequence.

Figure 5.11.   Virtual circuit and datagram operation.

only that packets arrive in proper sequence, but that all packets arrive correctly. For example, if a packet in a sequence fails to arrive at node 6, or arrives with an error, node 6 can request a retransmission of that packet from node 4. Finally, *flow control* is a technique for assuring that a sender does not overwhelm a receiver with data. For example, if station *E* is buffering data from *A* and perceives that it is about to run out of buffer space, it can request, via the virtual circuit facility, that *A* suspend transmission until further notice.

One advantage of the datagram approach is that the call setup phase is avoided. Thus if a station wishes to send only one or a few packets, datagram delivery will be quicker. Another advantage of the datagram service is that, because it is more primitive, it is more flexible. For example, if congestion develops in one part of the network, incoming datagrams can be routed away from the congestion. With the use of virtual circuits, packets follow a predefined route, and thus it is more difficult for the network to adapt to congestion. A third advantage is that datagram delivery is inherently more reliable. With the use of virtual circuits, if a node fails all virtual circuits that pass through that node are lost. With datagram delivery, if a node is lost, packets may find alternate routes.

chapter 6

Network Layer:
Internetwork Operation

Communication subnetworks, such as packet-switched networks and local networks, grew out of a need to allow the computer user to have access to resources beyond that available in a single system. In a similar fashion, the resources of a single subnetwork are often inadequate to meet users' needs. Because the subnetworks that might be of interest exhibit so many differences, and because they may be owned or managed by different organizations, it is impractical to consider merging them into a single subnetwork. Rather, what is needed is the ability to interconnect various subnetworks so that any two systems on any of the constituent subnetworks can communicate. Such an interconnected set of subnetworks is referred to as an *internet*.

Each constituent subnetwork in an internet supports communication among the devices attached to that subnetwork. In addition, subnetworks are connected by devices that we will refer to generically as *gateways*; the ISO literature also refers to them as *interworking units* (IWUs). Gateways provide a communication path and perform the necessary functions so that data can be exchanged between devices attached to different subnetworks in the internet.

We begin our examination of internetworking with a discussion of the principles that underlie all forms of internetworking facilities. We then examine a protocol, X.75, for one of the principle architectural approaches to internetworking, which is a connection-oriented approach. Next, we look at the more flexible connectionless approach, and examine the corresponding ISO protocol and ISO service definition. We are finally in a position to present the internal structure of the ISO network layer, which captures all of the concepts introduced in Chaps. 5 and 6. Two appendices address related matters.

6.1 PRINCIPLES OF INTERNETWORKING

Requirements

Although a variety of approaches have been taken to provide internetwork service, the overall requirements on the internetworking facility can be stated in general. These include:

1. Provide a link between networks. At minimum, a physical and link control connection is needed.
2. Provide for the routing and delivery of data between processes on stations attached to different networks.
3. Provide an accounting service that keeps track of the use of the various networks and gateways and maintains status information.
4. Provide the services listed above in such a way as not to require modifications to the networking architecture of any of the constituent networks. This means that the internetworking facility must accommodate a number of differences among networks. These include:
   a. *Different addressing schemes:* The networks may use different endpoint names and addresses and directory maintenance schemes. Some form of global network addressing must be provided, as well as a directory service.
   b. *Different maximum packet size:* Packets from one network may have to be broken up into smaller pieces for another. This process is referred to as segmentation.
   c. *Different network access mechanisms:* The network access mechanism between station and network may be different for stations on different networks.
   d. *Different timeouts:* Typically, a connection-oriented transport service will await an acknowledgment until a timeout expires, at which time it will retransmit its segment of data. In general, longer times are required for successful delivery across multiple networks. Internetwork timing procedures must allow successful transmission that avoids unnecessary retransmissions.

e. *Error recovery:* Intranetwork procedures may provide anything from no error recovery up to reliable end-to-end (within the network) service. The internetwork service should not depend on nor be interfered with by the nature of the individual network's error recovery capability.

f. *Status reporting:* Different networks report status and performance differently. Yet it must be possible for the internetworking facility to provide such information on internetworking activity to interested and authorized processes.

g. *Routing techniques:* Intranetwork routing may depend on fault detection and congestion control techniques peculiar to each network. The internetworking facility must be able to coordinate these to adaptively route data between systems on different networks.

h. *User access control:* Each network will have its own user access control technique (authorization for use of the network). These must be invoked by the internetwork facility as needed. Further, a separate internetwork access control technique may be required.

i. *Connection, connectionless:* Individual networks may provide connection-oriented (e.g., virtual circuit) or connectionless (datagram) service. It may be desirable for the internetwork service not to depend on the nature of the connection service of the individual networks.

These points are worthy of further comment but are best pursued in the context of specific architectural approaches.

Architectural Approaches

We have said that some kind of gateway function is needed to interconnect networks. The key issue in designing such a gateway deals with the communications architecture that is used. There are essentially two dimensions that determine this architecture:

- The nature of the interface
- The nature of the transmission service

There are two choices for the interface: two networks interface at either the node (network, DCE) or station (attached device, DTE) level (Fig. 6.1). An interface at the node level implies, at minimum, that the networks have a common network access interface (e.g., X.25). It does not necessarily imply that the networks have the same internal protocols. In any case, there is a standardized format for packets entering and leaving each network. The principal advantage of this approach is that, with the exception of an expanded address space, the stations are not aware that there are multiple networks. If the system is designed properly, no

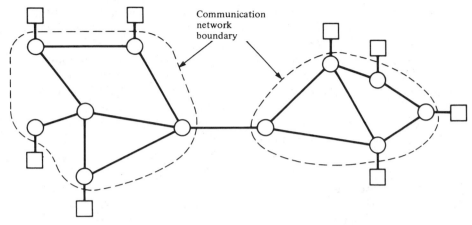

(a) Node–level interface

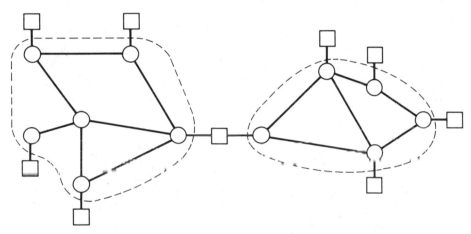

(b) Station–level interface

Figure 6.1. Internetwork interfacing.

changes need be made in the station software. If two stations can connect over a single network, they can connect via multiple networks with the same network access interface.

If it is not possible to standardize the network access interface, some form of protocol translation, or at least manipulation, is needed. At the worst, a specialized gateway for each pair of networks must be constructed. A better approach, as we shall see, is to standardize the objects that pass between networks. In any case, this function is performed by a station that attaches to two networks.

The other dimension for characterizing internetwork architecture is the nature of the transmission service, which can be either end to end or network by network. The end-to-end approach assumes only that all networks offer at least an unreliable datagram service; that is, if a sequence of packets is sent from one station to another on the same network, some but not necessarily all will get through, and there may be duplications and reordering of the sequence. The transmission across multiple networks requires a common end-to-end protocol for providing reliable end-to-end service. In the network-by-network approach, the technique is to provide reliable service within each network and then to splice together individual network connections across multiple networks.

Table 6.1 lists possible realizations of the four architectures that result from the 2×2 combination of interface and transmission service. One architecture that has been frowned on is network-by-network station level. The only way to achieve internetworking is for each gateway to be a true protocol translator between its two attached networks. This is generally an exercise in special-purpose software of little interest to the present discussion. However, this approach has recently received attention as a means of interconnecting local networks; its use in that context is explored in [STAL87].

The only type of approach that seems to fit neatly into the end-to-end node-level architecture is a configuration of multiple homogeneous networks. In this case, the internetworking task is rather simple, and the gateway device is referred to as a bridge. This mechanism is most commonly used to connect multiple homogeneous local networks (again, see [STAL87]).

The two remaining architectures are represented by radically different approaches taken by standards organizations. An example of a network-by-network node-level architecture is the X.75 standard, designed as an extension to X.25. X.75 specifies a protocol for exchange of packets between networks that allows a series of intranetwork X.25 virtual circuits to be spliced together. To two stations on different networks, it appears that they have a single virtual circuit connecting them. In fact, the virtual circuits terminate at the node gateways, which maintain the status information required to connect separate virtual circuits.

The end-to-end station-level architecture is implemented using a protocol above the network layer, called *Internet Protocol* (IP). IP was initially developed for the DARPA Internet Project and has been standardized by the Defense Department. A similar IP standard has been developed within ISO.

Table 6.1. ALTERNATIVE INTERNETWORKING APPROACHES

	Station (DTE) level	Node (DCE) level
Network-by-network	Protocol translator	X.75
End-to-End	Internet Protocol (IP)	Bridge

Table 6.2 compares IP and X.75 on a number of features. Because IP places no significant restrictions on internal network protocols, it is the more flexible approach.

Figure 6.2 depicts the protocol architecture that seems to be required for each of these four approaches. The figure depicts the gateway as a single system, which implements protocols appropriate to two networks. In fact, the gateway function is often split between two devices, although logically this is immaterial.

Let us briefly describe what is happening in this figure. In each case, we have two stations that wish to communicate across three networks by establishing a transport connection. In the first case, we assume that the networks differ and that the two stations have different transport protocols. Station A establishes a transport connection with gateway a. Each uses the network access protocols for network 1(N1, L1, P1). Gateway a must use another transport connection to gateway b. Gateway a also includes a relay mechanism (R12) that converts between the transport protocols of network 1(T1) and network 2(T2). This process continues on across to station B.

In the second case, we assume that stations A and B share a common transport protocol (T). Both stations and all gateways share a common internet protocol (I). Data units are transmitted from station 1 to gateway a across network 1, using that network's access protocols (N1, L1, P1). Gateway a takes the internet-level data unit and retransmits it across network 2.

In the first case (protocol translator), we are in effect splicing together transport connections. In the second case (internet protocol), there is a single transport connection, supported by a connectionless internet protocol that routes data units through the internet. Now consider the third case (bridge), in which all the networks are homogeneous. A relay function is used, in effect, to splice together the networks at the link level.

Finally, X.75 assumes that all networks use X.25 as the network

Table 6.2.   COMPARATIVE FEATURES OF IP AND X.75

IP	X.75
DTE-level gateway	DCE-level gateway
Datagram service	Virtual circuit service
Gateway must know IP, two network access schemes	Gateway must maintain state information about all virtual circuits
Adaptive routing easily implemented	Fixed routing typically; adaptive routing more difficult
All stations must have IP, may need common layer 4	All networks must be X.25

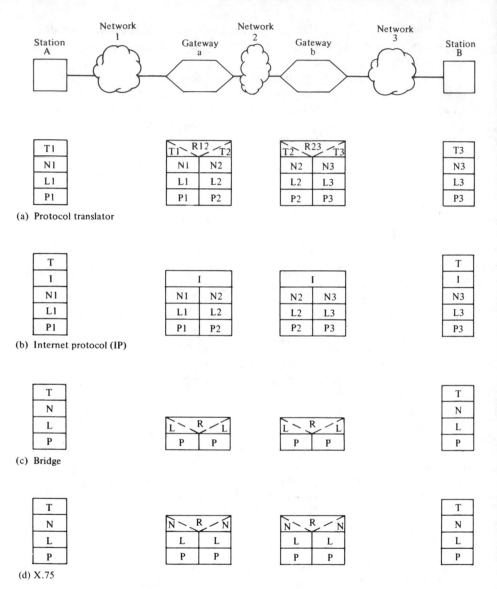

Figure 6.2. Internetwork architectures.

access standard. Virtual circuits are set up across each network and spliced together at the gateways by a relay mechanism.

6.2   X.75

The X.75 standard was developed by CCITT as a supplement to X.25. It is designed for use between public X.25 networks and is not likely to be used or even allowed as an interface between public and private networks. However, it could also be used to connect a collection of private X.25 networks in an internet that does not include public networks.

Figure 6.3 depicts the principle of X.75. As shown, X.25 specifies an interface between host equipment (DTE) and network equipment (DCE) that encompasses layers 1 through 3 and permits the set up, maintenance, and termination of virtual circuits between two DTEs. X.75

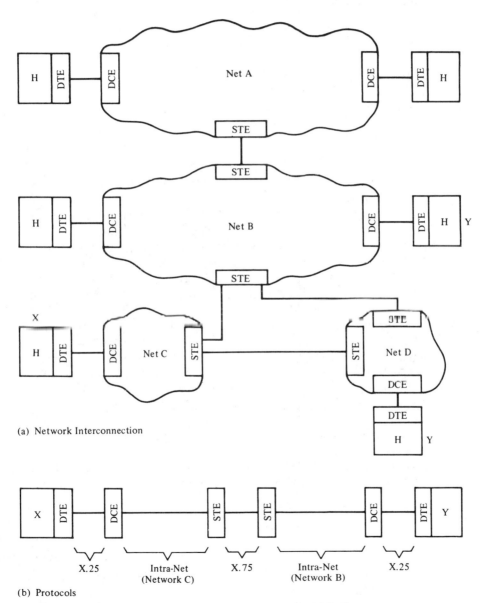

(a) Network Interconnection

(b) Protocols

Figure 6.3. Interconnection of X.25 networks via X.75 [POST80].

specifies signal terminating equipment (STE) that act as DCE-level gateways to connect two X.25 networks.

We begin with a description of the operation of an X.75 internet. We then look at some of the specific packet level characteristics of the standard.

Internetwork Operation

The interconnection of X.25 networks via X.75 provides a DTE–DTE virtual circuit that is spliced together from a series of virtual circuits:

- DCE to STE (intranetwork)
- STE to STE (internetwork)
- 0 or more:
  STE to STE (intranetwork)
  STE to STE (internetwork)
- STE to DCE

Each section is a distinct entity with a separate virtual circuit, flow control, and error control.

From the point of view of the DTE, however, it merely sees an enlarged X.25 network; X.75 is invisible. The DTE-DCE interface is still defined by X.25. As before, intranetwork protocols are undefined by the standard. The internetwork STE–STE interface is defined by X.75.

The transmission of a packet between two hosts can be explained with reference to Fig. 6.3b. Station X sends an X.25 data packet to its DCE with the virtual circuit number (group, channel) that it associates with a connection to Y. This packet is transmitted via network C to an STE. The STE uses the same format but modifies the virtual circuit number and flow control information for the appropriate STE–STE virtual circuit. The receiving STE then sends the packet to Y's DCE, which presents a packet to Y with the virtual circuit number that Y associates with a connection to X. Three important points about this process:

- There is no encapsulation by the STEs. The same layer 3 header format is reused.
- There is no end-to-end protocol. As in a single X.25 network, all information has local significance only (except when the D bit is set).
- Because of the 12-bit field, an STE–STE internet link can handle a maximum of 4096 connections.

Call request and clear request are handled step by step but must propagate end to end. Routing information must exist within DCEs and STEs to accomplish this. For example, a Call Request packet from X triggers the set up of a DCE–STE virtual circuit. Using the X.75 control packet format, which differs from X.25 only in the addition of a network-level utilities field, an STE–STE virtual circuit is set up between networks *C* and *B*. The Call Request packet then propagates to *Y*'s DCE, setting up another virtual circuit. Finally, a Call Indication packet is delivered to *Y*. The same procedure is used for Call Accepted and Clear Request packets.

Packet Level

As with X.25, the X.75 standard specifies three levels: *physical, link,* and *packet.* The link level employs both LAP-B and MLP, again as with X.25. In this section, we concentrate on the packet level.

The specification of the packet level of X.75 is almost the same as that of X.25. The general packet formats are identical (see Fig. 5.4), although fewer packet types are needed in X.75 (Table 6.3) because of the symmetry of the interface. The only other differences are those needed to accommodate internetwork administration and management functions of the STE. We consider these differences by examining the three phases of a virtual call:

- Call establishment
- Data transfer
- Call reset or termination

Call establishment is initiated by an STE using the CALL REQUEST packet. This packet, recall, contains information being prop-

Table 6.3. X.75 CONTROL PACKET TYPES AND PARAMETERS

Packet Types	Parameters
Call Request	Calling DTE address, Called DTE address, Network utilities, User facilities, Call user data
Call Connected	Calling DTE address, Called DTE address, Network utilities, User facilities, Called user data
Clear Request	Clearing cause, Diagnostic code, Calling DTE address, Called DTE address, Network utilities, User facilities, Clear user data
Clear Confirm	—
Interrupt	Interrupt user data
Interrupt Confirmation	—
RR	P(R)
RNR	P(R)
Reset Request	Resetting cause, Diagnostic code
Reset Confirmation	—
Restart Request	Restarting cause, Diagnostic code
Restart Confirmation	—

agated from the calling DTE to the called DTE. This includes, in particular, the facilities information. To accommodate STE–STE facilities, a utilities field is added to the packet. The facilities that can be requested are defined in Table 6.4. Most of the facilities either carry information related to DTE-requested services or are used for internetwork accounting and management functions. The called STE responds with a Call Connected packet.

Table 6.4.   X.75 NETWORK UTILITIES

Transit Network Identification	Used to name a transit network controlling a portion of the (perhaps partially established) virtual call. All of the networks in the complete or partially complete path are identified
Call Identifier	Used to uniquely identify the call by all the networks involved for accounting, auditing, and trouble reporting purposes
Throughput Class Indication	Used for negotiating the throughput class associated with this call. Any STE may reduce the throughput class requested for the call
Window Size Indication	Used for negotiating the window size at the STE–STE interface
Packet Size Indication	Used for negotiating the maximum data field length
Fast Select Indication	Indicates that the fast select facility applies for this call
Closed User Group Indication	Enables the establishment of calls by DTEs that are members of an international closed user group
Closed User Group with Outgoing Access Indication	Enables members of a closed user group to establish calls with nonmembers
Reverse Charging Indication	Indicates that reverse charging has been requested by the calling DTE
Called Line Address Modified Notification	Used in call connected and clear request packets when the called address differs from that specified in the call request packet. The reason, such as call redirection or hunt group, is indicated
Clearing Network Identification Code	Provides additional information about the origin of a clear request packet
Traffic Class Indication	Indicates service category (e.g., terminal, facsimile, maintenance). Its use is designated for further study
Transit Delay Selection	Signals the estimated transit delay for this call. Its use is designated for further study
Tariffs	For further study. May be used for billing information

The *data transfer* phase consists primarily of the exchange of data packets between STEs. These packets are, of course, intended for some destination DTE. Flow control is exercised by piggybacking and by using RR and RNR packets. If the D bit of a data packet is set to 0, acknowledgment has local significance: it is used to regulate STE–STE flow on a virtual circuit basis. However, if the sending DTE sets the D bit to 1, that bit remains set as the data packet propagates through the internet, and acknowledgment has end-to-end significance.

Call reset and termination is accomplished in the same manner as for X.25. Clear Request and Clear Confirmation packets are used to terminate a virtual call. Reset Request and Reset Confirmation reinitialize a virtual call by setting sequence numbers to 0 in both directions. Restart Request and Restart Confirmation reset all active virtual calls. X.75 specifies only local significance of these actions but, presumably, they correspond to global clear or reset events. Also, X.75 offers an international permanent virtual circuit service, used to splice together intranetwork permanent virtual circuits.

6.3   CONNECTIONLESS INTERNETWORKING ARCHITECTURE

A more flexible approach than the connection-oriented X.75 standard is the use of a connectionless protocol, which has been given the generic name of IP. ISO has specified such a protocol [DIS8473]. In this section, we examine the principles of the connectionless approach, and then turn to the ISO standards in the next two sections.

Operation of a Connectionless Internet

IP provides a connectionless or datagram service between stations. This contrasts with the connection-oriented X.75 service. There are a number of advantages to the connectionless approach:

- A connectionless internet facility is flexible. It can deal with a variety of networks, some of which are themselves connectionless. In essence, IP requires very little of the constituent networks.
- A connectionless internet service can be made highly robust. This is basically the same argument made for a datagram network service versus a virtual circuit service.
- A connectionless internet service is best for connectionless transport protocols.

As an example, Fig. 6.4 depicts the operation of IP for data exchange between station *A* on a LAN 1 and station *B* on a LAN 2 through a long-haul X.25 packet-switched network. These two stations share a

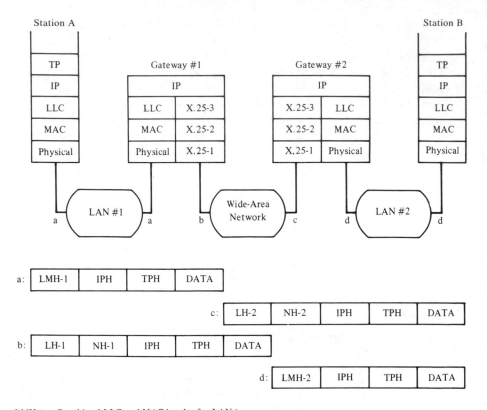

LMH-*i* : Combined LLC and MAC header for LAN i
LH-*j*   : Link Header (X.25 Layer 2) for DTE = Gateway *j*
NH-*k*   : Network Header (X.25 Layer 3) for DTE = Gateway k
IPH   : Internet Protocol Header
TPH   : Transport Protocol Header

Figure 6.4. Data encapsulation—IP approach.

common transport protocol. The data to be sent by *A* are encapsulated in an internet datagram with an IP header specifying a global network address (station *B*). This datagram is then encapsulated with the LAN 1 protocol and sent to a gateway that strips off the LAN 1 header. The datagram is then encapsulated with the X.25 protocol and transmitted across the network to a gateway. The gateway strips off the X.25 fields and recovers the datagram, which is then wrapped in LAN 2 headers and sent to *B*. If a connection-oriented service is required, *A* and *B* must share a common layer 4 protocol.

With this example in mind, we describe briefly the sequence of steps involved in sending a datagram between two systems on different networks. The process starts in the sending station. The station wants to send an IP datagram to a station in another network. The IP module in the station constructs the datagram with a global network address and recognizes that the destination is on another network. So the first step is to send the datagram to a gateway (example: station *A* to gateway 1 in Fig. 6.4). To do this, the IP module appends to the IP datagram a header appropriate to the network that contains the address of the gateway. For example, for an X.25 network, a layer 3 packet encapsulates the IP datagram to be sent to the gateway.

Next, the packet travels through the network to the gateway, which receives it via a DCE–DTE protocol. The gateway unwraps the packet to recover the original datagram. The gateway analyzes the IP header to determine whether this datagram contains control information intended for the gateway, or data intended for a station farther on. In the latter instance, the gateway must make a routing decision. There are four possibilities:

1. The destination station is attached directly to one of the networks to which the gateway is attached. This is referred to as *directly connected*. For example, in Fig. 6.5, all stations labeled SO are directly connected to gateway G1.
2. The destination station is on a network that has a gateway that directly connects to this gateway. This is known as a *neighbor gateway*. In Fig. 6.5, G2 is a neighbor gateway of G1, and all stations labeled S1 are one *hop* from G1.
3. To reach the destination station, more than one additional gateway must be traversed. This is known as a *multiple-hop* situation. In Fig. 6.5, all stations labeled S2 are in this category.
4. The gateway does not know the destination address.

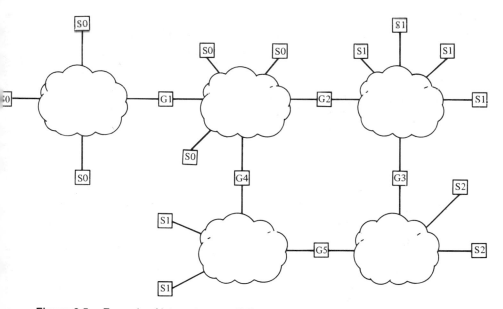

Figure 6.5. Example of internet connectivity.

In case 4, the gateway returns an error message to the source of the datagram. For cases 1 through 3, the gateway must select the appropriate route for the data, and insert them into the appropriate network with the appropriate address. For case 1, the address is the destination station address. For cases 2 and 3, the address is a gateway address. Remember, we are speaking here of a lower layer address, usually a layer 3 address or, in the case of local networks, a layer 2 address.

Before actually sending data, however, the gateway may need to segment the datagram to accommodate a smaller maximum packet size limitation on the outgoing network. Each segment becomes an independent IP datagram. Each new datagram is wrapped in a lower layer packet for transmission. The gateway then queues each packet for transmission. It may also enforce a maximum queue-length size for each network to which it attaches to avoid having a slow network penalize a faster one. In any case, once the queue limit is reached, additional datagrams are simply dropped.

The process described above continues through zero or more gateways until the datagram reaches the destination station. As with a gateway, the destination station recovers the IP datagram from its network wrapping. If segmentation has occurred, the IP module in the destination station buffers the incoming data until the original data field is reassembled. It then passes this block of data to a higher layer. The higher layer (e.g., transport) is responsible for the proper sequencing of a stream of datagrams and for end-to-end error and flow control.

Design Issues

With that thumbnail sketch of the operation of an IP-controlled internet, we can now go back and examine some design issues in greater detail:

- Addressing
- Routing
- Datagram lifetime
- Segmentation and reassembly
- Error control
- Flow control

Addressing.   A distinction is generally made among names, addresses, and routes. A name specifies what an object is; an address specifies where it is, and a route indicates how to get there. The distinction between names and addresses can be a useful concept, but it is also an arbitrary one. For a single network, an application program uses a name to identify a referent (process, station); the station translates the name into an address understood by the network; and the network may use a route to reach the referent.

In an internet, the distinction is less clear. Applications continue to use names and individual networks continue to use addresses and, if necessary, routes. To transfer data through a gateway, two entities must be identified: the destination network and the destination station. The gateway requires a network address to perform its function. This address can be specified in a number of ways:

- The application can refer to a network by a unique number; in effect, the name and address are the same.
- The internet logic in the station can translate a network name into a network address.
- A global station addressing scheme can be used. That is, there is a unique identifier for each station in the internet. For routing purposes, each gateway would need to derive network addresses from station addresses.

The latter technique has been proposed by the developers of Ethernet [DALA81]. They recommend a 48-bit station address. This is an address space sufficient to accommodate over 10^{14} unique referents, so it is likely to be sufficient for the foreseeable future. The primary advantages of this approach are that it permits stations to move from one network to another and that it allows address recognition at the station to be *hardwired*. The main disadvantages are that some central facility must manage the assignment of names and that unnecessarily long address fields must be carried across multiple networks.

A gateway will often receive an internet packet with a referent in the form *Net.Station*, where Net is a network address. The identifier *Station* is usually both a name and an address. To the higher-layer software in the station that generated the packet, *Station* is an address, translated from an application-level name. However, when it comes time for a gateway to deliver a datagram to a station on an attached network, *Station* must be translated into a layer 3 or 2 network address. This is so because different networks will have different address field lengths. Hence *Station* is treated as a name by the gateway.

The referent *Net.Station* can be considered a two-level hierarchical identifier of a host in the internet. The Ethernet developers (interestingly, the same ones interested in global station addresses) have proposed a third level of addressing to identify, at the internet level, an individual service access point (SAP) at a host [BOGG80, DALA82]. Thus the internet identifier would be of the form *Net.Station.SAP*. With this identifier, an internet protocol can be viewed as process to process rather than station to station. With *SAP* in the internet layer, the internet protocol is responsible for multiplexing and demultiplexing datagrams for software modules that use the internet service. The advantage of this approach is that the next higher layer could be simplified, a useful feature for small microprocessor devices. There are some problems in this approach, particularly when local networks are involved, where there is likely to be a proliferation of station types. Perhaps the most significant problem relates to the use of *well-known* ports that allow ready access to common services. If ports were implemented as SAPs at the IP level, the assignment of well-known ports would have to be centralized. For a further discussion, see volume III of this series.

Finally, an important service that must somehow be provided in the internet is a directory service. The station software must be able to determine the *Net.Station* identifier of a desired destination. One or more directory servers are needed, which themselves are well known. Each server would contain part or all of a name/address directory for internet stations.

An appendix to this chapter describes the ISO approach to internetwork addressing.

Routing.   Routing is generally accomplished by maintaining a routing table in each station and gateway that gives, for each possible destination network, the next gateway to which the IP datagram should be sent.

Table 6.5 shows the routing table for the BBN gateway, which is part of the DARPA internet. If a network is directly connected, it is so indicated. Otherwise, the datagram must be directed through one or more gateways (one or more hops). The table indicates the identity of the next gateway on the route (which must share a common network with this gateway or host) and the number of hops to the destination.

The routing table may be static or dynamic. A static table, however, could contain alternate routes if a gateway is unavailable. A dynamic table is more flexible in responding both to error and congestion situations. In the DARPA internet, for example, when a gateway goes down, all of its neighbors will send out a status report, allowing other gateways and hosts to update their routing tables. A similar scheme can be used to control congestion. This latter is particularly important because of the mismatch in capacity between local and long-haul networks. The interested reader may consult [DARP81], which specifies a variety of internet control messages used to facilitate routing.

Routing tables may also be used to support other internet services such as security and priority. For example, individual networks might be classified to handle data up to a given security classification. The routing mechanism must assure that data of a given security level is not allowed to pass through networks not cleared to handle such data.

Another routing technique is source routing. The source station specifies the route by including a sequential list of gateways in the datagram. This, again, could be useful for security or priority requirements.

Finally, we mention a service related to routing: route recording. To

Table 6.5.   INTERNET ROUTING TABLE[a]

Network name	Net address	Route[b]
SATNET	4	Directly connected
ARPANET	10	Directly connected
BBN-NET	3	1 hop via RCC 10.3.0.72 (ARPANET 3/72)
Purdue-Computer Science	192.5.1	2 hops via Purdue 10.2.0.37 (ARPANET 2/37)
INTELPOST	43	2 hops via Mills 10.3.0.17 (ARPANET 3/17)
DECNET-TEST	38	3 hops via Mills 10.3.0.17 (ARPANET 3/17)
Wideband	28	3 hops via RCC 10.3.0.72 (ARPANET 3/72)
BBN-Packet Radio	1	2 hops via RCC 10.3.0.72 (ARPANET 3/72)
DCN-COMSAT	29	1 hop via Mills 10.3.0.17 (ARPANET 3/17)
FIBERNET	24	3 hops via RCC 10.3.0.72 (ARPANET 3/72)
Bragg-Packet Radio	9	1 hop via Bragg 10.0.0.38 (ARPANET 0/38)
Clark Net	8	2 hops via Mills 10.3.0.17 (ARPANET 3/17)
LCSNET	18	1 hop via MIT LCS 10.0.0.77 (ARPANET 0/77)
BBN-Terminal Concentrator	192.1.2	3 hops via RCC 10.3.0.72 (ARPANET 3/72)
BBN-Jericho	192.1.3	3 hops via RCC 10.3.0.72 (ARPANET 3/72)
UCLNET	11	1 hop via UCL 4.0.0.60 (SATNET 60)
RSRE-NULL	35	1 hop via UCL 4.0.0.60 (SATNET 60)
RSRE-PPSN	25	2 hops via UCL 4.0.0.60 (SATNET 60)
San Francisco-Packet Radio-2	6	1 hop via C3PO 10.1.0.51 (ARPANET 1/51)

[a]Network table for BBN gateway.
[b]Names and acronyms identify gateways in the INTERNET system.
Source: [SHEL82].

record a route, each gateway appends its address to a list of addresses in the datagram. This feature is useful for testing and debugging purposes.

Datagram Lifetime.   If dynamic or alternate routing is used, the potential exists for a datagram or some of its segments to loop indefinitely through the internet. This is undesirable for two reasons. First, an endlessly circulating datagram consumes resources. Second, we will see in Chap. 7 that a reliable transport protocol may depend on there being an upper bound on datagram lifetime. To avoid these problems, each datagram can be marked with a lifetime. Once the lifetime expires, the datagram is discarded.

A simple way to implement lifetime is to use a hop count. Each time that a datagram passes through a gateway, the count is decremented. Alternatively, the lifetime could be a true measure of time. This requires that the gateways must somehow know how long it has been since the datagram or segment last crossed a gateway, and to know by how much to decrement the lifetime field. This would seem to require some global clocking mechanism.

The advantage of using a true time measure is that it can be used in the reassembly algorithm, which is described next.

Segmentation and Reassembly. Individual networks within an internet will generally be diverse and, in particular, specify different maximum (and sometimes minimum) packet sizes. It would be inefficient and unwieldy to try to dictate uniform packet size across networks. Thus gateways may need to segment incoming datagrams into smaller pieces before transmitting on to the next network.

If datagrams can be segmented (perhaps more than once) in the course of their travels, the question arises as to where they should be reassembled. The easiest solution is to have reassembly performed at the destination only. The principal disadvantage of this approach is that the packets can only get smaller as data moves through the internet. This may seriously impair the efficiency of some networks. On the other hand, if intermediate gateway reassembly is allowed, the following disadvantages result:

1. Large buffers are required at gateways, and there is a potential for reassembly deadlock (i.e., all buffer space is used up storing partial datagrams).
2. All segments of a datagram must pass through the same gateway. This inhibits the use of dynamic routing.

ISO IP specifies an efficient technique for segmentation with reassembly at the destination recommended. The technique requires the following parameters:

- ID
- Data Length
- Offset
- More flag

The *ID* is some means of uniquely identifying a station-originated datagram. In ISO IP, it consists of the source and destination addresses, and a sequence number supplied by that protocol layer. The *Data Length* is the length of the data field in octets, and the *Offset* is the position of a segment in the original datagram in multiples of 64 bits.

The source station IP layer creates a datagram with Data Length equal to the entire length of the data field, with Offset = 0, and a More Flag set to False. To segment a long datagram, an IP module in a gateway performs the following tasks:

1. Create two new datagrams and copy the header fields of the incoming datagram into both.
2. Divide the data into two approximately equal portions along a 64-bit boundary, placing one portion in each new datagram. The first portion must be a multiple of 64 bits.
3. Set the Data Length of the first datagram to the length of the inserted data, and set the More Flag to True. The Offset field is unchanged.
4. Set the Data Length of the second datagram to the length of the inserted data, and add the length of the first data portion divided by eight to the Offset field. The More Flag remains the same.

Table 6.6 gives an example. The procedure can be generalized to an *n*-way split.

To reassemble a datagram, there must be sufficient buffer space at the reassembly point. As segments with the same ID arrive, their data fields are inserted in the proper position in the buffer until the entire datagram is reassembled, which is achieved when a contiguous set of data exists starting with an *Offset* of zero and ending with data from a segment with a false *More Flag*.

One eventuality that must be dealt with is that one or more of the segments may not get through; the IP connectionless service does not guarantee delivery. Some means is needed to decide to abandon a reassembly effort to free up buffer space. The ISO IP standard suggests two possibilities. First, assign a reassembly lifetime to the first segment to arrive. This is a local, real-time clock assigned by the reassembly function and decremented while some, but not all, segments of the PDU are being

Table 6.6. SEGMENTATION EXAMPLE

Original datagram
   Data Length = 472
   Offset   = 0
   More   = 0
First segment
   Data Length = 240
   Offset   = 0
   More   = 1
Second segment
   Data Length = 232
   Offset   = 30
   More   = 0

---

buffered. If the time expires, all received segments are discarded. Second, the destination IP entity can make use of the datagram lifetime, which is part of the incoming PDU. The lifetime field continues to be decremented by the reassembly function as if the PDU were still in transit (in a sense, it still is).

Error Control. The internetwork facility does not guarantee successful delivery of every datagram. When a datagram is discarded by a gateway, the gateway should attempt to return some information to the source, if possible. The source internet protocol entity may use this information to modify its transmission strategy and may notify higher layers. To report that a specific datagram has been discarded, some means of datagram identification is needed.

   Datagrams may be discarded for a number of reasons, including lifetime expiration, congestion, and FCS error. In the latter case, notification is not possible because the source address field may have been damaged.

Flow Control. Internet flow control allows gateways and/or receiving stations to limit the rate at which they receive data. For the connectionless type of service we are describing, flow control mechanisms are limited. The best approach would seem to be to send flow control packets, requesting reduced data flow, to other gateways and source stations.

6.4   ISO CONNECTIONLESS-MODE NETWORK SERVICE DEFINITION

To accommodate the connectionless architecture that we have been describing, ISO has developed standards for both connectionless service and a connectionless protocol. In this section, we examine the network service definition for connectionless-mode service [DIS 8348/DAD 1].

   As Table 6.7 indicates, there are only two primitives required for this service (compare Table 4.3). The source and destination addresses are global internet addresses that uniquely identify end systems. The quality of service consists of a set of parameters drawn from the list of Table 6.8. Finally, the user data is a unit of data that is transmitted independently of any prior or succeeding NSDUs.

   Because no logical connection is set up between end users, there is no opportunity for a negotiation of quality of service involving the net-

Table 6.7.   ISO CONNECTIONLESS-MODE NETWORK SERVICE PRIMITIVES

N-UNITDATA.request (Source Address, Destination Address, Quality of Service, NS-User-Data)
N-UNITDATA.indication (Source Address, Destination Address, Quality of Service, NS-User-Data)

**Table 6.8.   QUALITY OF SERVICE PARAMETERS FOR THE ISO
                     CONNECTIONLESS-MODE NETWORK SERVICE**

Transit Delay	Expected value of the time between an N-UNITDATA.request and the corresponding N-UNITDATA.indication
Protection from Unauthorized Access	Four options are defined: (1) no protection features; (2) protection against passive monitoring; (3) protection against modification, replay, addition, or deletion; and (4) both (1) and (2)
Cost Determinants	Permits user to specify (1) that the service provider should use the least expensive means available; or (2) maximum acceptable cost
Residual Error Probability	Probability that a particular NSDU will be lost, duplicated, or incorrectly delivered
Priority	Specifies the relative priority of NSDUs with respect to: (1) the order in which NSDUs have their quality of service degraded, if necessary; and (2) the order in which NSDUs are to be discarded to recover resources, if necessary

work service and the two entities. Rather, there must be prior agreement or understanding between the service provider and each user of the quality of service available. In the request primitive, the requested service is based on this prior knowledge and should be within the range that the service provider can accommodate. If, because of changing conditions, the network service cannot provide the requested quality of service, then the network service will nevertheless attempt to deliver the data unit at whatever quality of service is available.

As with the connection-mode network service, the connectionless-mode service makes use of subnetwork services to attempt to satisfy the requested quality of service. The situation is complicated if the service is to be provided across an internet. One tool available to the network entity in the originating system is route selection. The network entity may be able to enumerate a complete list of the intermediate subnetworks and the gateways to be visited (complete source routing). For example, if a rather low transit delay is requested, the network entity may design a route that avoids satellite links. In some circumstances, the network entity may be able to enumerate some, but not all, of the intermediate systems to be visited (partial source routing). In this case, each system in the list must be visited in the order specified, but any path may be taken between listed systems. Such a list might be used when there are certain *don't care* branches that converge back to the desired path.

6.5   ISO INTERNETWORK PROTOCOL STANDARD

In this section, we look at the IP standard developed by ISO [DIS 8473, CALL83, PISC84, PISC86]. The IP protocol is designed to provide the ISO connectionless-mode network service and to provide an internetworking capability.

ISO IP Functions

Table 6.9 lists the functions that are provided by the ISO internetwork protocol. These are grouped into three types. Type 1 functions are mandatory; these must be supported by any implementation of the protocol. Type 1 functions can be further grouped into two subtypes. Most of the

Table 6.9.   ISO IP FUNCTIONS

Type 1—Mandatory	
PDU Composition	Construct protocol data unit header in response to an N-UNITDATA.request
PDU Decomposition	Remove and analyze header to generate an N-UNITDATA.indication
Header Format Analysis	Determines whether full protocol or subset is employed. Determines whether destination has been reached or PDU must be forwarded
PDU Lifetime Control	Enforces maximum PDU lifetime
Route PDU	Determines network-entity to which PDU should be forwarded and the underlying service that must be used to reach that network entity
Forward PDU	Forward PDU using subnetwork access protocol
Segmentation	Segment PDU when required by subnetwork service used for forwarding
Reassembly	Reconstruct initial PDU from segments
Discard PDU	Discard PDU when one of a list of designated conditions is met
Type 1—Mandatory and selectable	
Error Reporting	An attempt to return an Error Report PDU to the source network entity when a PDU is discarded
PDU Header Error Detection	Uses a checksum computed on the entire PDU header. Checksum is verified at each point at which the PDU header is processed, and modified each time the header is modified

Table 6.9   (continued)

Type 2—Optional/discard	
Security	Indicates the provision of protection services (e.g., data origin authentication, data confidentiality, data integrity of a single NSDU)
Complete Source Routing	List of network entities (in the OSI sense) to be visited in path from source to destination. The entities must be visited in the designated order, and no other entities may be visited
Complete Route Recording	Path taken by PDU is recorded as it traverses the internet. Record consists of a list of all network entities visited. Prohibits intermediate reassembly of segments that followed different paths

Type 3—Optional/ignore	
Partial Source Routing	List of network entities (in the OSI sense) to be visited in path from source to destination. The entities must be visited in the designated order. However, a PDU may take any path to arrive at the next entity on the list, including a path that visits other network entities
Partial Route Recording	Path taken by PDU is recorded as it traverses the internet. Record consists of a list of all network entities visited. When intermediate reassembly of segments that followed different paths occurs, the route recorded in any one of the segments may be placed in the reassembled PDU
Priority	Provides a means whereby the resources of network entities, such as outgoing transmission queues and buffers, can be used preferentially to process higher priority PDUs ahead of lower priority PDUs
Quality of Service Maintenance	Provides information to network entities along route that may be used to make routing decisions and subnetwork service requests to provide a requested quality of service
Congestion Notification	Intermediate systems may inform the destination network entity of congestion. This information is provided to the network service user
Padding	Allows space to be reserved in the PDU header for aligning the data field to a boundary convenient for the originating network entity (e.g., computer word boundary)

type 1 functions are always provided. Two of the type 1 functions, which relate to error handling, must be implemented, but they are only provided when selected by the sending network service user. The remaining functions are considered less important than the type 1 functions, and may or may not be supported. This allows the implementer the flexibility to deploy reduced versions of the protocol for efficiency or resource conservation. Type 2 functions are those optional functions that, if requested, are considered essential to the successful delivery of a PDU. Thus, if an intermediate system receives a PDU that requests a type 2 function not supported by that intermediate system, then the PDU is discarded. Finally, type 3 functions are those optional functions that, if requested, are considered desirable but not essential. Thus, if an intermediate system receives a PDU that requests a type 3 function not supported by that intermediate system, then the PDU is processed exactly as though the function had not been selected.

Most of the functions listed in Table 6.9 were discussed in Sec. 6.3; a few warrant further elaboration. The first of these is the PDU lifetime control. This function serves two purposes: to ensure against unlimited looping of PDUs and to support transport layer requirements. As we shall see, it is easier for the transport protocol to deal with a lost PDU than with an excessively delayed PDU. Because of the service to the transport layer, the maximum PDU lifetime must be expressible in units of time; a transport entity cannot count hops. The IP protocol standard provides some guidance on this point:

> It is not necessary for each intermediate system to subtract a precise measure of the time that elapsed since an NPDU visited the previous intermediate system. It is sufficient to subtract an overestimate of the actual time taken. In most cases, an intermediate system may simply subtract a constant value which depends upon the typical near maximum delays that are encountered in a specific underlying service. It is only necessary to make an accurate estimate on a per NPDU basis for those subnetworks which have both a relatively large maximum delay, and a relatively large variation in delay.

The discard PDU function allows a gateway to discard an incoming PDU. If error reporting has been selected for the given PDU, then the intermediate system that discards the PDU will generate an Error Report PDU. The Error Report PDU is transmitted back to the originating network entity, using the same protocol. Thus, there is no guarantee that the error report will get through, and nonreceipt of an error report does not imply successful delivery of a Data PDU.

ISO IP PDU Formats

Two PDU types are defined in the standard: data PDUs and error report PDUs; the formats are illustrated in Fig. 6.6. The data PDU header con-

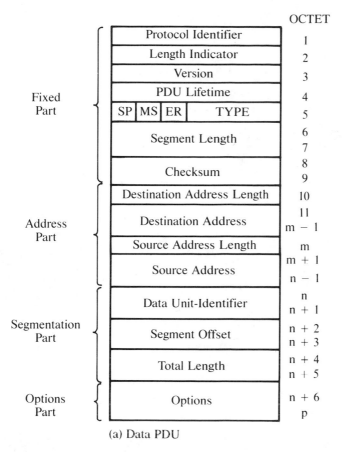

(a) Data PDU

Figure 6.6. ISO IP header formats.

sists of four parts. The fixed part is always present and is of fixed length. It contains the following fields:

- *Protocol identifier:* When the source and destination stations are connected to the same network, an internet protocol is not needed. In that case, the internet layer is null and the header consists of this single field of 8 bits.
- *Length indicator:* Length of the header in octets.
- *Version:* Included to allow evolution of the protocol. Either header format or semantics might change.
- *PDU Lifetime:* Expressed as a multiple of 500 ms. It is determined and set by the source station. Each gateway that the IP data unit visits decrements this field by 1 for each 500 ms of estimated delay for that hop (transit time to this gateway plus processing time).
- *Flags:* The SP flag indicates whether segmentation is permitted. The MS flag is the more flag described earlier. The ER flag indicates whether an error report is desired by the source station if an IP data unit is discarded.

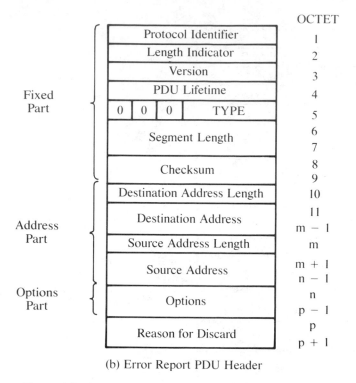

(b) Error Report PDU Header

Figure 6.6   (continued)

- *Type:* Indicates whether this is a Data (contains user data) or Error (contains error report) PDU.
- *PDU Segment Length:* Total data unit length, including header, in octets.
- *PDU checksum:* Result of a checksum algorithm (defined in an appendix to this chapter) computed on the entire header. As some header fields may change (e.g., time to live, segmentation-related fields), this is reverified and recomputed at each gateway.

The address part of the header is a variable length and is always present. Because addresses may be of variable length, an address length field precedes both the source and destination addresses.

If the SP flag is set to 1, then the header includes a segmentation part, with the following fields:

- *Data unit identifier:* Intended to uniquely identify the PDU. Thus, the originating network entity must assign values that are unique for the PDUs destination and for the maximum time that the PDU may remain in the internet.

- *Segment offset:* Indicates where in the initial PDU this segment (fragment) belongs, measured in 64-bit units. This implies that fragments other than the last one must contain user data fields that are a multiple of 64 bits ir length.
- *Total length:* Specifies the total length of the original PDU, including header and data.

Finally, an optional part may be included in the header, and is used to convey optional parameters. Each option is encoded in three fields: parameter code, parameter length, and parameter value. The parameters that may be specified are:

- *Padding:* Used to lengthen the PDU header to a convenient size.
- *Security:* Defined by the user. The security classification system is not specified in the standard.
- *Source Routing:* Lists the network entities to be visited.
- *Recording of Route:* Traces the route the PDU has taken so far.
- *Quality of service:* Specifies reliability and delay values.
- *Priority:* Values 0 through 14 may be specified.

The Error Report PDU has substantially the same format as the Data PDU. The fixed part includes the same fields. In the case of the Error Report PDU, the three flags (SP, MS, ER) are set to 0; there is no segmentation of error reports, and if an error report is discarded, this does not generate another error report. In the address part, the source address specifies the originator of the error report, and the destination address specifies the originator of the discarded PDU. Because an Error Report PDU cannot be segmented, there is no segmentation part in the header. The options part of the error report header is determined by the options that are present in the corresponding Data PDU. If the system generating the Error Report PDU does not support an option in the corresponding Data PDU, then that option will not be placed in the header. Otherwise, the following rules apply—

- Priority and security parameter values are the same as in the Data PDU.
- Complete source routing is used to retrace the path taken by the Data PDU.
- Padding, partial source routing, and record route may be provided and may be based on the values in the Data PDU, but this is not a requirement.

The last field in the header is the Reason for Discard. Table 6.10 lists the reasons that may be specified. The body of the PDU contains the entire header of the discarded Data PDU, and may contain some or all of the data field of the discarded PDU.

Table 6.10. REASONS FOR DISCARD

Parameter Value		Class of Error	Meaning
Octet 1	Octet 2		
0000	0000	GENERAL	REASON NOT SPECIFIED
	0001		PROTOCOL PROCEDURE ERROR
	0010		INCORRECT CHECKSUM
	0011		PDU DISCARDED DUE TO CONGESTION
	0100		HEADER SYNTAX ERROR (CANNOT BE PARSED)
	0101		SEGMENTATION NEEDED BUT NOT PERMITTED
	0110		INCOMPLETE PDU RECEIVED
	0111		DUPLICATE OPTION
1000	0000	ADDRESS	DESTINATION ADDRESS UNREACHABLE
	0001		DESTINATION ADDRESS UNKNOWN
1001	0000	SOURCE ROUTING	UNSPECIFIED SOURCE ROUTING ERROR
	0001		SYNTAX ERROR IN SOURCE ROUTING FIELD
	0010		UNKNOWN ADDRESS IN SOURCE ROUTING FIELD
	0011		PATH NOT ACCEPTABLE
1010	0000	LIFETIME	LIFETIME EXPIRED WHILE DATA UNIT IN TRANSIT
	0001		LIFETIME EXPIRED DURING REASSEMBLY
1011	0000	PDU DISCARDED	UNSUPPORTED OPTION NOT SPECIFIED
	0001		UNSUPPORTED PROTOCOL VERSION
	0010		UNSUPPORTED SECURITY OPTION
	0011		UNSUPPORTED SOURCE ROUTING OPTION
	0100		UNSUPPORTED RECORDING OF ROUTE OPTION
1100	0000	REASSEMBLY	REASSEMBLY INTERFERENCE

6.6 INTERNAL ORGANIZATION OF THE NETWORK LAYER

The purpose of the network layer is to provide the transport layer above it with the capability to transfer data units from one end system to another independent of the operational characteristics of any of the subnetworks along the route. As we have seen, because of the variety of subnetwork capabilities and interfaces, the network layer protocols needed to provide the network layer service may be quite complex.

Because of this potential complexity, ISO has chosen to develop a model of the network layer that is similar in intent to the overall OSI model. This model specifies a three-sublayer architecture for the network layer [DIS 8648, HEMR84], and is referred to as the internal organization of the network layer. The network layer model describes the types of protocols and different strategies that might be used for OSI interconnection of *real world* networks. Like the OSI model, the network layer model does not standardize specific protocols or services. Rather, it provides a framework within which network-level protocols can be developed and standardized.

The network layer model deals with three types of real world entities:

- *Real subnetworks:* Such as local networks, packet-switched networks, and ISDN.
- *Real end systems:* Open systems that communicate with one another, either over a direct link or through one or more real subnetworks.
- *Interworking units:* Pieces of equipment used to connect different real subnetworks together; we have referred to these as gateways.

With these concepts in mind ISO considers a number of strategies by which the network layer service may be provided. These may be grouped into three general strategies:

1. If two end systems are connected through a single subnetwork, then the DTE–DCE protocol that is used for subnetwork attachment is used to support the network service. If the service offered by the subnetwork is insufficient, then it is enhanced by means of a protocol above the level of the DTE–DCE protocol.
2. If two end systems are connected by means of multiple subnetworks, then a hop-by-hop strategy can be used. The service available from each subnetwork (each hop) is used and, if necessary, enhanced individually to the level of the OSI network service to be provided. The X.75 scheme is an example of this approach.
3. If two end systems are connected by means of multiple subnetworks, then an internetworking protocol approach can be used.

The connectionless IP scheme is an example of this approach for providing the connectionless-mode network service.

With these concepts in mind, a three-sublayer model has been developed by ISO (Fig. 6.7). At each sublayer, there may be a protocol that fulfills a particular role:

- *Subnetwork access protocol* (SNAcP) role
- *Subnetwork-dependent convergence protocol* (SNDCP) role
- *Subnetwork-independent convergence protocol* (SNICP) role

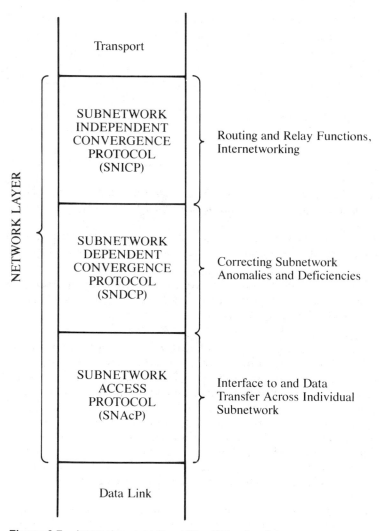

Figure 6.7.   Internal organization of the ISO network layer.

In a given situation, it is not necessary that a separate protocol be used for each role. In many cases, there will be only one or two protocols at the network layer. However, it is useful to organize the network layer into these three sublayers to understand the requirements for providing the network service and the protocols needed to satisfy those requirements.

The SNAcP is the protocol that operates between a network entity in the subnetwork and a network entity in the end system (a DTE–DCE protocol). The SNAcP entity in the end system directly makes use of the services of the subnetwork and performs three key functions:

- *Data transfer:* NSDUs are presented to the subnetwork for transfer to another end system or gateway.
- *Connection management:* If a connection-oriented subnetwork service is available and required, the connection is established and maintained.
- *Quality of service selection:* The end system requests the required quality of service from the network.

All information (e.g., quality of service, flow control) needed to provide the OSI network service is carried in the fields of the SNAcP. An example of SNAcP is the X.25 packet level protocol [ISO 8208].

In addition to the SNAcP, ISO defines two types of convergence protocols. A convergence protocol operates over top of a subnetwork service and utilizes it. Some of the information needed to provide the OSI network service is transferred as transparent user data in the SNAcP over the subnetwork being used.

The SNDCP is defined for, and requires beneath it, a particular type of subnetwork. Such a protocol can be used to enhance a SNAcP to provide a particular network service to transport entities. An example of a SNDCP is found in the provision of the OSI connection-mode network service over a subnetwork that employs the 1980 version of CCITT X.25. The 1980 version is still in use on a number of networks, but does not provide all the facilities so that the OSI network service can be directly supported by the SNAcP. The deficiencies in the 1980 X.25 are primarily the absence of elements in the protocol for conveying some of the parameter information needed to support OSI network connection establishment and release (e.g., complete NSAP addresses, quality of service parameters, and reason codes). ISO has defined a SNDCP [DIS 8878] that makes use of 1980 X.25 as far as possible, and carries the rest of the required information as user data in X.25 packets. To support connection establishment, the convergence protocol defines two different procedures. Over subnetworks where the fast select facility is available, that facility is used to convey as user data the parameter information not accommodated by fields in the X.25 call set-up packet. Where fast select is not available, or where more than 128 octets are needed to carry the remaining parameter information, the SNDCP uses X.25 data packets with the Q bit set to 1, transferred immediately following the virtual call establishment. To provide connection release, the SNDCP makes use of Clear Request and Clear Confirmation packets, and in some circumstances must precede the virtual call clearing procedure with a transfer of parameter information by means of a data packet with the Q bit set to 1.

An SNICP is intended for use over a wide variety of different subnetwork types, and thus is defined to require a minimal subnetwork service underneath. The ISO IP protocol is an example.

APPENDIX 6A.   NETWORK LAYER ADDRESSING

It is at the network layer that the end systems involved in a communication must be identified. The key function involved is addressing. ISO describes this function as follows [ISO 7498/PDAD 3]:

> The task of the addressing functions of the Network Layer is, for any instance of communication, to use the called and calling NSAP addresses, together with other information, to determine which Network entities participate in the communication (i.e., to determine the route to be taken within the Network Layer).

Two concepts need to be distinguished here. The NSAP address is the abstract term used by OSI to refer to points where the service of the Network Layer is made available to its users. In practical terms, NSAPs can be considered addressable points within a system, and they represent the endpoints of communication through the network layer. Instances of NSAP addresses include the Called Address, Calling Address, and Responding Address in the N-CONNECT primitives (see Table 5.8) and the Source Address and Destination Address in the N-UNITDATA primitives (see Table 6.7). In contrast, the subnetwork address is the information that a real subnetwork needs to identify a particular end system or gateway, and thus represents a point of attachment to the subnetwork. In general, the relationship between subnetwork addresses and NSAP addresses is many-to-many, as an end system may be attached to more than one subnetwork and may have more than one NSAP address.

The ISO defines three properties that NSAP addresses must possess [ISO 7498/PDAD 3]:

- *Global nonambiguity:* An NSAP identifies a unique entity. Synonyms are permitted; that is, an NSAP may have more than one NSAP address.
- *Global applicability:* It is as possible at any NSAP to identify any other NSAP, in any end-system, by means of the NSAP address

of the other NSAP. This does not imply that a communication to a given NSAP can always be made. Restrictions can occur because of lack of physical media, lack of directory information needed to determine the subnetwork address, or security requirements.

- *Route independence:* Network service users cannot derive routing information from NSAP addresses. They cannot control the route chosen by the network service by the choice of synonym and they cannot deduce the route taken by an incoming NSDU from the NSAP address. However, as pointed out in the CCITT document [X.213], NSAP addresses should be constructed, when possible, in such a way as to facilitate routing through an internet. That is, the network service providers, especially gateways, may be able to take advantage of the address structure to achieve economical processing of routing aspects.

In addition to defining these properties of NSAPs, ISO has developed an NSAP addressing scheme to provide these properties [ISO 8348/ DAD 2, HEMR85]. The scheme is based on two concepts: a hierarchical arrangement of addressing domains and the existence of multiple, cooperating addressing authorities.

An address domain is a set of addresses related to one another by virtue of being administered by the same addressing authority. The addressing authority is responsible for ensuring that addresses from the domain are assigned uniquely. The set of all addresses in the OSI environment is referred to as the *global network addressing domain*. This domain is divided into *network addressing domains* in a hierarchical fashion (Fig. 6.8). Every NSAP address is part of a network addressing domain that is administered directly by one and only one addressing authority. If that network addressing domain is part of a hierarchically higher addressing domain, the authority for the lower domain is authorized by the authority for the higher domain to assign NSAP addresses from the lower domain. All domains are ultimately part of the global network addressing domain, for which the addressing authority is ISO 8348/DAD 2.

The ISO specification explicitly defines six subdomains of the global network addressing domain:

- A set of four domains, each of which corresponds to a type of public telecommunication network (i.e., packet-switched, Telex, telephone, and ISDN) and which is administered by CCITT.
- An ISO geographic domain that is allocated and corresponds to individual countries. ISO member bodies within each country are responsible for assigning these addresses.
- An ISO international organization domain that is allocated and corresponds to different international organizations (e.g., NATO).

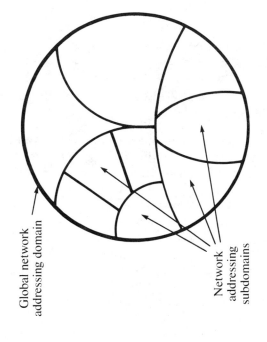

Global network
addressing domain

Network
addressing
subdomains

a) Partitioning of the Domain into Subdomains

170

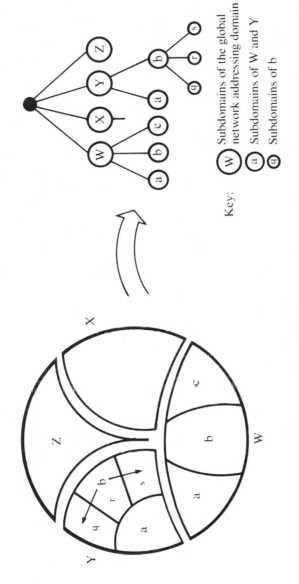

Key:

W   Subdomains of the global
    network addressing domain

a   Subdomains of W and Y

g   Subdomains of b

b) Hierarchical Relationship Among Subdomains

Figure 6.8.   Partitioning of the global Network Addressing domain and subdomain hierarchy.

171

In addition, the specification makes accommodation for the future definition of other domains at the second level in the hierarchy.

The ISO specification only defines the abstract syntax and semantics of the NSAP addresses. The actual encoding of the address information is left for specification by the specific network layer protocol standard. The structure is shown in Fig. 6.9. The address consists of an *Initial Domain Part* (IDP) and a *Domain Specific Part* (DSP). The IDP, in turn, consists of an *Authority and Format Identifier* (AFI) and an *Initial Domain Identifier* (IDI).

The AFI represents the first partitioning in the NSAP address space and is used to identify one of the second-level address domains listed above. In addition, the AFI specifies the format of the IDI part and the structure of the DSP part. For example, an AFI value of 36 indicates that the address is for a system attached to a public packet-switched network, that the IDI part of the address consists of up to 14 decimal digits providing a subnetwork address, and that the DSP part, if any, will be represented in decimal digits. The IDI part is the initial (and perhaps only) part of the actual address, and is interpreted according to the value of the AFI. Finally, the DSP part, if needed, provides address information below the second level of the addressing hierarchy. For example, if a local network is attached to a public X.25 network, the IDI provides the subnetwork address (DTE address) of the entire local network, and the DSP provides the address of individual end systems on the local network.

The ISO network addressing specification provides the framework for an ambitious scheme to provide unique, cooperatively-defined addresses for every present and future NSAP in the OSI environment. This specification certainly does not solve all the technical and administrative problems associated with OSI addressing, but it succeeds in structuring the problem so that future work can be coordinated.

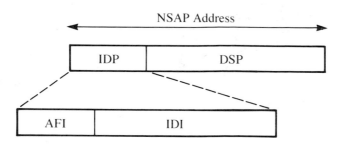

IDP: Initial Domain Part
AFI: Authority & Format Identifier
IDI: Initial Domain Identifier
DSP: Domain Specific Part

Figure 6.9.   NSAP address structure.

APPENDIX 6B.   ISO CHECKSUM ALGORITHM

The Class 4 transport protocol uses a checksum algorithm originally specified in [FLET82]. The algorithm is much easier to implement in software than a CRC, yet has error-detection properties that are almost the equal of those of CRC.

The mechanism employed is a 16-bit checksum included as a parameter in each internet PDU. The checksum is initially calculated by the sender and placed in the outgoing PDU. The receiver applies the same algorithm to the entire header, now including the 16-bit checksum, and should get a zero result if there are no errors.

The algorithm is as follows. For transmission, let

$$L = \text{length of header in octets}$$
$$B_i = \text{value of } i^{\text{th}} \text{ octet}$$
$$n, n + 1 = \text{octet positions for checksum}$$

Initially, B_n and B_{n+1} are set to zero. Two checksum octets, R and S, are calculated by processing the B_i one at a time:

$$R_i = R_{i-1} + B_i$$
$$S_i = S_{i-1} + R_i$$

Addition is performed modulo 255 (one's complement arithmetic). On completion, we have

$$R = R_L = \sum_{i=1}^{L} B_i$$

$$S = S_L = \sum_{i=1}^{L} (L - i + 1)B_i$$

These numbers were computed with $B_n = B_{n+1} = 0$. Now we must put the appropriate values in these octets so that the algorithm yields zero on reception. Some thought reveals that we must have

$$B_n + B_{n+1} = -R$$

$$(L - n + 1)B_n + (L - n)B_{n+1} = -S$$

Solving, we obtain

$$B_n = (L - n)R - S$$
$$B_{n+1} = (L - n + 1)(-R) + S.$$

chapter 7

Transport Layer

The transport layer can be thought of as the highest of the lower layer protocols. Transport and below and concerned with the transmission of data between end systems across a communications facility. Above the transport layer, the concerns are focused on user requirements and applications. It is the purpose of the transport layer to provide a data transfer service that shields the upper layers from the details of the communications facility employed. Accordingly, the interface between transport and session, as embodied in the transport service, is rather simple. On the other hand, the transport protocol may need to be very complex, as it must deal with a variety of network characteristics and capabilities.

The chapter begins, as usual, with the OSI definition of the layer. Then we examine the protocol mechanisms required to provide a connection-oriented service. Next, the ISO connection-oriented transport service and protocol standards are examined, followed by a look at the connectionless counterparts. Finally, the relationship between transport and network services is examined.

7.1   OSI DEFINITION

The OSI document [ISO 7498] characterizes the transport layer as providing transparent transfer of data between session entities. It relieves session entities from any concern with the detailed way in which reliable and cost-effective data transfer is achieved. All protocols at this layer have end-to-end significance between transport entities in end systems.

Table 7.1 lists the services and functions of the transport layer. The OSI document is curiously reticent about the services at this layer (compare with other layers, Appendix A). The transport service provides the means to establish, maintain, and release transport connections on behalf of session entities. Two session entities in different end systems can establish more than one transport connection between them. Reference is made in the document to the ability to request a particular quality of service on each transport connection. Data transfer can be normal or expedited.

Most of the functions listed for the transport layer are self-explanatory, but a few comments are in order. In terms of addressing, transport addresses are *transport service access points* (TSAPs) and network addresses are the *network service access points* (NSAPs). The TSAP identifies a particular session entity, and a transport entity may support more than one such TSAP. It is the job of the transport layer to map the TSAP into an NSAP. The NSAP, recall is a global network address that uniquely

Table 7.1.   SERVICES AND FUNCTIONS OF THE TRANSPORT LAYER

Services
Transport connection establishment

Data transfer

Transport connection release

Functions
Mapping transport addresses onto network addresses

Multiplexing transport connections onto network connections

Establishment and release of transport connections

End-to-end sequence control on individual connections

End-to-end error detection and any necessary monitoring of the quality of service

End-to-end error recovery

End-to-end segmenting, blocking, and concatenation

End-to-end flow control on individual connections

Supervisory functions

Expedited TSDU transfer

identifies another end system. We will have more to say about this mapping later in the chapter. Transport connections are carried on network connections; both upward and downward multiplexing may be used.

7.2 CONNECTION-ORIENTED TRANSPORT PROTOCOL MECHANISMS

In most cases, it is desired to provide a reliable, connection-oriented service at the transport layer. This service must be provided independent of the type and quality of network and internetwork facilities available. The result is that a connection-oriented transport protocol can be very complex. Thus, it is useful to examine the mechanisms used in such protocols before directly considering the ISO transport protocol. For purposes of clarity, we present the transport protocol mechanisms in an evolutionary fashion. We begin with a network service that makes life easy for the transport protocol and define the required mechanisms. As the network service is made progressively less capable, the transport protocol becomes progressively more complex.

ISO has defined three types of network service [ISO 8073]:

- *Type A:* Network connections with acceptable residual error rate and acceptable rate of signaled failures.
- *Type B:* Network connections with acceptable residual error rate but unacceptable rate of signaled failures.
- *Type C:* Network connections with residual error rate not acceptable to the transport service user.

In this context, an error is defined as a lost or duplicated network protocol data unit. If the error is caught and corrected by the network service in a fashion that is transparent to the transport entity, no damage is done. If the network service detects an error, cannot recover, and signals the transport entities, this is known as a signaled failure. An example would be notification by X.25 that a RESET has occurred. Finally, there are residual errors—those that are not corrected and for which the transport entity is not notified.

Type A provides a reliable network service. This makes life easy for the transport protocol designer. It is well to examine this case, because it helps to clarify the basic transport mechanisms. We will then see that most of the complexity of a transport protocol occurs when the underlying service is unreliable.

Following [MCQU78], we consider three subcases of Type A, which present progressively greater difficulties to the transport service:

- Reliable, sequencing network service with arbitrary message size

  - Reliable, nonsequencing network service with arbitrary message size
  - Reliable, nonsequencing network service with maximum message size

An example of the first case would be reliable X.25 service. The second and third cases might, for example, be reliable datagram services.

In what follows, we will concern ourselves primarily with the most stringent requirement for a transport protocol: The user of the transport service requires a reliable, sequenced, connection-oriented service. It should be clear to the reader what the implications would be of less stringent requirements.

We now consider each of the five types of network service (three subcases of Type A; Type B; Type C).

Reliable Sequencing Network Service

In this case, we assume that the network service will accept messages of arbitrary length and will, with virtually 100 percent reliability, deliver them in sequence to the destination. These assumptions allow the development of the simplest possible transport protocol. Four issues need to be considered:

  - Addressing
  - Multiplexing
  - Flow Control
  - Connection establishment/termination

Addressing.   The issue concerned with addressing is simply this: a user of a given transport entity wishes to either establish a connection with or make a connectionless data transfer to a user of some other transport entity. The target user needs to be specified by all of the following:

  - User identification
  - Transport entity identification
  - End-system identification

The user is identified by a TSAP. Each user of the transport layer accesses the transport services via a unique TSAP. This TSAP must be communicated to the transport entity at the other end so that received data can be routed to the proper transport user. Usually, there will be a single transport entity in each end system, so a transport entity identification is not needed. Finally, the end system identification is a NSAP. Since routing and relaying are not the concern of the transport layer, it simply passes the NSAP down to the network service. TSAP is included in the transport header, to be used at the destination by the destination transport entity.

One question remains to be addressed: How does the initiating transport user know the address of the destination transport user? Two static and two dynamic strategies suggest themselves:

1. The user must know the address it wishes to use ahead of time. This is basically a system configuration function.
2. Some commonly used services are assigned *well-known addresses*.
3. A name server is provided. The user requests a service by some generic or global name. The request is sent to the name server, which does a directory lookup and returns an address. The transport entity then proceeds with the connection.
4. In some cases, the target user is to be a process that is spawned at request time. The initiating user can send a process request to a well known address. The user at that address is a privileged system process that will spawn the new process and return an address.

To see that these are distinct cases, we give an example of each:

1. A process may be running that is only of concern to a limited number of transport users. For example, a process in a station may collect statistics on performance. From time to time, a central network management routine connects to the process to obtain the statistics. These processes generally are not, and should not be, well known and accessible to all.
2. Examples of commonly used services are time sharing and word processing.
3. Some services may be commonly used, but their location may change from time to time. For example, a data entry process may be moved from one station to another on a local network to balance load. The names of such *movable* processes can be kept in a directory, with the addresses updated when a move occurs.
4. A programmer has developed a private application (e.g., a simulation program) that will execute on a remote mainframe but be invoked from a local minicomputer. An RJE-type request can be issued to a remote job-management process that spawns the simulation process.

Multiplexing.   We now turn to the concept of multiplexing, which was discussed in general terms in Sec. 2.2. With respect to the interface between the transport protocol and higher level protocols, the transport protocol performs a multiplexing/ demultiplexing function. That is, multiple users employ the same transport protocol, and are distinguished by TSAP.

The transport entity may also perform a multiplexing function with respect to the network services that it uses. Recall that we defined upward multiplexing as the multiplexing of multiple (N) connections on a single (N-1) connection, and downward multiplexing as the splitting of a single (N) connection among multiple (N-1) connections.

Consider, for example, a transport entity making use of an X.25 service. Why should the transport entity employ upward multiplexing? There are, after all, 4095 virtual circuits available. In the typical case, this is more than enough to handle all active transport users. However, most X.25 networks base part of their charge on virtual circuit connect time, because each virtual circuit consumes some node buffer resources. Thus, if a single virtual circuit provides sufficient throughput for multiple transport users, upward multiplexing is indicated.

On the other hand, downward multiplexing or splitting might be used to improve throughput. If, for example, each X.25 virtual circuit is restricted to a 3-bit sequence number, only seven packets can be outstanding at a time. A larger sequence space might be needed for high-delay networks. Of course, throughput can only be increased so far. If there is a single station-node link over which all virtual circuits are multiplexed, the throughput of a transport connection cannot exceed the data rate of that link.

Flow Control. The OSI document [ISO7498] defines flow control as a function for the control of the data flow within a layer or between adjacent layers. Whereas flow control is a relatively simple mechanism at the link layer, it is a rather complex mechanism at the transport layer, for two main reasons:

- Flow control at the transport level involves the interaction of transport users, transport entities, and the network service.
- The transmission delay between transport entities is generally long compared to actual transmission time and, what is worse, variable.

Figure 7.1 illustrates the first point. Transport user *A* wishes to send data to transport user *B* over a transport connection. We can view the situation as involving four queues. *A* generates data and queues it up to send. *A* must wait to send that data until

- It has permission from *B* (peer flow control), and
- It has permission from its own transport entity (interface flow control).

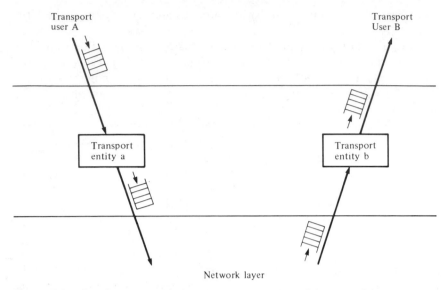

Figure 7.1.   Queuing representation of connection-oriented data transfer.

As data flows down from *A* to transport entity *a*, *a* queues the data until it has permission to send it on from *b* and the network service. The data are then handed to the network layer for delivery to *b*. The network service must queue the data until it receives permission from *b* to pass them on. Finally, *b* must await *B*'s permission before delivering the data to their destination.

To see the effects of delay, consider the possible interactions depicted in Fig. 7.2. When a user wishes to transmit data, it sends these data to its transport entity (e.g., using a SEND call). This triggers two events. The transport entity generates one or more transport protocol data units (TPDUs) and passes these on to the network service. It also in some way acknowledges to the user that it has accepted the data for transmission. At this point, the transport entity can exercise flow control across the user-transport interface by simply withholding its acknowledgment. The transport entity is most likely to do this if the entity itself is being held up by a flow control exercised by either the network service or the target transport entity.

In any case, once the transport entity has accepted the data, it sends out a TPDU. Some time later, it receives an acknowledgment that the data has been received at the remote end. It may then send a confirmation to the sender.

At the receiving end, a TPDU arrives at the transport entity. It unwraps the data and sends it on (e.g., by an Indication primitive) to the destination user. When the user accepts the data, it issues an acknowledgment (e.g., in the form of a RESPONSE primitive). The user can exercise flow control over the transport entity by withholding its response.

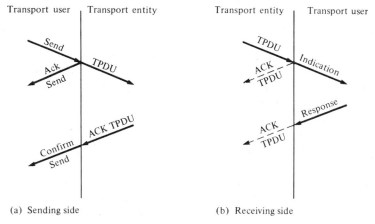

Transport user | Transport entity   Transport entity | Transport user

(a) Sending side   (b) Receiving side

Figure 7.2. User–transport interaction.

Now, the target transport entity has two choices regarding acknowledgment. Either it can issue an acknowledgment as soon as it has correctly received the TPDU (the usual practice), or it can wait until it knows that the user has correctly received the data before acknowledging. The latter course is the safer. In the latter case, the send confirmation is in fact a confirmation that the destination user received the data. In the former case, it merely confirms that the data made it through to the remote transport entity.

With the discussion above in mind, we can cite two reasons why one transport entity would want to restrain the rate of TPDU transmission over a connection from another transport entity:

- The user of the receiving transport entity cannot keep up with the flow of data.
- The receiving transport entity itself cannot keep up with the flow of TPDUs.

How do such problems manifest themselves? Well, presumably a transport entity has a certain amount of buffer space. Incoming TPDUs are added to the buffer. Each buffered TPDU is processed (i.e., examine the transport header) and the data are sent to the user. Either of the two problems mentioned above will cause the buffer to fill up. Thus the transport entity needs to take steps to stop or slow the flow of TPDUs to prevent buffer overflow. This requirement is not so easy to fulfill, because of the annoying time gap between sender and receiver. We return to this point in a moment. First, we present four ways of coping with the flow control requirement. The receiving transport entity can:

1. Do nothing.
2. Refuse to accept further TPDUs from the network service.

3. Use a fixed sliding-window protocol.
4. Use a credit scheme.

Alternative 1 means that the TPDUs that overflow the buffer are discarded. The sending transport entity, failing to get an acknowledgment, will retransmit. This is a shame, as the advantage of a reliable network is that one never has to retransmit. Furthermore, the effect of this maneuver is to exacerbate the problem! The sender has increased its output to include new TPDUs plus retransmitted old TPDUs.

The second alternative is a backpressure mechanism that relies on the network service to do the work. When a buffer of a transport entity is full, it refuses additional data from the network service. This triggers flow control procedures within the network that throttle the network service at the sending end. This service, in turn, refuses additional TPDUs from its transport entity. It should be clear that this mechanism is clumsy and coarse-grained. For example, if multiple transport connections are multiplexed on a single network connection (virtual circuit), flow control is exercised only on the aggregate of all transport connections. Remarkably, there is at least one transport protocol that uses this strategy: the EHKP4 protocol standard developed in West Germany [MEIJ82].

The third alternative is already familiar to you from our discussions of link layer protocols. The key ingredients, recall, are:

• The use of sequence numbers on data units.
• The use of a window of fixed size.
• The use of acknowledgments to advance the window.

With a reliable network service, the sliding window technique would actually work quite well. For example, consider a protocol with a window size of 7. Whenever the sender receives an acknowledgment to a particular TPDU, it is automatically authorized to send the succeeding seven TPDUs (of course, some may already have been sent). Now, when the receiver's buffer capacity gets down to seven TPDUs, it can withhold acknowledgment of incoming TPDUs to avoid overflow. The sending transport entity can send at most seven additional TPDUs and then must stop. Because the underlying network service is reliable, the sender will not time out and retransmit. Thus, at some point, a sending transport entity may have a number of TPDUs outstanding for which no acknowledgment has been received. Since we are dealing with a reliable network, the sending transport entity can assume that the TPDUs will get through and that the lack of acknowledgment is a flow control tactic. This tactic would not work well in an unreliable network, since the sending transport entity would not know whether the lack of acknowledgment is due to flow control or a lost TPDU.

The fourth alternative, a credit scheme, provides the receiver with a greater degree of control over data flow. Although it is not strictly necessary with a reliable network service, a credit scheme should result in a smoother traffic flow. Furthermore, it is a more effective scheme with an unreliable network service, as we shall see.

The credit scheme decouples acknowledgment from flow control. In fixed sliding-window protocols, such as X.25, the two are synonymous. In a credit scheme, a TPDU may be acknowledged without granting new credit, and vice versa. Figure 7.3 illustrates the protocol (compare Fig. 4.5). For simplicity, we show a data flow in one direction only. In this

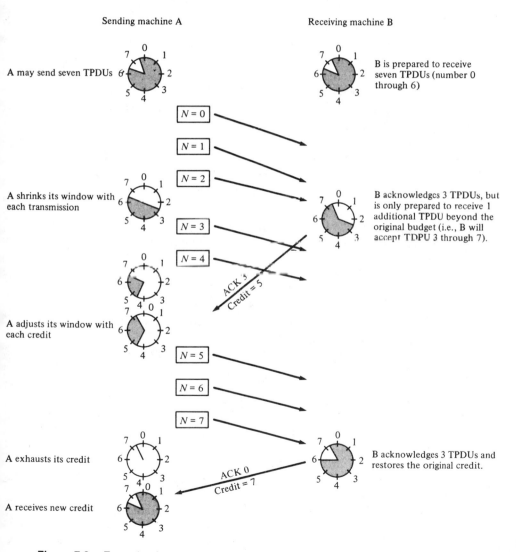

Figure 7.3. Example of a credit allocation protocol.

example, TPDUs are numbered sequentially modulo 8. Initially, through the connection establishment process, the sending and receiving sequence numbers are synchronized and A is granted a credit allocation of 7. A advances the trailing edge of its window each time that it transmits, and advances the leading edge only when it is granted credit.

In both the credit allocation scheme and the sliding window scheme, the receiver needs to adopt some policy concerning the amount of data it permits the sender to transmit. The conservative approach is to only allow new TPDUs up to the limit of available buffer space. If this policy were in effect in Fig. 7.3, the first credit message implies that B has five free buffer slots, and the second message that B has seven free slots.

A conservative flow control scheme may limit the throughput of the transport connection in long-delay situations. The receiver could potentially increase throughput by optimistically granting credit for space it does not have. For example, if a receiver's buffer is full but it anticipates that it can release space for two TPDUs within a round-trip propagation time, it could immediately send a credit of 2. If the receiver can keep up with the sender, this scheme may increase throughput and can do no harm. If the sender is faster than the receiver, however, some TPDUs may be discarded, necessitating a retransmission. Since retransmissions are not otherwise necessary with a reliable network service, an optimistic flow control scheme will complicate the protocol.

Connection Establishment and Termination. Even with a reliable network service, there is a need for connection establishment and termination procedures to support connection-oriented service. Connection establishment serves three main purposes:

- It allows each end to assure that the other exists.
- It allows negotiation of optional parameters (e.g., TPDU size, window size, quality of service).
- It triggers allocation of transport entity resources (e.g., buffer space, entry in connection table).

Connection establishment is by mutual agreement and can be accomplished by a simple set of user commands and control TPDUs, as shown in the state diagram of Fig. 7.4. To begin, a user is in an IDLE state (with respect to the transport entity). The user can signal that it will passively wait for a request with a LISTEN command. A server program, such as time sharing or a file transfer application, might do this. The user may change its mind by sending a CLOSE command.

After the LISTEN command is issued, the transport entity creates a connection object of some sort (i.e., a table entry) that is in the LSTN state. If a RFC (request for connection) TPDU is received that specifies

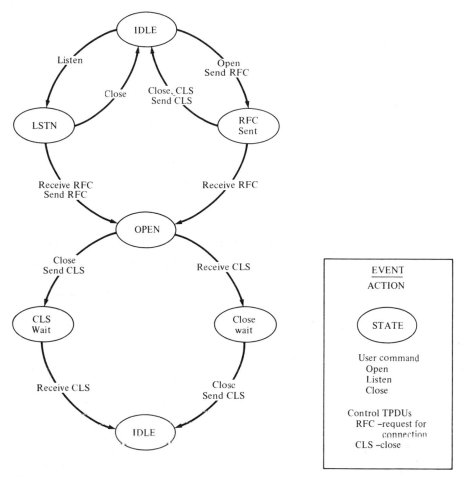

Figure 7.4. Simple connection state diagram.

the listening user, then a connection is opened. To do this, the transport entity:

- Signals the user that a connection is open.
- Sends an RFC as confirmation to the remote transport entity.
- Puts the connection object in an OPEN state.

A user may open a connection by issuing an OPEN command, which triggers the transport entity to send an RFC. The reception of a matching RFC establishes the connection. The connection is prematurely aborted if the local user issues a CLOSE command or the remote transport entity refuses the connection by sending a CLS TPDU.

Figure 7.5 shows the robustness of this protocol. Either side can

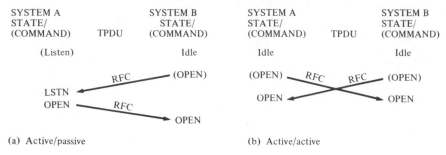

Figure 7.5.   Connection establishment sequence of events.

initiate a connection. Furthermore, if both sides initiate the connection at about the same time, it is established without confusion.

The reader may ask what happens if an RFC comes in while the requested user is idle (not listening). Three courses may be followed:

- The transport entity can reject the request by sending a CLS.
- The request can be queued until a LISTEN is issued by the user.
- The transport entity can interrupt or otherwise signal the user to notify it of a pending request.

Note that if the latter mechanism is used, a Listen command is not strictly necessary, but may be replaced by an Accept command, which is a signal from the user to the transport entity that it accepts the request for connection. This is the ISO approach.

Connection termination is handled similarly. Either side, or both sides, may initiate a close. The connection is closed by mutual agreement. This strategy allows for either abrupt or graceful termination. To achieve the latter, a connection in the CLS WAIT state must continue to accept data TPDUs until a CLS is received.

Reliable Nonsequencing Network Service

In this case, we assume that the network service will accept messages of arbitrary length and will, with virtually 100 percent reliability, deliver them to the destination. However, we now assume that the TPDUs may arrive out of sequence. This seemingly trivial change has a number of consequences.

The first consequence is that sequence numbers are required on TPDUs for connection-oriented service. We employ them with a reliable sequencing network service for flow control purposes. Here they are required to permit the transport entity to deliver data in sequence.

Equally important, the transport entity must keep track of control TPDUs, both in relationship to each other and to data TPDUs. Examples of this requirement are seen in flow control and in connection establishment and termination.

First, consider flow control. A transport entity may sometimes find it desirable to decrease outstanding offered credit on a connection, because expected resources did not become available, or because resources had to be reallocated to serve another connection. If sequencing is not guaranteed, a situation such as that shown in Fig. 7.6 might arise. After transport entity *A* has sent TPDU 1, *B* responds with a new credit allocation of 5. A short time later, and before additional TPDUs arrive, *B* discovers a potential shortfall and sends a reduced credit allocation of 3. However, this allocation overtakes the earlier one and arrives first. It appears to *A* that *B* has initially granted an allocation of 3 and then obtained additional resources, and increased the allocation to 5. Thus, while *B* is not prepared to receive any more TPDUs at this point, *A* feels entitled to send two additional TPDUs. The solution to this problem is to number credit allocations sequentially.

Now consider connection establishment. Figure 7.4 shows that after a transport entity has sent an RFC, it expects to receive either a CLS (connection reject) or RFC (connection accept) from the target entity. The target transport entity, having received the opening RFC, might respond with RFC, followed by a number of TPDUs. One of these TPDUs could arrive back at the initiating entity prior to the RFC. The best policy would seem to be for the initiating transport entity to queue these TPDUs until the RFC is received that confirms the connection.

Just as data may arrive before a connection is officially open, they may also arrive after the connection has closed. The following may occur. After a transport entity has sent its last data TPDU, it sends a CLS. The

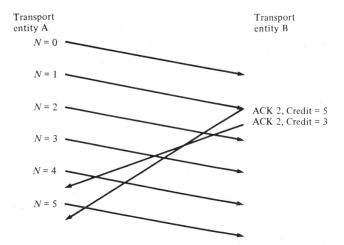

Figure 7.6.   Example of flow control with a nonsequenced network service.

CLS may arrive before the last data TPDU. One way to avoid a problem is for the CLS TPDU to contain the next sequence number after the last data TPDU sent on this connection. Then, the receiving transport entity, upon receiving a CLS, will wait if necessary for late-arriving data TPDUs before closing the connection.

Reliable Nonsequencing Network Service with Maximum TPDU Size

We now add another limitation to the capability of the network service: It will only accept TPDUs of some maximum size for transfer. Presumably, this size is chosen to optimize network performance.

We need to distinguish two types of data transfer required by the user: stream oriented and block oriented. A stream-oriented interface between transport and the user accepts data as if they were a continuous stream of bits and reproduces the stream at the other end without conveying any information about the breakpoints in the stream submitted by the sender. This interface might serve voice and real-time applications.

A more common occurrence is a transport user that sends data in blocks. Following OSI convention, we refer to a block of data presented to transport as a TSDU. If a TSDU exceeds the maximum allowable TPDU size, the transport entity must segment the TSDU before transmission, to be reassembled at reception before delivery to the user. Because our network is nonsequencing, segments may arrive out of order. Worse, segments from different TSDUs may be interchanged en route.

A simple solution to this problem is to number each TSDU sequentially and to number each segment sequentially within each TSDU. This, however, is an unnecessary duplication of the TPDU sequence numbering function. A moment's thought should make it clear that all that is required is an end-of-transmission (EOT) flag. As TPDUs arrive at the destination transport entity, they are reordered. Each sequential set of TPDUs, starting with the first TPDU after an EOT, and including all TPDUs through the next EOT, are treated as a unit. The data from this unit, stripped of transport headers, is delivered as a single TSDU to the user.

Failure-Prone Network Service

We now turn to what may strike the reader as an unusual sort of network. This is a connection-oriented network service and, while it delivers data reliably (though not necessarily in sequence), it suffers from network failures that cause it to reset or restart network connections. Thus TPDUs may be lost, but the loss is reported to the transport entities affected. The reader might visualize an X.25 network service being provided by a relatively unreliable underlying network.

In any case, the transport entity must now cope with the problem of recovering from known loss of data and/or network connections. The sequence numbering scheme provides an effective tool. In the normal course of events, TPDUs need not be acknowledged, because the network service is reliable. However, acknowledgment takes place from time to time in connection with the flow control scheme. We show this mechanism also deals with network failure.

First, consider a connection reset, such as the X.25 RESET command will cause. The network service will signal the transport entity that a reset has occurred on one or more transport connections. The transport entity realizes that it has perhaps lost some incoming TPDUs in transit, and that some already-transmitted TPDUs may not reach their destination. Two actions are indicated:

- Issue a control TPDU to the other end that acknowledges a reset condition and gives the number of the last TPDU received.
- Refrain from issuing new data TPDUs until a corresponding reset control TPDU is received from the other end.

A more serious condition is the loss of an underlying network connection, such as an X.25 RESTART causes. In this case, the side that first initiated the connection should issue a request to the network service for a new network connection and then issue a control TPDU to the other side that identifies the new network connection for the ongoing transport connection. Following this, both sides must resynchronize with the use of reset control TPDUs.

Unreliable Network Service

The most difficult case for a transport protocol is that of an unreliable network service. The problem is not just that TPDUs are occasionally lost, but that TPDUs may arrive out of sequence due to variable transit delays. As we shall see, elaborate machinery is required to cope with these two interrelated network deficiencies. We shall also see that a discouraging pattern emerges. The combination of unreliability and nonsequencing creates problems with every mechanism we have discussed so far. Generally, the solution to each problem raises new problems. Although there are problems to be overcome for protocols at all levels, it seems that there are more difficulties with a reliable connection-oriented transport protocol than any other sort of protocol.

Six issues need to be addressed:

- Retransmission strategy
- Duplicate detection
- Flow control
- Connection establishment
- Connection termination
- Crash recovery

Retransmission Strategy.   Two events necessitate the retransmission of a TPDU. First, the TPDU may be damaged in transit but nevertheless arrive at its destination. If a frame check sequence is included with the TPDU, the receiving transport entity can detect the error and discard the TPDU. The second contingency is that a TPDU fails to arrive. In either case, the sending transport entity does not know that the TPDU transmission was unsuccessful. To cover this contingency, we require that a positive acknowledgment (ACK) scheme be used: The receiver must acknowledge each successfully received TPDU. For efficiency, we do not require one ACK per TPDU. Rather, a cumulative acknowledgment can be used, as we have seen many times in this book. Thus the receiver may receive TPDUs numbered 1, 2, and 3, but only send ACK 4 back. The sender must interpret ACK 4 to mean that number 3 and all previous TPDUs have been successfully received.

If a TPDU does not arrive successfully, no ACK will be issued and a retransmission is in order. To cope with this situation, there must be a timer associated with each TPDU as it is sent. If the timer expires before the TPDU is acknowledged, the sender must retransmit.

So the addition of a timer solves that problem. Next problem: At what value should the timer be set? If the value is too small, there will be many unnecessary retransmissions, wasting network capacity. If the value is too large, the protocol will be sluggish in responding to a lost TPDU. The timer should be set at a value a bit longer than the round trip delay (send TPDU, receive ACK). Of course this delay is variable even under constant network load. Worse, the statistics of the delay will vary with changing network conditions.

Two strategies suggest themselves. A fixed timer value could be used, based on an understanding of the network's typical behavior. This suffers from an inability to respond to changing network conditions. If the value is set too high, the service will always be sluggish. If it is set too low, a positive feedback condition can develop, in which network congestion leads to more retransmissions, which increase congestion.

An adaptive scheme has its own problems [ZHAN86]. Suppose that the transport entity keeps track of the time taken to acknowledge data TPDUS and sets its retransmission timer based on the average of the observed delays. This value cannot be trusted for three reasons:

- The peer entity may not acknowledge a TPDU immediately. Recall that we gave it the privilege of cumulative acknowledgments.
- If a TPDU has been retransmitted, the sender cannot know whether the received ACK is a response to the initial transmission or the retransmission.
- Network conditions may change suddenly.

Each of these problems is a cause for some further tweaking of the transport algorithm, but the problem admits of no complete solution.

There will always be some uncertainty concerning the best value for the retransmission timer.

Incidentally, the retransmission timer is only one of a number of timers needed for proper functioning of a transport protocol. These are listed in Table 7.2, together with a brief explanation. Further discussion will be found in what follows.

Duplicate Detection. If a TPDU is lost and then retransmitted, no confusion will result. If however, an ACK is lost, one or more TPDUs will be retransmitted and, if they arrive successfully, be duplicates of previously received TPDUs. Thus the receiver must be able to recognize duplicates. The fact that each TPDU carries a sequence number helps but, nevertheless, duplicate detection and handling is no easy thing. There are two cases:

- A duplicate is received before the close of the connection.
- A duplicate is received after the close of the connection.

Notice that we say *a* duplicate rather than *the* duplicate. From the sender's point of view, the retransmitted TPDU is the duplicate. However, the retransmitted TPDU may arrive before the original TPDU, in which case the receiver views the original TPDU as the duplicate. In any case, two tactics are needed to cope with a duplicate received before the close of a connection:

- The receiver must assume that its acknowledgment was lost and therefore must acknowledge the duplicate. Consequently, the sender must not get confused if it receives multiple ACKs to the same TPDU.
- The sequence number space must be long enough so as not to *cycle* in less than the maximum possible TPDU lifetime.

Table 7.2. TRANSPORT PROTOCOL TIMERS

Retransmission timer	Retransmit an unacknowledged TPDU
Reconnection timer	Minimum time between closing one connection and opening another with the same destination address
Window timer	Maximum time between ACK/CREDIT TPDUs
Retransmit-RFC timer	Time between attempts to open a connection
Persistence timer	Abort connection when no TPDUs are acknowledged
Inactivity timer	Abort connection when no TPDUs are received

Figure 7.7 illustrates the reason for the latter requirement. In this example, the sequence space is of length 8. For simplicity, we assume a sliding-window protocol with a window size of 3. Suppose that *A* has transmitted TPDUs 0, 1, and 2 and receives no acknowledgments. Eventually, it times out and retransmits TPDU 0. *B* has received 1 and 2, but 0 is delayed in transit. Thus *B* does not send any ACKs. When the duplicate TPDU 0 arrives, *B* acknowledges 0, 1, and 2. Meanwhile, *A* has timed out again and retransmits 1, which *B* acknowledges with another ACK 3. Things now seem to have sorted themselves out and data transfer continues. When the sequence space is exhausted, *A* cycles back to sequence number 0 and continues. Alas, the old TPDU 0 makes a belated appearance and is accepted by *B* before the new TPDU 0 arrives.

It should be clear that the untimely emergence of the old TPDU would have caused no difficulty if the sequence numbers had not yet wrapped around. The problem is: How big must the sequence space be? This depends on, among other things, whether the network enforces a maximum packet lifetime, and the rate at which TPDUs are being trans-

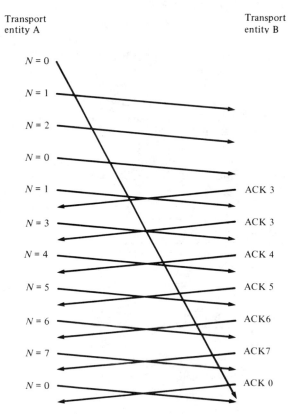

Figure 7.7. Example of incorrect duplicate detection.

mitted. Fortunately, each addition of a single bit to the sequence number field doubles the sequence space, so it is rather easy to select a safe size. As we shall see, the standard transport protocol allows stupendous sequence spaces.

A more subtle problem is posed by TPDUs that continue to rattle around after a transport connection is closed. If a subsequent connection is opened between the same two transport entities, a TPDU from the old connection could arrive and be accepted on the new connection! Similarly, a delayed ACK can enter a new connection and cause problems.

There are a number of approaches to this particular problem. We mention several of the more promising. First, the sequence numbering scheme can be extended across connection lifetimes. This requires that a transport entity remember the last sequence number that it used on transmission for each terminated connection. Then, when a new connection to a transport entity is attempted, the RFC contains the sequence number to be used to begin data transfer. Of course, this procedure is symmetric, with each side responsible for declaring the sequence number with which it will commence transmission.

A second approach is to provide a separate transport connection identifier, and use a new identifier with each new connection.

The procedures above work fine unless a system crash occurs. In that case, the system will not remember what sequence number or connection identifier was used last. An alternative is to simply wait a sufficient time between connections to assure that all old TPDUs are gone. Then, even if one side has experienced a crash, the other side can refuse a connection until the reconnection timer expires. This, of course, may cause unnecessary delays.

Flow Control.   The credit allocation flow control mechanism described earlier is quite robust in the face of an unreliable network service and requires little enhancement. We assume that the credit allocation scheme is tied to acknowledgments in the following way: To both acknowledge TPDUs and grant credit, a transport entity sends a control TPDU of the form (ACK N + 1, CREDIT M), where ACK N + 1 acknowledges all data TPDUs through number N, and CREDIT M allows TPDUs number N + 1 though N + M to be transmitted. This mechanism is quite powerful. Consider that the last control TPDU issued by B was (ACK N + 1, CREDIT M). Then:

- To increase or decrease credit to X when no additional TPDUs have arrived, B can issue (ACK N + 1, CREDIT X).
- To acknowledge a new TPDU without increasing credit, B can issue (ACK N + 2, CREDIT M − 1).

If an ACK/CREDIT TPDU is lost, little harm is done. Further acknowledgments will resynchronize the protocol. Further, if no new acknowledgments are forthcoming, the sender times out and retransmits a data TPDU, which triggers a new acknowledgment. However, it is still possible for deadlock to occur. Consider a situation in which B sends (ACK N, CREDIT 0), temporarily closing the window. Subsequently, B sends (ACK N, CREDIT M), but this TPDU is lost. A is awaiting the opportunity to send data and B thinks that it has granted that opportunity. To overcome this problem, a window timer can be used. This timer is reset with each outgoing ACK/CREDIT TPDU. If the timer ever expires, the protocol entity is required to send an ACK/CREDIT TPDU, even if it duplicates a previous one. This breaks the deadlock and also assures the other end that the protocol entity is still alive.

An alternative or supplemental mechanism is to provide for acknowledgments to the ACK/CREDIT TPDU. With this mechanism in place, the window timer can have a quite large value without causing much difficulty.

Connection Establishment.   As with other protocol mechanisms, connection establishment must take into account the unreliability of a network service. Recall that a connection establishment calls for the exchange of RFCs, a procedure sometimes referred to as a *two-way handshake*. Suppose that A issues an RFC to B. It expects to get an RFC back, confirming the connection. Two things can go wrong: A's RFC can be lost or B's answering RFC can be lost. Both cases can be handled by use of a retransmit-RFC timer. After A issues an RFC, it will reissue the RFC when the timer expires.

This gives rise, potentially, to duplicate RFCs. If A's initial RFC was lost, there are no duplicates. If B's response was not lost, then B may receive two RFCs from A. Further, if B's response was not lost, but simply delayed, A may get two responding RFCs. All of this means that A and B must simply ignore duplicate RFCs once a connection is established.

Now, consider that a duplicate RFC may survive past the termination of the connection. Figure 7.8 depicts the problem that may arise. An old RFC X (request for connection, sequence number begins at X) arrives at B after the connection is terminated. B assumes that this is a fresh request and responds with RFC Y. Meanwhile, A has decided to open a new connection with B and sends RFC Z. B discards this as a duplicate. Subsequently, A initiates data transfer with a TPDU numbered Z. B rejects the TPDU as being out of sequence.

The way out of this problem is for each side to acknowledge explicitly the other's RFC and sequence number. The procedure is known as a *three-way handshake* [TOML75]. The revised connection state diagram is shown in the upper part of Fig. 7.9. A new state (RFC Received) is added. In this state, the transport entity hesitates during connection opening to assure that any RFC which was sent has also been acknowledged

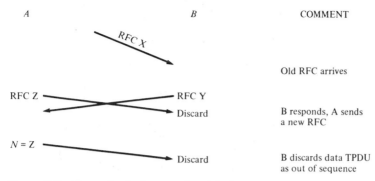

Figure 7.8.   Example of a two-way handshake.

before the connection is declared open. In addition to the new state, there is a new control TPDU (RST) to reset the other side when a duplicate RFC is detected.

Figure 7.10 illustrates typical three-way handshake operations. Under normal conditions, an RFC includes the sending sequence number. The responding RFC acknowledges that number and includes the sequence number for the other side. The initiating transport entity acknowledges the RFC/ACK in its first data TPDU. Next is shown a situation in which an old RFC X arrives at *B* after the close of the relevant connection. *B* assumes that this is a fresh request and responds with RFC Y, ACK X. When *A* receives this message, it realizes that it has not requested a connection and therefore sends a RST, ACK Y. Note that the ACK Y portion of the RST message is essential so that an old duplicate RST does not abort a legitimate connection establishment. The final example shows a case in which an old RFC, ACK arrives in the middle of a new connection establishment. Because of the use of sequence numbers in the acknowledgments, this event causes no mischief.

The upper part of Fig. 7.9 does not include transitions in which RST is sent. This was done for simplicity. The basic rule is: Send an RST if connection state is not yet OPEN and an invalid ACK (one that does not reference something that was sent) is received. The reader should try various combinations of events to see that this connection establishment procedure works in spite of any combination of old and lost TPDUs.

Connection Termination.   As with connection establishment, the connection termination procedure must cope with old and lost control TPDUs. Figure 7.9 indicates that a similar solution is adopted. Each side must explicitly acknowledge the CLS TPDU of the other. To avoid confusion, sequence numbers are used as follows:

- CLS contains the sequence number plus one of the last data TPDU sent.
- ACK contains the sequence number received in the CLS.

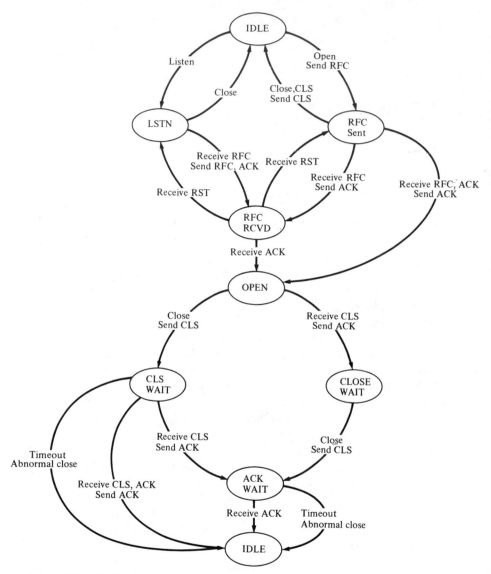

Figure 7.9. Revised connection state diagram.

Timeout procedures are included to allow a transport entity to complete its closing if the other side appears uncooperative. The problem may be lost TPDUs rather than a failure at the other end. Therefore, one or more retransmissions are advisable before signaling an abnormal close.

Crash Recovery. When the system upon which a transport entity is running fails and subsequently restarts, the state information of all active

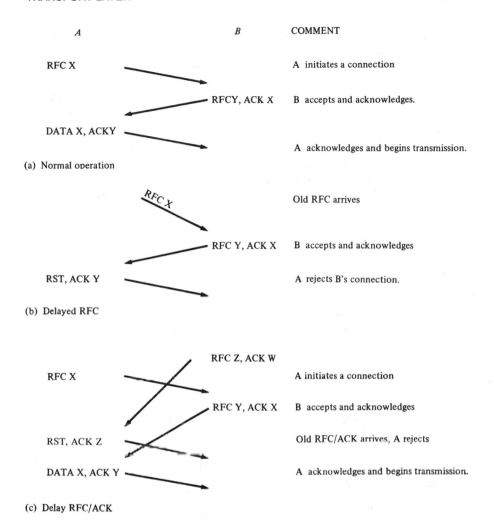

Figure 7.10. Examples of three-way handshake.

connections is lost. The affected connections become *half-open* as the side that did not fail does not yet realize the problem.

The still active side of a half-open connection can close the connection using a give-up timer. This timer measures the time the transport machine will continue to await an acknowledgment (or other appropriate reply) of a transmitted TPDU after the TPDU has been retransmitted the maximum number of times. When the timer expires, the transport entity assumes that the other transport entity or the intervening network has failed, closes the connection, and signals an abnormal close to the transport user.

In the event that a transport entity fails and quickly restarts, half-open connections can be terminated more quickly by the use of the RST TPDU. The failed side returns a RST X to every TPDU X that it receives.

When the RST X reaches the other side, it must be checked for validity based on the sequence number X, as the RST could be in response to an old TPDU. If the reset is valid, the transport entity performs an abnormal termination.

These measures clean up the situation at the transport level. The decision as to whether to reopen the connection is up to the transport users. The problem is one of synchronization. At the time of failure, there may have been one or more outstanding TPDUs in either direction. The transport user on the side that did not fail knows how much data it has received, but the other user may not, if state information were lost. Thus, there is the danger that some user data will be lost or duplicated.

7.3 ISO CONNECTION-ORIENTED TRANSPORT SERVICE DEFINITION

ISO has issued a standard for a connection-oriented transport service [ISO 8072], with an identical specification being issued by CCITT [X.214]. Key characteristics of the transport service, as listed in the standard are:

- *Quality of service selection:* The transport service optimizes the use of available communications resources to provide the requested quality of service at minimum cost.
- *Independence of underlying communications resources:* Transport users need not be aware of the quality of service provided by the network service.
- *End-to-end significance:* Data is transferred between transport service users in end systems.
- *Transparency of transferred information:* The transport service does not restrict the content, format, or coding of the user data.
- *User addressing:* A system of addressing is used that allows transport service users to refer unambiguously to one another.

The standard specifies a set of parameters that define the quality of service as observed by transport service users over a transport connection. The list of parameters (Table 7.3) is almost identical to that for the ISO connection-oriented network service (see Table 5.7). The definitions correspond, with the following exceptions:

- *Throughput:* The transport parameters specify average and maximum throughput. The transport service will attempt to provide the lowest-cost service that satisfies these parameters.
- *Transport connection (TC) protection:* One of four options: (1) no protection features, (2) protection against passive monitoring, (3)

**Table 7.3.   QUALITY OF SERVICE PARAMETERS FOR THE TRANSPORT
                     SERVICE**

TC Establishment Delay

TC Establishment Failure Probability

Throughput

Transit Delay

Residual Error Rate

Transfer Failure Probability

TC Release Delay

TC Release Failure Probability

TC Protection

TC Priority

Resilience of the TC

> protection against modification, replay, addition, or deletion, and
> (4) both (2) and (3).
> * *Resilience of the TC:* Probability of a TC release initiated by a
>   transport service (TS) provider.

As in the case of the network service, most of the parameters deal with
the speed or accuracy/reliability characteristics during the three phases
of a connection (see Table 5.6).

As usual, the service definition is in the form of a set of primitives
and their parameters; these are listed in Table 7.4. The T-CONNECT
primitives are used to establish a connection. Quality of service parameters are negotiated as follows:

* In the request primitive, any defined value for each parameter is
  allowed.
* In the indication primitive, for each requested parameter, the
  value is equal to or poorer than the value in the request primitive,
  except for the protection parameter, which must have the same
  value.
* In the response primitive, for each requested parameter, the value
  is equal to or poorer than the value in the indication primitive.
* In the confirm primitive, for each requested parameter, the value
  is equal to or poorer than the value in the response primitive.

The expedited data service is negotiated as follows. If the calling user
does not request this service, it is not available to either user for this
connection. If the calling user requests this service, the called user may
agree to its use on this connection, in which case the transport service

Table 7.4.   ISO TRANSPORT SERVICE PRIMITIVES

T-CONNECT.request (Called Address, Calling Address, Expedited Data Option, Quality of Service, Data)

T-CONNECT.indication (Called Address, Calling Address, Expedited Data Option, Quality of Service, Data)

T-CONNECT.response (Quality of Service, Responding Address, Expedited Data Option, Data)

T-CONNECT.confirm (Quality of Service, Responding Address, Expedited Data Option, Data)

T-DISCONNECT.request (Data)

T-DISCONNECT.indication (Disconnect Reason, Data)

T-DATA.request (Data)

T-DATA.indication (Data)

T-EXPEDITED-DATA.request (Data)

T-EXPEDITED-DATA.indication (Data)

---

provider will provide it. If the called user refuses this service, it will not be provided on this connection.

The T-DISCONNECT primitives provide for abrupt connection termination (TSDUs may be lost) and are also used for connection rejection, by either the transport service or the called user. In either case, the indication primitive includes a reason parameter, with one of the following values:

- Remote user invoked
- Lack of local or remote resources of the TS provider
- Quality of service below minimum level
- Misbehaviour of TS provider
- Called TS user unknown
- Called TS user unavailable
- Unknown reason

The T-DATA primitives provide for the transfer of TSDUs in a way that preserves the integrity, sequence, and boundaries of the TSDUs. The T-EXPEDITED-DATA primitives provide for the transfer of expedited TSDUs. The transport service provider guarantees that an expedited data TSDU will be delivered before subsequently submitted data TSDUs. However, the amount of previously submitted normal data that is bypassed, if any, cannot be predicted. Figure 7.11 displays the sequences in which these primitives may be used.

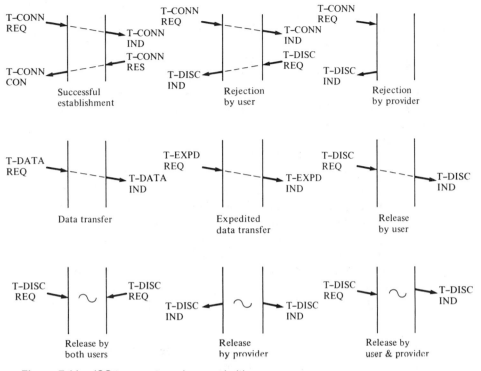

Figure 7.11. ISO transport services—primitive sequences.

7.4 ISO CONNECTION-ORIENTED TRANSPORT PROTOCOL

ISO has issued a standard for a family of connection-oriented transport protocols [ISO 8073]. An identical specification has been issued by CCITT [X.224].

The Transport Protocol Family

To handle a variety of user service requirements and available network services, ISO has defined five classes of transport protocol:

- *Class 0:* Simple class
- *Class 1:* Basic error recovery class
- *Class 2:* Multiplexing class
- *Class 3:* Error recovery and multiplexing class
- *Class 4:* Error detection and recovery class

These classes are related to the three types of network service defined in Sec. 7.2. Classes 0 and 2 are used with Type A networks; Classes 1 and

3 are used with Type B networks; and Class 4 is used with Type C networks. Table 7.5 lists the functions of the various protocol classes, and Table 7.6 defines them.

Class 0 was developed by CCITT and is oriented for teletex, a text-transmission upgrade to Telex (T.70). It provides the simplest kind of transport connection. It provides a connection with flow control based on network-level flow control, and connection release based on the release of the network connection.

Class 1 was also developed by CCITT and is designed to run on an X.25 network and provide minimal error recovery (network-signaled errors). The key difference from Class 0 is that TPDUs are numbered. This allows the protocol to resynchronize after an X.25 RESET and to reassign a transport connection after an X.25 RESTART. Flow control is still provided by the network layer. Expedited data transfer is also provided.

Class 2 is an enhancement to Class 0 that still assumes a highly reliable network service. The key enhancement is the ability to multiplex multiple transport connections onto a single network connection. A corollary enhancement is the provision of explicit flow control, because a single network connection flow control mechanism does not allow individual flow control of transport connections. A credit allocation scheme is used.

Class 3 is basically the union of the Class 1 and 2 capabilities. It provides the multiplexing and flow control capabilities of Class 2. It also contains the resynchronization and reassignment capabilities needed to cope with failure-prone networks.

Class 4 assumes that the underlying network service is unreliable. Thus most, if not all, of the mechanisms described in Sec. 7.2 must be included.

Protocol Formats

The ISO protocol makes use of 10 types of transport protocol data units (TPDUs):

- *Connection request* (CR)
- *Connection confirm* (CC)
- *Disconnect request* (DR)
- *Disconnect confirm* (DC)
- *Data* (DT)
- *Expedited data* (ED)
- *Acknowledgment* (AK)
- *Expedited acknowledgment* (EA)
- *Reject* (RJ)
- *TPDU error* (ER)

Table 7.5.　FUNCTIONS OF ISO TRANSPORT PROTOCOL CLASSES[a]

Protocol mechanism	Variant	0	1	2	3	4
Assignment to network connection		*	*	*	*	*
TPDU transfer		*	*	*	*	*
Segmenting and reassembling		*	*	*	*	*
Concatenation and separation			*	*	*	*
Connection establishment		*	*	*	*	*
Connection refusal		*	*	*	*	*
Normal release	Implicit	*				
	Explicit		*	*	*	*
Error release		*		*		
Association of TPDUs with transport connection		*	*	*	*	*
DT TPDU numbering	Normal		*	m(1)	m	m
	Extended			o(1)	o	o
Expedited data transfer	Network normal		m	*(1)	*	*
	Network expedited		ao			
Reassignment after failure			*		*	
Retention until acknowledgment of TPDUs	Conf. receipt		ao			
	AK		m		*	*
Resynchronization			*		*	
Multiplexing and demultiplexing				*	*	*
Explicit flow control						
With				m	*	*
Without		*	*	o		
Checksum						
Use of					m	*
Nonuse of		*	*	*	*	o
Frozen references			*		*	*
Retransmission on timeout						*
Resequencing						*
Inactivity control						*
Treatment of protocol errors		*	*	*	*	*
Splitting and recombining						*

[a]Symbols used in this table are as follows:

*Procedure always included in class.

mNegotiable procedure whose implementation in equipment is mandatory.

oNegotiable procedure whose implementation in equipment is optional.

aoNegotiable procedure whose implementation in equipment is optional and where use depends on availability within the network service.

(1)Not applicable in Class 2 when nonuse of explicit flow control is selected.

Table 7.6.   DEFINITION OF FUNCTIONS OF THE ISO PROTOCOL CLASSES

Assignment to Network Connection	A transport entity may assign a new transport connection to a new network connection or an existing network connection with adequate quality of service. For Classes 1 and 3, an existing transport connection can be reassigned after the failure of a network connection
TPDU Transfer	A TPDU is transferred as the user data parameter of a NSDU
Segmenting and Reassembly	A TSDU shall be sent as an ordered sequence of TPDUs, ending with a TPDU with an EOT set to 1
Concatenation and Separation	Multiple TPDUs can be conveyed in one NSDU. Not performed in Class 0
Connection Establishment	Includes the negotiation of optional facilities
Connection Refusal	Used by a transport entity to refuse a connection request
Normal Release	In Class 0, a transport entity releases a connection by requesting release of the corresponding network connection. In all other classes, an explicit release, using the DR TPDU, is used
Error Release	For Classes 0 and 2, if an N-DISCONNECT or N-RESET is received, the transport connection is released. In all other classes, error recovery procedures are invoked
Association of TPDUs with Transport Connections	Use of source and destination references to identify a connection
Data TPDU Numbering	Provided for ordered delivery, flow control, and error control. Not used in Class 0. Not used in Class 2 when the explicit flow control option is not selected. All transport connections begin with sequence number 0
Expedited Data Transfer	In Class 1, an ED TPDU may be transferred using a network expedited data service, if available. In Classes 2 through 4, ED TPDUs are transferred using the normal network data transfer service
Reassignment After Failure	In Classes 1 and 3, if an N-DISCONNECT. indication is received, the transport connection is reassigned to another network connection, and any lost TPDUs are retransmitted
Retention until Acknowledgment of TPDUs	In Class 1, acknowledgment may be achieved using the network-service confirmation of receipt, if available. Otherwise, an AK TPDU is used

Table 7.6 (continued)

Resynchronization	After a network connection reset and after a network connection failure and reassignment, the transport entity retransmits unacknowledged TPDUs
Multiplexing and Demultiplexing	Several transport connections may share a network connection
Explicit Flow Control	Uses the credit allocation technique
Checksum	Applies to the entire TPDU when used
Frozen References	When a transport connection is released the reference number that had been used is not reused for a specified length of time
Retransmission on Timeout	To cope with unsignaled loss of TPDUs
Resequencing	To cope with misordering of TPDUs
Inactivity Control	To cope with unsignaled termination of a network connection
Treatment of Protocol Errors	A transport entity that receives a TPDU that can be associated to a transport connection and is invalid or constitutes a protocol error shall transmit an ER TPDU or reset or close the network connection
Splitting and Recombining	A transport connection may make use of multiple network connections

By this time, the use of these TPDUs should be self-explanatory. In this subsection we confine ourselves to a discussion of the formats and field values of the various TPDUs. In the next subsection, we discuss the protocol mechanisms that are implemented with these TPDU types.

Each TPDU consists of three parts: a fixed header, a variable header, and a data field. The latter two optionally may not be present in a TPDU. The fixed header contains the frequently occurring parameters (Fig. 7.12), and the variable header contains optional or infrequently occurring parameters (Table 7.7).

The fixed headers of the various TPDU types are similar. The fields, not all of which occur in all types, can be defined briefly:

- *Length indicator (LI) (8 bits):* Length of the header (fixed plus variable) excluding the LI field, in octets
- *TPDU code (4 bits):* Type of TPDU
- *Credit (CDT) (4 bits):* Flow control credit allocation. Initial credit is granted in CR and CC, subsequent credit is granted in AK. As an option, a 16-bit credit field is used with AK, and is appended after the YR-TU-NR field.
- *Source reference (16 bits):* Reference used by the transport entity to identify the transport connection uniquely in its own system

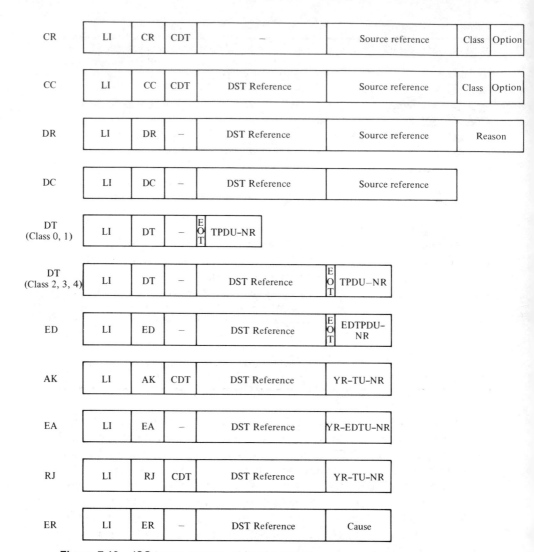

Figure 7.12.   ISO transport protocol fixed header formats.

- *Destination reference (16 bits):* Reference used by the peer transport entity to identify the transport connection uniquely in its own system
- *Class (4 bits):* Protocol class
- *Option (4 bits):* Specifies normal (7-bit sequence number, 4-bit credit) or extended (31-bit sequence number, 16-bit credit) flow control fields. Also specifies whether explicit flow control is to be used in Class 2.
- *Reason (8 bits):* Reason for requesting a disconnect or rejecting a connection request. The reasons are listed in Table 7.8.

Table 7.7. ISO TRANSPORT PROTOCOL VARIABLE HEADER PRIMITIVES[a]

	CR	CC	DR	DC	DT	ED	AK	EA	RJ	ER
Calling TSAP ID	X	X								
Called TSAP ID	X	X								
TPDU size	X	X								
Version number	X	X								
Security parameter	X	X								
Checksum	4	4	4	4	4	4	4	4		
Additional option selection	X	X								
Alternative protocol class	X	X								
Acknowledge time	4	4								
Throughput	X	X								
Residual error rate	X	X								
Priority	X	X								
Transmit delay	X	X								
Reassignment time	1, 3	1, 3								
Additional information			X							
Subsequence number							4			
Flow control confirmation							4			
Invalid TPDU									X	

[a]4, Class 4 only; 1, 3, Classes 1 and 3 only.

- *EOT (1 bit):* Used when a TSDU has been segmented into multiple TPDUs. It is set to 1 on the last TPDU.
- *TPDU-NR (7 bits):* Send sequence number of a DT TPDU. It is normally modulo 2^7, but may be extended by three octets to be modulo 2^{31}.
- *EDTPDU-NR (7 bits):* Send sequence number of a ED TDPU
- *YR-TU-NR (8 bits):* The next expected DT sequence number
- *YR-EDTU-NR (8 bits):* The next expected ED sequence number
- *Cause (8 bits):* Reason for rejection of a TPDU (Table 7.8)

The variable header consists of a sequence of additional parameters. Each parameter field consists of three subfields: a parameter code (8 bits), a parameter length (8 bits), and the parameter value (one or more octets). Most of the parameters are used by CC and CR in the connection establishment process. The parameters are:

- *Calling TSAP ID:* Service access point that identifies the calling transport user
- *Called TSAP ID:* Service access point that identifies the called transport user
- *TPDU size:* Maximum TPDU size in octets. The range of options is from 128 to 8192 in powers of 2.
- *Version number:* Version of protocol to be followed. This accommodates future revisions to the standard.
- *Security parameter:* User-defined
- *Checksum:* Result of checksum algorithm (Appendix 6B) for the

Table 7.8.   ISO TRANSPORT PARAMETER VALUES

Reason for disconnect request	Reason for TPDU error
Not specified	Not specified
Congestion at TSAP	Invalid parameter code
Session entity not attached to TSAP	Invalid TPDU type
Address unknown	Invalid parameter value
Normal user-initiated disconnect	
Remote transport entity congestion	**Negotiated Options**
Connection negotiation failed	Network expedited in Class 1
Duplicate source reference	Acknowledgment in Class 1
Mismatch references	Checksum in Class 4
Protocol error	Transport expedited data service
Reference overflow	
Request refused on this network connection	
Header or parameter length invalid	

entire TPDU. The checksum is used only for Class 4 and, within that class, it is mandatory for all CR TPDUs, and for all TPDUs when the checksum option is selected.

- *Additional option selection:* Used to specify use or nonuse of certain options (Table 7.8)
- *Alternative protocol class:* Specifies whether only the requested protocol class is acceptable, or that some other class is also acceptable.
- *Acknowledge time:* An estimate of the time taken by the entity to acknowledge a DT TPDU. This helps the other entity select a value for its retransmission timer.
- *Throughput:* Specifies the user's throughput requirements in octets per second. Eight values are specified: the target and minimum acceptable values for both maximum throughput and average throughput, in both the calling–called direction and the called–calling direction.
- *Residual error rate:* Expresses the target and minimum rate of unreported user data loss
- *Priority:* Priority of this connection
- *Transit delay:* Specifies the user's delay requirements in milliseconds. Four values are specified: the target and maximum acceptable transit delay in both directions.
- *Reassignment time:* Amount of time an entity will persist in attempts to reconnect after a network connection is broken.
- *Additional information:* Related to the clearing of the connection. User defined.
- *Subsequence number:* Number of the AK. It is used to assure that AKs with the same YR-TU-NR are processed in correct sequence.
- *Flow control confirmation:* Echoes parameter values in the last AK TPDU received. It contains the values of the YR-TU-NR, CDT, and Subsequence Number fields.
- *Invalid TPDU:* The bit pattern of the rejected TPDU up to and including the octet that caused the rejection.

Protocol Mechanisms

The purpose of this section is to highlight the key transport protocol mechanisms. Much of what was discussed in Sec. 7.2 is applicable, so only a brief commentary is provided. The following topics are considered:

- Connection establishment
- Data transfer
- Connection termination

Connection Establishment. The connection establishment phase requires, at minimum, the exchange of a CR and a CC TPDU (Fig. 7.12). This two-way handshake suffices for Classes 0 through 3. For Class 4, a third TPDU is needed to acknowledge the CC; this may be an AK, DT, or ED.

The purpose of this phase is to establish a transport connection with agreed-upon characteristics. If the establishment attempt is successful, these characteristics are defined by the parameters of the CC. Prior to success, there may be a period of negotiation. In some cases, the calling entity specifies options (e.g., other classes are acceptable), and the called entity selects one in the CC. In other cases, the calling entity proposes a value (e.g., maximum TPDU size), and the calling entity may accept it (CC) or reject it (DR). The parameters involved in this latter process are listed in Table 7.8.

A transport connection involves three different types of identifiers:

- TSAP
- NSAP
- Transport connection identifier

As there may be more than one user of the transport entity, a TSAP is needed to allow the transport entity to multiplex data transfers to multiple users. This identifier must be passed down from the transport user, and included in CC and CR TPDUs. The NSAP identifies the system on which the transport entity is located. This address, or a corresponding name, is passed down from the transport user. The address is not needed in any TPDU, but must be passed down to the network protocol entity for its use. Finally, each transport connection is given a unique identifier (similar to an X.25 virtual-circuit number) by each of the two transport entities involved. This identifier is used in all TPDUs. It allows the transport entity to multiplex multiple transport connections on a single network connection.

Data Transfer. Normal data transfer over a connection is accomplished using DTs. Each data unit may be self-contained. Alternatively, if the TSDU plus DT header exceeds the maximum packet size, the transport entity may segment the TSDU and send it out as a sequence of TPDUs. The last TPDU in sequence has the EOT bit set.

DTs are numbered sequentially. This is used in Classes 2 through 4 for flow control. A credit-allocation scheme is used. The initial credit is set in the CC and CR TPDUs. Subsequent credit is granted with an AK. Note that acknowledgments are in separate TPDUs, and never piggy-backed onto DTs. At first glance, this might seem inefficient because an entire TPDU is needed for flow control. This is not so for two reasons:

- The transport entity may choose not to acknowledge every single DT, but only acknowledge in bunches. Thus no overhead for pig-gybacking is wasted in the DT.

- A sort of piggybacking is possible. A transport entity may concatenate multiple TPDUs (e.g., a DT and an AK) into one unit to be passed to the network service. Thus several TPDUs will be efficiently handled as a single packet by the network.

In Class 4, sequence numbers are also used for resequencing DTs that arrive out of order. Another mechanism unique to Class 4 is the DT checksum. If an error is detected, an ER is returned. Other reasons for ER, for all classes, are listed in Table 7.8.

Expedited data transfer uses the ED and EA data units. Sequence numbers are used, but only one ED may be outstanding at a time. The sender must receive an EA before sending another ED. The reader may ask how a transport entity expedites data. The answer may strike some as clumsy and inefficient, but it is just one more example of the limitations and complexities with which a transport protocol must cope. In Classes 1 through 4, an ED is sent before any DTs queued for that connection. In Class 4, we must contend with the problem that being sent out first does not mean being delivered first. Therefore, the Class 4 entity also suspends the transfer of new DTs (although pending DTs will go out) until an EA is received. In effect, the connection is shut down to accommodate this one piece of data.

Connection Termination.   An abrupt termination is achieved by the exchange of a DR and a DC. When a transport entity receives a disconnect request from its user, it discards any pending DTs and issues the DR. The entity that receives the DR issues a DC, discards any pending DTs, and informs its user.

7.5 CONNECTIONLESS OPERATION

As supplements to the initial standards, ISO has issued standards for both a connectionless transport service [ISO 8072/DAD 1] and a connectionless transport protocol [DIS 8602].

Connectionless Transport Service

Only two primitives are defined for the connectionless-mode service: T-UNITDATA.request and T-UNITDATA.indication. Each primitive has four parameters:

- Source address
- Destination address
- Quality of service
- TS-user-data

Thus, the connectionless transport service primitives have the identical structure to that of the connectionless network primitives (see Table 6.7). In the case of the transport service, the source and the destination addresses uniquely identify TSAPs, and the quality of service parameters are:

- Transit delay
- Protection
- Residual error probability
- Priority

These have meaning that correspond to those of the connectionless network service (see Table 6.8).

Connectionless Transport Protocol

The connectionless transport service is not expected to provide ordered delivery, flow control, or error control. Hence, the connectionless transport protocol is very simple. A single protocol data unit (PDU) is used: the UNITDATA (UD) TPDU. The structure of the UD TPDU is shown in Fig. 7.13. The fields in the TPDU are as follows:

- *Length indicator (LI):* Length of TPDU in octets, excluding the LI and user-data fields
- *TPDU code:* Indicates that this is a UD TPDU
- *Parameter code:* Code of a particular parameter, which include checksum, Source TSAP-ID, Destination TSAP-ID, and user-data
- *Parameter length:* Length of following parameter value field in octets

    A TPDU is constructed and sent in response to a T-UNITDATA.request. The source and destination addresses received from the transport user are used to determine the source and destination NSAPs, which are passed down to the network service, and the source and destination TSAPs, which are placed in the TPDU. The quality of service requested in the T-UNITDATA.request is used to determine if a checksum should be included in the TPDU. If so, the algorithm in Appendix 6B is used. The TS-User-Data parameter in the T-UNITDATA.request is a TSDU, and this becomes the User-Data field in the TPDU; it is not possible to segment the TSDU.

    The resulting TPDU is sent by the network service to the destination transport entity. If the TPDU contains a checksum and a checksum verification yields a false, then the TPDU is discarded. If the checksum is valid or not present, then the transport entity constructs a T-UNITDATA.indication and provides it to the transport user identified by the Destination TASP-ID.

Octet

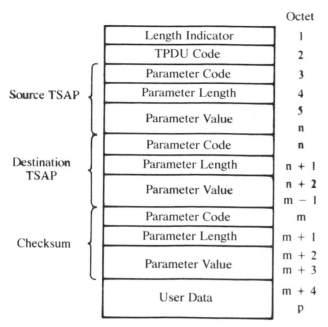

	Octet
Length Indicator	1
TPDU Code	2

Source TSAP: Parameter Code (3), Parameter Length (4), Parameter Value (5, n)

Destination TSAP: Parameter Code (n), Parameter Length (n + 1), Parameter Value (n + 2, m − 1)

Checksum: Parameter Code (m), Parameter Length (m + 1), Parameter Value (m + 2, m + 3)

User Data (m + 4, p)

Figure 7.13. Transport UNITDATA TPDU format.

7.6   RELATIONSHIP BETWEEN TRANSPORT AND NETWORK SERVICES

Figure 2.15 indicates that the transport service can be either connection-oriented or connectionless, and that either can be provided by the use of a connection-oriented or a connectionless network service. The mapping of the transport service onto the network service is the job of the transport protocol. A variety of ISO documents address the way in which this mapping is to be done. There are four cases:

- *Connectionless transport and network* [DIS 8602]
- *Connectionless transport, connection-oriented network* [DIS 8602]
- *Connection-oriented transport and network* [ISO 8073]
- *Connection-oriented transport and connectionless network* [ISO 8073 PDAD 2]

We examine each of these cases in turn.

Connectionless Transport and Network Services

Each UNITDATA (UD) TPDU is mapped into an N-UNITDATA primitive (see Table 6.7). On transmission, the N-UNITDATA.request primitive is invoked. The source and the destination address parameters, which are NSAPs, are derived from the transport user. The quality of service is passed down from that in the T-UNITDATA.request. The NS-User-Data is the TPDU. The TPDU is then transmitted by the network service and is received by the other transport entity in the form of a N-UNIT-DATA.indication.

Connectionless Transport, Connection-Oriented Network Services

The connectionless transport protocol makes use of only a subset of the connection-oriented network service primitives (see Table 5.8). To transmit TPDUs, a network connection is needed, and it must be one dedicated to that task. That is, a network connection that is being used to support transport connections may not be used to transmit connectionless TPDUs.

When a T-UNITDATA.request is received by the transport entity, the address and the quality of service parameters are handled as before. If a network connection to the destination NSAP that can be used for connectionless TPDUs does not exist, an N-CONNECT.request is issued. If an N-DISCONNECT.indication is received in response (rejecting the network connection request), then the transport user data is discarded. If a N-CONNECT.confirm is received, or a network connection already exists, then a UD TPDU is constructed and included as NS-User-Data in an N-DATA.request.

To receive a UD TPDU, a suitable network connection must already exist, having been set up previously by the calling or called transport entity. Each TPDU is received as NS-User-Data in the N-DATA.indication primitive.

Whenever an N-DISCONNECT.indication is received on an active network connection, the transport entity recognizes that the connection is terminated. Whenever an N-RESET.indication is received, the transport entity responds with an N-RESET.response.

Connection-Oriented Transport and Network Services

The connection-oriented transport protocol makes use of all of the connection-oriented network service primitives (see Table 5.8). All TPDUs are carried as data in the N-DATA and N-EXPEDITED-DATA primitives.

Let us consider each of the three phases of a transport connection in turn, beginning with transport connection establishment, in response to a T-CONNECT.request. A transport connection, recall, is initiated by the transmission of a CR TPDU. Before sending the CR TPDU, the initiator must assign the transport connection to be created to a network connection. The transport entity may use an existing network connection or create a new one; the requirement is that the network connection be compatible with the requested transport connection (quality of service, expedited data option). All of the TPDUs that might be used in the connection establishment procedure (CR, CC, DR, ER) are transmitted as NS-User-Data of the N-DATA primitives.

Once a transport connection is established, TPDUs are exchanged over the network connection. In most cases, the N-DATA primitives are used. The N-EXPEDITED-DATA primitives are used for ED and EA TPDUs in Class 1 transport. Also, the N-DATA-ACKNOWLEDGE primitives may be used in Class 1 transport.

A transport connection is terminated implicitly in Class 0 transport by terminating the corresponding network connection using N-DISCONNECT. In the other classes, a transport connection is terminated explicitly using a DR TPDU in an N-DATA primitive. After the release of the last transport connection on a network connection, the network connection may be released or retained for future use.

Connection-Oriented Transport and Connectionless Network Services

Of the connection-oriented transport protocols, only Class 4 can make use of a connectionless network service. The connectionless network service primitives (see Table 6.7), N-UNITDATA.request and N-UNITDATA.indication, are used. All TPDUs, including those used for connection establishment, are contained as user data in the network service primitives.

chapter 8

Session Layer

This chapter examines the session layer. As always, we begin with the OSI description of the session layer. The following two sections examine the standard developed by ISO [EMM083]. In describing this standard, we will notice a marked contrast with the discussion of transport protocols in the preceding chapter. Our primary concern at the transport layer was the complexity of the transport protocol mechanisms required to provide a reliable service. At the session layer, such elaborate mechanisms are not needed; when a session protocol data unit is sent, we are guaranteed that it will be delivered reliably. Instead, the focus at the session layer is with defining a variety of data exchange services that might (or might not) be useful to applications. Accordingly, although the session protocol is straightforward, the ISO session services are rich and complex.

8.1 OSI DEFINITION

The purpose of the session layer is to provide the means for cooperating presentation entities to organize and synchronize their dialogue and to manage the data exchange. To do this, the session layer establishes a session connection and imposes a structure on the interaction or dialogue between session users.

Table 8.1 defines the services and functions of the session layer. Some of these warrant further elaboration. Whereas transport connection release is abrupt, session connection release is orderly. When a connection release is requested, the connection is not released until all outstanding Session Service Data Units (SSDUs) in both directions have been delivered. The OSI document [ISO7498] also specifies the provision of a quarantine service. This service allows a sending session user to supply a number of SSDUs to the session service and request that the session service refrain from delivering any of the data until explicitly released by the user, at which time all of the quarantined data is delivered. The sending user may also request that all quarantined data be discarded. This service places a buffering requirement on the session service, in effect removing that requirement from the application layer. Interestingly, the ISO session service standard does not include this service.

The session layer may be asked to manage the interaction or dialogue between users. Three possible modes are provided: two-way si-

Table 8.1.   SERVICES AND FUNCTIONS OF THE SESSION LAYER

Services	
Session connection establishment	Connection of presentation entities
Session connection release	Release in an orderly way without loss of data
Normal data exchange	Exchange of SDUs
Quarantine service	Allows presentation entity to request quarantining of one or more SSDUs
Expedited data exchange	Expedited handling of SDUs
Interaction management	Two-way simultaneous, two-way alternate, or one-way interaction
Session connection synchronization	Allows presentation entities to define synchronization points and resynchronize to those points
Exception reporting	Notification of presentation entity
Functions	
Session connection to transport connection mapping	One-to-one mapping
Session connection flow control	No peer flow control; backpressure on transport connection
Expedited data transfer	Supports expedited data service
Session connection recovery	Reestablish transport connection after failure
Session connection release	Supports release service
Session layer management	Management activities related to the session layer

multaneous, two-way alternate, and one-way. The two-way simultaneous is a full-duplex type of operation; both sides can simultaneously send data. Once this mode is agreed upon in the session negotiation phase, there is no specific interaction management task required. This will probably be the most common mode of dialogue. In two-way alternate, the two session users must take turns sending data. An example of the use of this mode is for inquiry/response applications. The session entity enforces the alternating interaction by informing each user when it is its turn. This is actually a three-step process:

- The session user who has the turn informs its session entity when it has completed its turn.
- The sending session entity sends any outstanding data to the receiving entity and then informs the receiving entity that the turn is being passed.
- The receiving entity passes up any outstanding data to its user and then informs the user that it is its turn.

One-way interaction requires that user data flow in one direction only. An example of this is if data are to be sent to a temporarily inactive user, and are accepted by a *receiver server*, whose only task is to accept data on behalf of other local users and store them. This mode is not supported in the ISO standard.

The session-connection synchronization service is a recovery support service similar to the checkpoint/restart mechanisms used in file management. This service allows the user to define synchronization points in the data stream and to be able to back up the dialogue to that point. The session entity is not itself responsible for recovery. In particular, the session entity will not save previously transmitted SSDUs for later retransmission after a backup. It merely provides a marking service to support recovery at the application layer.

Now consider the session protocol functions. A key function is the mapping of session connections to transport connections. At any given instant, there is a one-to-one relationship between session connections and transport connections. This relieves the session layer of a peer flow control responsibility, since the flow control can be exercised by the transport protocol (analogous to Class 0 or 1 transport over a network connection). However, the lifetime of session and transport connections can be distinguished, as indicated in Fig. 8.1. A transport connection may be used to support several session connections, in sequence, or a single session connection can make use of a sequence of transport connections. There is a note in the OSI document that the multiplexing of session connections over a single transport connection is for future consideration. This would reduce the processing burden and amount of state information required of the transport entity. We note, however, that caution must be

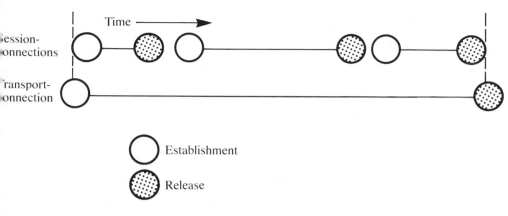

(a) Several consecutive session-connections

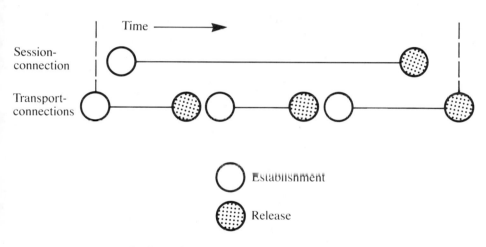

(b) Several consecutive transport-connections

Figure 8.1. Relationship between session connections and transport connections.

observed. For example, a session connection supporting inquiry/response should not be multiplexed with a session connection supporting a file transfer, as the sending of the inquiry text may be significantly delayed when entering a long transport queue of file text from the other session.

8.2 ISO SESSION SERVICE

In this section, we look at the definition of ISO session service developed and standardized by ISO [DIS 8326], and issued in identical form by CCITT [X.215].

Session Services

Table 8.2 lists all of the services provided by ISO session. The ISO document sums up the services provided to a session-service user (SS-user) by the session service as consisting of the following:

1. Establish a connection with another SS-user, exchange data with that user in a synchronized manner, and release the connection in an orderly manner.
2. Negotiate for the use of tokens to exchange data, synchronize and release the connection, and arrange for data exchange to be half-duplex or full-duplex.
3. Establish synchronization points within the dialogue and, in the event of errors, resume the dialogue from an agreed synchronization point.
4. Interrupt a dialogue and resume it later at a prearranged point.

We examine the use of tokens in the next subsection. The remainder of the above points are explained in this subsection.

Table 8.2.   ISO SESSION SERVICES

Session Connection Establishment Phase	
Session Connection	Used to establish a connection between two users. Allows users to negotiate tokens and parameters to be used for the connection. Parameters include quality of service and the use of session services
Data Transfer Phase	
Data-Transfer Related	
Normal Data Transfer	Allows the transfer of normal Session Service Data Units (SSDUs) over a session connection, in either half-duplex or full-duplex mode
Expedited Data Transfer	Allows the transfer of expedited SSDUs containing up to 14 octets of user data over a session connection, free from the token and flow control constraints of the other data transfer services
Typed Data Transfer	Allows the transfer of SSDUs over a session connection, independent of the assignment of the data token. Thus, data may be sent against the normal flow in half-duplex mode

Table 8.2   (continued)

Capability Data Exchange	Used when activity services are available. Allows users to exchange up to 512 octets of data while not within an activity
Token-Management Related	
Give Token	Used to surrender one or more specific tokens to the other user
Please Token	Allows a user to request a token currently assigned to the other user. Thus, this service is only used for a particular token when the other user possesses that token
Give Control	Allows a user to surrender all available tokens to the other user. This service is part of the activity management service
Synchronization Related	
Minor Synchronization Point	Allows the user to define minor synchronization points in the flow of SSDUs. The requestor may request explicit confirmation that the minor synchronization point has been received by the other user
Major Synchronization Point	Allows the user to define major synchronization points in the flow of SSDUs, which completely separates the flow before and after the major synchronization point. No additional data SSDUs may be sent until after a confirmation is received
Resynchronize	Used to set the session connection to a previous synchronization point, but no further back than the last major synchronization point. The state of the connection at that point is restored
Exception-Reporting Related	
Provider-Initiated Exception Reporting	Notifies the users of exception conditions or session protocol errors
User-Initiated Exception Reporting	Allows a user to report an exception condition when the data token is assigned to the other user
Activity Related	
Activity Start	Used to indicate that a new activity is entered
Activity Resume	Used to indicate that a previously interrupted activity is re-entered

Table 8.2 (continued)

Activity Interrupt	Allows an activity to be abnormally terminated with the implication that the work so far achieved is not to be discarded and may be resumed later
Activity Discard	Allows an activity to be abnormally terminated with the implication that the work so far achieved is to be discarded
Activity End	Used to end an activity
Session Connection Release Phase	
Orderly Release	Allows the session connection to be released after all in-transit data have been delivered and accepted by both users. If the negotiated release option is selected during connection setup, the user receiving a release request may refuse the release and continue the session
User-Initiated Abort	Releases a session in a way that will terminate any outstanding service request. This service will cause loss of undelivered SSDUs
Provider-Initiated Abort	Used by the session service provider to indicate the release of a connection for internal reasons. This service will cause loss of undelivered SSDUs

In addition to providing for the establishment, maintenance, and termination of connections, the ISO session service provides a variety of ways of structuring the dialogue that takes place over a session connection. The simplest of these facilities is the ability to choose two-way simultaneous (full-duplex) or two-way alternate (half-duplex) operation.

The ISO session service also provides an optional facility for labeling the data stream with *synchronization points*, which serve two purposes. First, synchronization points can be used to clearly isolate portions of the dialogue. Second, synchronization points can be used in error recovery. Two types of synchronization points are defined: *major synchronization points* and *minor synchronization points*. The relationship is illustrated in Fig. 8.2a. Major synchronization points are used to structure the exchange of data into dialogue units. The characteristic of a dialogue unit is that all data within it is completely separated from all data before and after it. When a user defines a major synchronization point, the user may not send more data until that synchronization point is acknowledged by the destination user. For recovery purposes, it is not possible to back up beyond the last major synchronization point. Thus, the two purposes

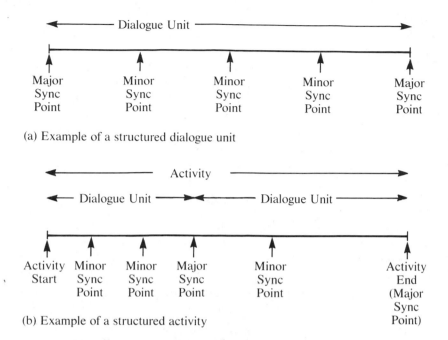

(a) Example of a structured dialogue unit

(b) Example of a structured activity

Figure 8.2. Session interaction structure.

mentioned above are achieved. First, as the completion of one dialogue unit must be acknowledged before the next begins, the dialogue unit can be used by the session user to define application-oriented functions. For example, if a sequence of files is to be transferred, each file could be segregated into a separate dialogue unit. Thus the sender could be assured that a particular file had been received and accepted before attempting to send another file. Second, the dialogue units define the limit of recovery. For example, in a transaction processing application, each transaction could be equated with a dialogue unit. When a transaction is complete and acknowledged, each side can purge any recovery information that had been saved for the purpose of permitting backup to the beginning of that transaction.

Minor synchronization points are used to structure the exchange of data within a dialogue. They provide more flexibility in the recovery facility. A session user may define one or more minor synchronization points within a dialogue unit, and need not wait for acknowledgment before proceeding. At any point, it is possible to resynchronize the dialogue to any previous minor synchronization point within the current dialogue unit, or, of course, to resynchronize to the beginning of the dialogue unit (most recent major synchronization point). This permits the session user to make a tradeoff: With frequent synchronization points, backup and recovery can be speeded up at the expense of saving frequent checkpoints.

In the ISO standard, it is not the responsibility of the session layer to save any data that has already been transmitted. The session service will simply mark the data stream as requested with a serial number; numbers are assigned sequentially. When resynchronization occurs, the session layer decrements the sequence number back to the point of resynchronization. If it is desired to retransmit data that had been previously transmitted, it is the responsibility of the session user to have saved that data and to present it to the session service again.

One additional level of structuring is available as an option: the activity. An activity is defined as a logical unit of work, consisting of one or more dialogue units (Fig. 8.2b). The key feature of the activity is that it can be interrupted and later resumed. For example, if a very long data base transfer is taking place and one machine or the other needs to interrupt this process (e.g., to go down for system maintenance or to handle a higher priority task), then the activity is stopped by the session service, which remembers the last serial number used so that the activity may be resumed later with the same structure of synchronization points intact. Again, it is the responsibility of the session user to save any other context information that will be needed for resumption.

The relationship between an activity and a session connection is not fixed. As indicated in Fig. 8.3a, it is possible to make a one-to-one correspondence. In this case, a new activity begins a new session connection, and when the activity is completed, the session connection is terminated. It is also possible to perform multiple activities in sequence over a single session connection (Fig. 8.3b). This approach may be desirable if session establishment is time-consuming or resource-consuming. If two session users know that they will engage in a sequence of activities, then it make sense to maintain the session connection. Finally, a single activity can span multiple session connections (Fig. 8.3c). If an activity is interrupted, and it is not anticipated that it will be resumed immediately, then it makes sense to break the connection to free up resources and begin a new connection when the users are prepared to resume the activity.

A final feature illustrated in Fig. 8.3 is the use of *capability data*. If two users choose to make use of the activity option, then data may normally only be exchanged when an activity is in progress. Capability data is a mechanism by which such users can exchange a small amount of acknowledged data over a session connection when no activity is in progress. For example, this feature could be used to transmit control information without going through the overhead of setting up an activity.

The Use of Tokens

In the context of the ISO standard, a token is an attribute of a session connection that is dynamically assigned to one user at a time and that grants that user the exclusive right to invoke certain services. Put another

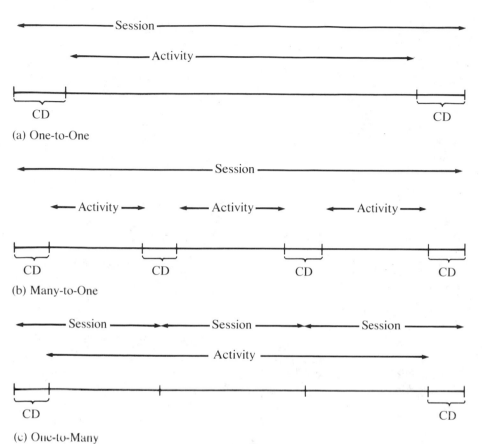

CD = Capability Data may be sent

Figure 8.3. Relationship of activities and sessions.

way, there are certain services that can only be invoked by the current token holder. A simple example is a token that grants the right to transmit data. As illustrated in Fig. 8.4, this token enforces a half-duplex mode of operation. Only the holder of the token can send data. At any time, the token holder can pass the token to the other user, at which time the other user becomes the possessor of the right to transmit.

The token mechanism is used in the ISO session service to structure the dialogue. Four tokens are defined:

- *Data token:* Used to manage a half-duplex connection
- *Synchronize-minor token:* Used to govern the setting of minor synchronization points
- *Major/activity token:* Used to govern the setting of major synchronization points and to manage the activity structure
- *Release token:* Used to govern the release of connections

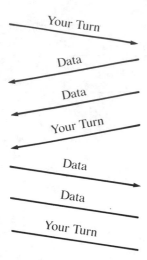

Figure 8.4.   Simplified token exchange.

Associated with the token mechanism are three services. The give-token service allows a user to pass a token to the other user of a session connection. The please-token service allows a user who does not possess a token to request it. The give-control service is used to pass all tokens from one user to another.

Figure 8.5 shows the use of the data token to provide the half-duplex mode of operation. In this example, the token is initially possessed by User A, who is free to transmit data. User B may not transmit normal data, but may transmit a small amount of what is referred to as typed data. An example of typed data would be the transmission of a break character from a terminal to halt the flow of data from an application. User B may request the data token at any time, but the token is relinquished only at User A's discretion.

Each of the four tokens is always in one of two states:

- *Not available:* All four of the tokens are optional and their use must be negotiated during connection establishment. In the case of the data and release tokens, their unavailability means that the corresponding services (data transfer, release) are always available to both users. In the case of the synchronization-minor and major/activity tokens, their unavailability means that the corresponding services (synchronization, activities) are unavailable to both users.
- *Available:* An available token is assigned to one of the two users, who then has the exclusive right to use the associated service.

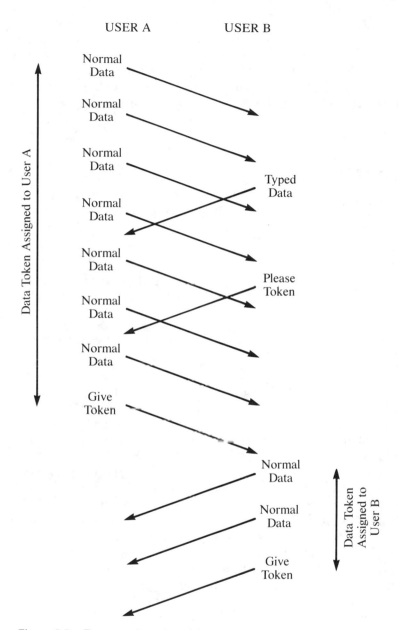

Figure 8.5. Two-way alternate service.

Table 8.3 summarizes the use of the session tokens and their relationship to session services. Note that, with the exception of the release service, each service listed in the table requires the use of a particular token, and may require the use of additional tokens if they are available. The restrictions appear to be reasonable ones. For example, in the case of half-duplex operation, only the holder of the data token can set synchronization points.

Quality of Service

Associated with each session connection is a quality of service, defined by the values of a list of parameters (Table 8.4). For the most part, these parameters are passed down to the transport service, and were defined in Sec. 7.3. There are two additional parameters:

- *Extended control:* Allows a user to make use of the resynchronize, abort, activity interrupt, and activity discard services when normal flow is congested.
- *Optimized dialogue transfer:* Permits the session protocol to concatenate multiple session service requests (SSDUs) and send them as a unit.

All of the quality-of-service parameters fall into two categories: prearranged and negotiated. The value of each prearranged parameter is selected and/or known prior to connection establishment and is not negotiated. The standard does not specify how this is to be done; it is a local implementation matter. Note, however, that all of the parameters in this category are directly supported by the transport service. Thus, their use must be agreed to by the transport service. The transport service standard indicates that each of the transport quality-of-service parameters can be either negotiated or prearranged. In the case of a session service that has a different set of prearranged parameter values with different session users, then these parameters could be requested on a per-transport-connection basis and negotiated at the transport level. If the session service is providing the same set of prearranged parameter values to all session users, it would seem to be appropriate to prearrange these values with the transport service; however, the session service standard does not provide explicit guidance on these points [CANE86].

The remainder of the quality-of-service parameters are negotiated during the session connection establishment phase, as described later. Once the session connection is established, the selected parameters are not renegotiated during the lifetime of the session connection. If changes occur in the quality of service, these are not signaled to the session users.

Table 8.3. THE USE OF ISO SESSION TOKENS

Function	Token			
	Data	Minor Synchronization	Major Synchronization	Release
Transfer SSDU (half-duplex)	M	—	—	—
Transfer capability data	I	I	M	—
Set minor synchronization point	I	M	—	—
Set major synchronization point	I	I	M	—
Start activity	I	I	M	—
Resume activity	I	I	M	—
Interrupt activity	—	—	M	—
Discard activity	—	—	M	—
End activity	I	I	M	—
Release connection	I	I	I	I

M = Mandatory; token must be available and assigned to user to perform function.
I = If available; if token is available, it must be assigned to user to perform function.

Table 8.4.   ISO SESSION QUALITY OF SERVICE PARAMETERS

Parameter	Negotiate/ prearranged	Performance/ other	Passed to transport
SC establishment delay	P	P	Yes
SC establishment failure probability	P	P	Yes
Throughput	N	P	Yes
Transit delay	N	P	Yes
Residual error rate	N	P	Yes
Transfer failure probability	P	P	Yes
SC release delay	P	P	Yes
SC release failure probability	P	P	Yes
SC protection	N	O	Yes
SC priority	N	O	Yes
SC resiliance	P	P	Yes
Extended control	N	O	No
Optimized dialogue transfer	N	O	No

SC = Session Connection

Service Primitives and Parameters

Associated with each of the services listed in Table 8.2 is one type of primitive, as listed in Table 8.5. As usual, each type of primitive appears in one or more of variations (request, indication, response, confirm), depending on the requirements of the service.

Figure 8.6 indicates the ways that these variations may be combined in the session service. A service action on the part of one of the session users usually results in action between the two session protocol entities at the two ends of the session connection. This protocol action is invisible to the session user and only manifests itself as a resultant service primitive (indication or confirm). *Confirmed services* are those for which the user invoking the service expects an acknowledgment from the peer user at the other end of the connection. Examples are connection establishment, synchronization actions, and activity-related actions. In the case of connection establishment, the interaction is used for parameter negotiation as well as acknowledgment. *Nonconfirmed services* require no acknowledgment. An example of this is data transfer. In this case, the data are delivered to the session service provider by a request primitive and delivered by the service provider to the other user by an indication prim-

Table 8.5.   ISO SESSION PRIMITIVES AND PARAMETERS

S-CONNECT.request (identifier, calling SSAP, called SSAP, quality of service, requirements, serial number, token, data)

S-CONNECT.indication (identifier, calling SSAP, called SSAP, quality of service, requirements, serial number, token, data)

S-CONNECT.response (identifier, called SSAP, result, quality of service, requirements, serial number, token, data)

S-CONNECT.confirm (identifier, called SSAP, result, quality of service, requirements, serial number, token, data)

S-DATA.request (data)

S-DATA.indication (data)

S-Expedited-Data.request (data)

S-Expedited-Data.indication (data)

S-Typed-Data.request (data)

S-Typed-Data.indication (data)

S-Capability-Data.request (data)

S-Capability-Data.indication (data)

S-Token-Give.request (tokens)

S-Token-Give.indication (tokens)

S-Token-Please.request (token, data)

S-Token-Please.indication (token, data)

S-CONTROL-GIVE.request

S-CONTROL-GIVE.indication

S-Sync-Minor.request (type, serial number, data)

S-Sync-Minor.indication (type, serial number, data)

S-Sync-Minor.response (serial number, data)

S-Sync-Minor.confirm (serial number, data)

S-Sync-Major.request (serial number, data)

S-Sync-Major.indication (serial number, data)

S-Sync-Major.response (data)

S-Sync-Major.confirm (data)

S-Resynchronize.request (type, serial number, tokens, data)

S-Resynchronize.indication (type, serial number, tokens, data)

S-Resynchronize.response (serial number, tokens, data)

S-Resynchronize.confirm (serial number, tokens, data)

S-P-Exception-Report.indication (Reason)

S-U-Exception-Report.request (Reason, data)

S-U-Exception-Report.indication (Reason, data)

Table 8.5   (continued)

S-Activity-Start.request (activity ID, data)

S-Activity-Start.indication (activity ID, data)

S-Activity-Resume.request (activity ID, old activity ID, serial number, old SC ID, data)

S-Activity-Resume.indication (activity ID, old activity ID, serial number, old SC ID, data)

S-Activity-Interrupt.request (reason)

S-Activity-Interrupt.indication (reason)

S-Activity-Interrupt.response

S-Activity-Interrupt.confirm

S-Activity-Discard.request (reason)

S-Activity-Discard.indication (reason)

S-Activity-Discard.response

S-Activity-Discard.confirm

S-Activity-End.request (serial number, data)

S-Activity-End.indication (serial number, data)

S-Activity-End.response (data)

S-Activity-End.confirm (data)

S-Release.request (data)

S-Release.indication (data)

S-Release.response (result, data)

S-Release.confirm (result, data)

S-U-Abort.request (data)

S-U-Abort.indication (data)

S-P-Abort.indication (reason)

itive. The session protocol, making use of transport guarantees the delivery of the data and, therefore, there is no need to confirm that delivery to the sender of the data. *Provider-initiated services* are initiated by the session provider in response to an exception condition that it has detected.

Connection Establishment Phase

For the connection establishment phase, the S-CONNECT primitives are used. The parameters that are provided are (Fig. 8.7):

- *Identifier:* A unique identifier of this connection
- *Calling and called SSAP:* Service access points that serve as the addresses of the session users

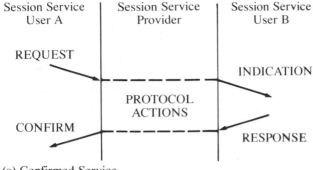

(a) Confirmed Service

(b) Non-confirmed Service

(c) Provider Initiated

Figure 8.6.   Session service primitives.

- *Quality of service:* A list of parameters that are negotiated as part of the connection establishment process
- *Requirements:* A list of functional units of the session service that may be requested. Functional units are logical groupings of related services (Table 8.6) defined for the purpose of (1) negotiation of user requirements during the session connection establishment phase and (2) reference by higher layer standards.
- *Serial number:* When synchronization services are to be employed, this is the proposed initial serial number. This number will be assigned to the first major or minor synchronization point that is defined. Serial numbers are in the range 0 to 999999.
- *Token:* A list of the initial side to which the available tokens are assigned
- *Result:* Used in the response and confirm primitives, to indicate the success or failure of the connection establishment request
- *Data:* Up to 512 octets of user data

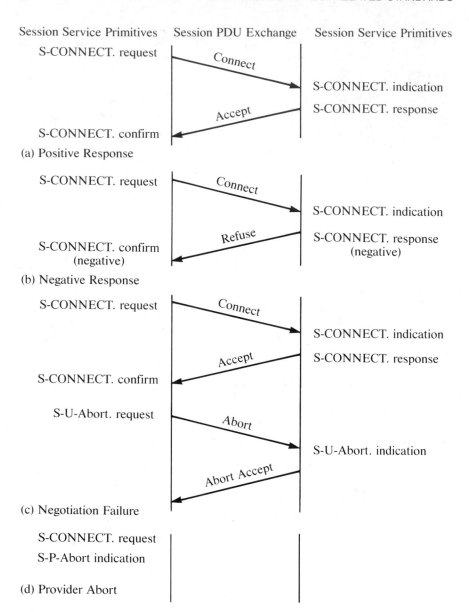

Figure 8.7. Session connection establishment.

Table 8.6.   ISO SESSION FUNCTIONAL UNITS

Functional unit	Service(s)	Token use
Kernel (non-negotiable)	Session connection Normal data transfer Orderly release U-Abort P-Abort	
Negotiated release	Orderly release Give tokens Please tokens	Release token
Half-duplex	Give tokens Please tokens	Data token
Duplex	No additional service	
Expedited data	Expedited data transfer	
Typed data	Typed data transfer	
Capability data exchange	Capability data exchange	
Minor synchronize	Minor synchronization point Give tokens Please tokens	Synchronize- minor token
Major synchronize	Major synchronization point Give tokens Please tokens	Major/activity token
Resynchronize	Resynchronize	
Exceptions	Provider exception reporting User exception reporting	
Activity management	Activity start Activity resume Activity interrupt Activity discard Activity end Give tokens Please tokens Give control	Major/activity token

The connection establishment phase involves negotiation of a number of these parameters. The quality-of-service (QOS) parameters are negotiated as follows:

1. In the S-CONNECT.request primitive, the calling user can specify:
   a. For SC protection and SC priority, a single parameter value that is the desired QOS; for extended control and optimized dialogue transfer, one of the two values "desired" or "not desired"
   b. For residual error rate, and for each direction of throughput

and transit delay, two values, which are the "desired" and the "lowest acceptable" QOS
2. In the S-CONNECT.indication primitive, for each of the negotiated parameters, an "available" value is conveyed that is specified as follows:
   a. For SC protection, if the service provider agrees to provide the desired value, then that value is used; if the service provider does not agree, it issues an S-CONNECT.confirm with a result of "connection rejected"
   b. For SC priority, a value that is equal to or better than the requested value
   c. For residual error rate, and for each direction of throughput and transit delay, if the service provider agrees to provide a value that is at least equal to the "lowest acceptable" requested value, then the provider's value is used; if the service provider does not agree, it rejects the connection
   d. For extended control and optimized data transfer, if the "desired" value is requested and the provider does not agree, it sets the value to "not desired;" otherwise, the provider conveys the same value as the one requested
3. In the S-CONNECT.response primitive, for each of the negotiated parameters, an "agreed" value is conveyed that is specified as follows:
   a. For optimized data transfer, if the called user agrees to the indicated value, it specifies that value; if the indicated value is "desired" and the user does not agree, it specifies "not desired"; if the indicated value is "not desired" and the user does not agree, it may reject the connection
   b. For each of the other parameters, if the called user agrees to the indicated value, it specifies that value; if the user does not agree, it may reject the connection
4. In the S-CONNECT.confirm primitive, the value from the response primitive is conveyed.

For the session requirements parameter, those functional units that are proposed in both the indication and the response and that are supported by the service provider are the ones selected for use on the session connection. Finally, for each available token, the initial assignment of token parameter can have one of the following values in the request/indication: requestor side, acceptor side, acceptor chooses. If the last value is selected, then the initial token setting is indicated by the called user in the response/confirm primitives; otherwise the value chosen by the calling user is selected.

Data Transfer Phase

The data transfer phase involves primitives for the transfer of data and for the structuring of the dialogue. Each data unit that is delivered to the session service provider is to be delivered to the other user as quickly as possible. Thus, there is no quarantining service provided.

The primitives used in the data transfer phase are largely self-explanatory. Those involved in synchronization and resynchronization warrant elaboration. Minor and major synchronization points are set by the S-Sync-Minor and S-Sync-Major primitives, respectively. Each point has an associated serial number that is unique within a given session connection. Although the serial number parameter appears in the request primitives, it is actually set by the session service provider, to one more than the previous serial number. Major synchronization points are consecutively numbered in the same sequence space as the minor synchronization points to facilitate resynchronization by the service provider. The type parameter in the S-SYNC-Minor request/indication primitives indicates whether an explicit acknowledgment is required. Major synchronization points are always acknowledged.

The type parameter in the S-Resynchronize primitives is used to indicate the type of value to be assigned to the serial number; it selects one of three options (Fig. 8.8):

- *Abandon:* Any unused value greater than the current serial number
- *Restart:* Any previously used value greater than the synchronization point serial number that identifies the last acknowledged major synchronization point
- *Set:* Any value

The restart option is used for recovery to a previous point in the dialogue. However, it is up to the session user to perform any SSDU retransmission or other recovery function; the session service merely changes the value of the serial number. The set and abandon options are used in contexts in which recovery is not desired but the current dialogue is to be aborted without aborting the connection. Again, the semantics of these options is up to the session user.

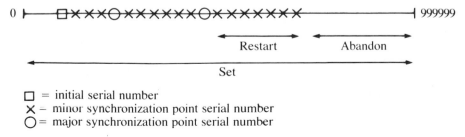

= initial serial number
X = minor synchronization point serial number
O = major synchronization point serial number

Figure 8.8.   Serial number assignment.

Connection Release Phase

The connection release service is orderly. Release is performed cooperatively between the two session users of the connection. All in-transit data is delivered and accepted prior to the release. If the negotiated release option was selected, then the user receiving a release indication may refuse the release and continue the session connection without loss of data.

Session Service Subsets

As you might be able to gather, the session service tries to be all things to all people. The result is that a full-blown implementation of the session standard is not only complex but unnecessary for virtually all applica-

Table 8.7.   ISO SESSION SERVICE SUBSETS

Service	Kernel	BCS	BSS	BAS
Session connection	X	X	X	X
Normal data transfer	X	X	X	a
Expedited data transfer	—	—	—	—
Typed data transfer	—	—	X	X
Capability data transfer	—	—	—	X
Give tokens	—	X	X	X
Please tokens	—	X	X	X
Give control	—	—	—	X
Minor synchronization point	—	—	X	X
Major synchronization point	—	—	X	—
Resynchronize	—	—	X	—
Provider-initiated exception reporting	—	—	—	X
User-initiated exception reporting	—	—	—	X
Activity start	—	—	—	X
Activity resume	—	—	—	X
Activity interrupt	—	—	—	X
Activity discard	—	—	—	X
Activity end	—	—	—	X
Orderly release	X	X	b	X
User-initiated abort	X	X	X	X
Provider-initiated abort	X	X	X	X

BCS = Basic Combined Subset
BSS = Basic Synchronized Subset
BAS = Basic Activity Subset
a = Half-duplex only
b = Negotiated Release option available

tions. Thus, it is likely that only subsets of the session service will be provided by particular implementations. The standard anticipates this and tries to impose some order by defining four subsets of the session service. The services supported by each of these subsets are listed in Table 8.7, and the relationship between service subsets and functional units is shown in Table 8.8.

The minimum implementation is the kernel, and this must be provided in any implementation. In essence, it provides for the transparent use of transport connections, with none of the special features associated with the session layer. The kernel alone would be useful for very small systems such as microcomputers [DOLA84]. The *basic combined subset* (BCS) adds support for half-duplex operation. This subset is useful if the principal additional operation is terminal-host interaction. The basic synchronized subset (BSS) provides dialogue synchronization and negotiated release (release only when both sides agree). BSS is intended for applications such as reliable file transfer and transaction processing. It is likely that most users will implement at least BCS and that many will implement BSS.

The most highly structured set is the basic activity subset (BAS), which has most of the services defined in the standard, including those relating to activity management; it lacks full-duplex operation, minor synchronization, resynchronization, and negotiated release. The BAS is used in CCITT applications to separate a document from operator control information and message text from control information; the specification of the BAS is compatible with a similar description in CCITT recommendation T.62. Outside of this specialized application area, there may be few uses for BAS.

Table 8.8. ISO SESSION SERVICE SUBSETS AND FUNCTIONAL UNITS

Functional Unit	BCS	BSS	BAS
Kernel	X	X	X
Negotiated release		X	
Half-duplex	X	X	X
Duplex	X	X	
Expedited data			
Typed data		X	X
Capability data exchange			X
Minor synchronization		X	X
Major synchronization		X	
Resynchronize		X	
Exceptions			X
Activity management			X

8.3   ISO SESSION PROTOCOL

The ISO session protocol bridges the gap between the services provided by the transport layer and the services required by the session user. In essence, the transport layer provides three services:

* Establishment and maintenance of a transport connection with certain quality-of-service characteristics
* Reliable transfer of data
* Reliable transfer of expedited data

The session service, as we have seen, provides a variety of services relating to the managing and structuring of the exchange of data. Hence, it is the job of the session protocol to provide those structuring mechanisms on top of the rather straightforward transport service. In this section, we examine the session protocol standard developed by ISO [DIS 8327] and also adopted by CCITT [X.225]. In some ways, it will appear far more elaborate than the ISO transport protocol standard. For example, the transport protocol includes 10 types of transport protocol data units, whereas the session protocol includes 34 types of session protocol data units. This is, however, misleading. In the transport protocol, elaborate mechanisms were needed to deal with the unreliability and variable delay problems that are faced. The session protocol is provided with a reliable service. Hence, the session protocol provides a rather straightforward mapping of session service primitives into session protocol data units, and makes use of the comparatively simple interface (see Table 7.4) to transport.

Protocol Mechanisms

The session protocol is reasonably simple to explain. The best way to start is by listing the *session protocol data units* (SPDUs), which we do in Table 8.9. For the most part, these SPDUs represent a one-to-one mapping with session service primitive pairs. Figure 8.6 defines these pairings: request-indication and response-confirm.

   As an example of the relationship between session service primitives and session protocol data units, let us look at the most complicated instance, namely session connection establishment. Figure 8.7 depicts the possible sequences of events. A request for a connection by a user triggers a Connect SPDU by the user's session protocol entity. The SPDU contains those parameters that were contained in the S-CONNECT.request and that need to be communicated to the other users. These include connection ID, serial number, token selections, requirements parameters, calling and called SSAP, and finally, those quality-of-service parameters that are negotiated between the users (extended control and optimized dialogue), referred to as protocol options. This information is transmitted via the SPDU to the other session protocol entity, which delivers the connection request and associated parameters in an S-CONNECT.indication primitive. The user accepts the connection and negotiates the parameters with a response primitive, which triggers the transmission of an Accept SPDU back to the other side, where a confirm primitive is generated.

A session user may refuse a connection because of congestion, unavailability of the desired application, or other reasons. This is reported to the session protocol entity with a response primitive in which the result parameter indicates the reason for refusal. The session protocol then sends a Refuse SPDU back to the calling side, which sends a confirm primitive to the calling user, indicating that the connection is refused and specifying the reason.

A third alternative sequence is that the called session user accepts the connection request, but proposes session parameters (e.g., no use of synchronization) unacceptable to the calling user. In this case, the calling user will abort the connection as soon as it is confirmed, and the called user will be informed. Note in Fig. 8.7c that both an Abort and an Abort-accept SPDU are used. The latter is needed so that the session protocol entity that initiated the abort knows that the other side is ready for a new session connection and, if desired, that the transport connection can now be terminated.

Finally, a session provider can refuse to establish a connection, either because of inability to set up a transport connection, inability to provide the desired quality of service, or some other reason. In this case, no SPDUs are employed, as the action is purely local.

Most of the other SPDUs are largely self-explanatory, however, some additional comments will be useful. In the case of the data transfer SPDU, the typical case is that each unit of data (session service data unit, SSDU) received from a session user is encapsulated with a session header and transmitted. If, however, there is a size restriction on data units to be presented to the transport layer (TSDUs), as indicated in the Connect and Accept SPDUs, then the session entity may need to segment the user's data and send it out in two or more Data-transfer SPDUs. In this latter case, the enclosure item parameter is used to indicate whether or not a Data-transfer SPDU is the last one of a group that carries a single SSDU. The receiving session entity will buffer the user data from incoming SPDUs until the last one in a group is received and then transfer all of the data to the user in an S-Data.indication primitive.

The Prepare SPDU is only used when the transport expedited flow option is available. It notifies the recipient session protocol entity of the imminent arrival of a certain SPDU. The SPDUs that may be so signaled include Resynchronize, Activity Interrupt, Activity Discard, and Activity End. In some cases, this alert will allow the session entity to discard some

Table 8.9. SESSION PROTOCOL DATA UNITS, PARAMETERS, AND FUNCTIONS

SPDU	Parameters	Function
Connect	Connection ID, protocol options, version number, serial number, token setting, maximum TSDU size, requirements, calling SSAP, called SSAP, User data	Initiate session connection
Accept	Same as Connect parameters	Establish session connection
Refuse	Connection ID, transport disconnect, requirements, version number, reason	Reject connection request
Finish	Transport disconnect, User data	Initiate orderly release
Disconnect	User data	Acknowledge orderly release
Not Finished	User data	Reject orderly release
Abort	Transport disconnect, protocol error code, User data	Abnormal connection release
Abort Accept	—	Acknowledge abort
Data Transfer	Enclosure item, User data	Transfer normal data
Expedited	User data	Transfer expedited data
Typed Data	Enclosure item, User data	Transfer typed data
Capability Data	User data	Transfer capability data
Capability Data ACK	User data	Acknowledge capability data
Give Tokens	Tokens	Transfer tokens
Please Tokens	Tokens, User data	Request token assignment
Give Tokens Confir	—	Transfer all tokens
Give Tokens ACK	—	Acknowledge all tokens

Minor Sync Point	Confirm required flag, serial number, User data	Define minor sync point
Minor Sync ACK	Serial number, User data	Acknowledge minor sync point
Major Sync Point	End of activity flag, serial number, User data	Define major sync point
Major Sync ACK	Serial number, User data	Acknowledge major sync point
Resynchronize	Token settings, resync type, serial number, User data	Resynchronize
Resynchronize ACK	Token settings, serial number, User data	Acknowledge resynchronize
Prepare	Type	Notify type SPDU is coming
Exception Report	SPDU bit pattern	Protocol error detected
Exception Data	Reason, User data	Put protocol in error state
Activity Start	Activity ID, User data	Signal beginning of activity
Activity Resume	Connection ID, old activity ID, new activity ID, User data	Signal resumption of activity
Activity Interrupt	Reason	Interrupt activity
Activity Interrupt ACK	—	Acknowledge interrupt
Activity Discard	Reason	Cancel activity
Activity Discard ACK	—	Acknowledge cancellation
Activity End	Serial number, User data	Signal activity end
Activity End ACK	Serial number, User data	Acknowledge activity end

incoming SPDUs that arrive prior to the anticipated SPDU. In all cases, it is useful as a means of preparing the recipient for the occurrence of an important event.

Session Protocol Formats

As can be seen from Table 8.9, the number of parameters that is sent with an SPDU varies widely. Furthermore, the length of parameters is variable. The ISO standard provides a flexible formatting scheme to accommodate these variations. Unfortunately, because the final standard represents the merger of several independent efforts (ISO work plus T.62), the scheme is unnecessarily complex.

Figure 8.9 shows the general structure of an SPDU. Each SPDU has up to four fields. The first field is the SPDU identifier (SI), which specifies one of the 34 types of SPDUs. The next field is the length indicator, which specifies the length of the header. If the SPDU contains any parameters, then the next field contains these parameters, using a structure described later. Finally, there may be a field for session user information.

The parameter field may take on one of several general forms, depending on the way in which particular parameters are expressed. In its

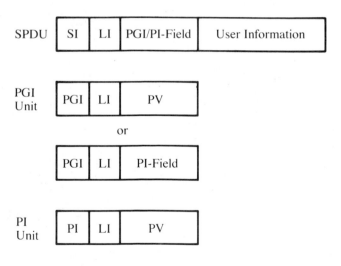

SI = SPDU identifier
LI = Length indicator
PGI/PI-Field = One or more PGI and/or PI units
PGI = Parameter Group Identifier
PV = Parameter Value
PI-Field = One or more PI units
PI = Parameter Identifier

Figure 8.9. SPDU structure.

simplest form, a parameter is expressed with three subfields: a parameter identifier, a length indicator, and the parameter value. This form is known as a PI unit, and the SPDU may contain one or more such units. Alternatively, related parameters may be expressed in a PGI unit, which consists of a parameter group identifier, a length indicator, and either a single parameter value or one or more PI units. As was said, this is a complicated way of achieving a simple purpose, namely the listing of parameters within a single SPDU. Figure 8.10 gives examples of the formats that appear within the standard.

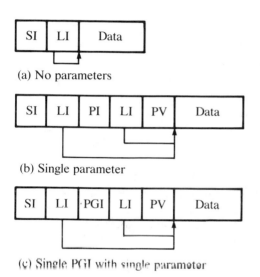

(a) No parameters

(b) Single parameter

(c) Single PGI with single parameter

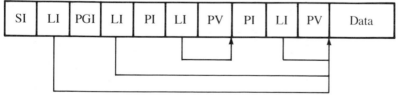

(d) Single PGI with several parameters

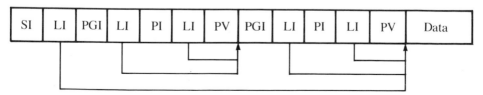

(e) Two PGIs

Figure 8.10. SPDU encoding examples.

Transport Connections

Session connections must be mapped into transport connections by the session protocol entity. The ISO standard contains specific guidance on the way this is to be done. Most important is the requirement that a transport connection be dedicated to a single session connection. There seems good justification for this restriction. For one thing, different session connections may require different quality of service, which will influence the parameters used to set up the transport connection. Also, if several session connections share a transport connection, neither the session user nor the session protocol entity has much control over how the transport service allocates resources to meet the dynamic data transfer demands of several session connections.

A transport connection must be available prior to the exchange of SPDUs. If a transport connection provides expedited service, then Abort, Abort Accept, Expedited Data, and Prepare SPDUs are sent using that service (T-EXPEDITED-DATA primitives). If this service is not available, the Abort and Abort Accept are sent using normal transport data transfer service (T-DATA primitives), and the Expedited Data and the Prepare SPDUs cannot be sent. All other SPDUs, including those associated with connection establishment and release, are transmitted using T-DATA primitives.

When a session is terminated, the session protocol entity that initially set up the corresponding transport connection has the option of terminating that connection or not. If the transport connection is retained, then it may be used to support a new session connection request, provided that it meets the required quality of service.

chapter *9*

Presentation Layer

With the presentation layer, several significant new concepts are introduced. First, we see a tighter coupling between the presentation layer and the session layer than we have between other layers. This is primarily because the presentation layer is providing only a limited and specific set of services to the application layer, and these services do not build on or add value to the data exchange services of the lower layers. Therefore, the presentation layer must allow the application entities to have detailed access to session services. Second, we see a concern with the way in which user data is represented and how it can be encoded for transmission.

As usual, we begin with the OSI definition of the presentation layer. This is followed by a discussion of key concepts and a description of the ISO service and protocol standards. Finally, standards relating to syntax and representation are discussed.

9.1 OSI DEFINITION

The presentation layer deals with the representation of information of concern to application entities. Two aspects of representation are cited in the OSI document [ISO 7498]:

- Data to be transferred between application entities. This is the end-user information.
- The data structure that application entities refer to in their communication. This is the structure of the application service data unit (ASDU).

The purpose of the presentation layer is to assure that end systems may successfully communicate even if they use different representations. It does this by providing a common representation to be used in communication and by converting from the local representation to this common representation.

Table 9.1 lists the services and functions of the presentation layer. Two services are provided. To clarify these, consider that there are three syntactic versions of the information to be exchanged between application entities: the syntax used by the originating application entity, the syntax used by the receiving application entity, and the syntax used between presentation entities. This last is referred to as the *transfer syntax*. It is possible that all three or any two of these may be identical. The presentation layer is responsible for translating the representation of the information between the transfer syntax and each of the other two syntaxes as required.

There is not a single predetermined transfer syntax for all of OSI. The transfer syntax to be used on a particular presentation connection is negotiated between the correspondent presentation entities. Each side attempts to select a transfer syntax for which it can readily make a transformation to and from its user's syntax. In addition, the selected transfer syntax may reflect other service requirements, such as the need for compression.

The functions of the presentation layer fall into two categories: those dealing with the session layer and those dealing with syntax. Each presentation connection is mapped one-to-one onto a session connection.

Table 9.1.   SERVICES AND FUNCTIONS OF THE PRESENTATION LAYER

Services
Transformation of syntax
Selection of syntax

Functions
Session establishment request
Data transfer
Negotiation and renegotiation of syntax
Transformation of syntax including data transformation, formatting, and special purpose transformations
Session termination request

In setting up a connection, a transfer syntax is negotiated; the syntax to be used may change during the lifetime of the connection. Note that the presentation protocol is concerned only with the transfer syntax; the syntaxes used by the application entities are not mentioned in the protocol dialogue. However, each presentation entity is responsible for converting between its user's syntax and the transfer syntax.

9.2 PRESENTATION LAYER CONCEPTS

Before looking at the details of the ISO standards for the presentation layer, it is useful to elaborate on the concepts introduced in the preceding section. Figure 9.1, which shows the context of the presentation layer, and Table 9.2, which defines some key terms, summarize the concepts to be discussed.

As we cross the boundary from the session layer to the presentation layer, there is a significant change in the way that data is viewed. For the session layer and below, the user data parameter of a service primitive is specified as the binary value of a sequence of octets. This binary value can be directly assembled into service data units (SDUs) for passing between layers and into protocol data units (PDUs) for passing between protocol entities within a layer. The application layer, however, is concerned with the user's view of data. In general, that view is one of a structured set of information, such as text in a document, a personnel file, an integrated data base, or a visual display of videotex information.

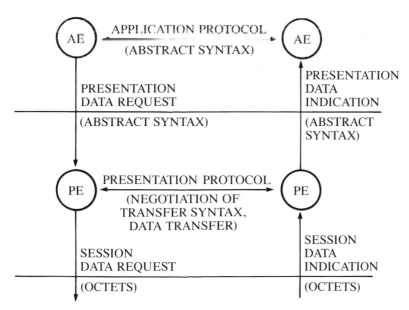

Figure 9.1. Presentation layer context.

Table 9.2.   PRESENTATION LAYER TERMS

Abstract Syntax	Describes the generic structure of data independent of any encoding technique used to represent the data. The syntax allows data types to be defined and values of those types to be specified
Data Type	A named set of values. A type may be simple, which is defined by specifying the set of its values, or structured, which is defined in terms of other types
Encoding	The complete sequence of octets used to represent a data value
Encoding Rules	A specification of the mapping from one syntax to another. Specifically, encoding rules determine algorithmically, for any set of data values defined in an abstract syntax, the representation of those values in a transfer syntax
Presentation Context	A combination of abstract syntax and transfer syntax that can be used for the transfer of data using the presentation service
Transfer Syntax	Concerned with the way in which data is actually represented in terms of bit patterns while in transit between presentation entities

The user is concerned only with the meaning of the data values in use, that is, in the semantics of the data. The presentation layer must provide a representation of this data that is or can be converted to binary values; that is, it must be concerned with the syntax of the data.

In practical terms, it is impossible to completely separate syntax and semantics. If the application layer has no knowledge of syntax, and the presentation layer has no knowledge of semantics, there is no way to accomplish the coupling of a set of semantics with a syntax that can be used to produce a concrete representation of data values for the session service.

The approach taken by ISO to provide the linkage between semantics and syntax is as follows. At the application layer, information is represented in an abstract syntax that deals with data types and data values. The abstract syntax formally specifies data independently from any specific representation. Thus, an abstract syntax has many similarities to the data type definition aspects of conventional programming languages like Pascal, C, and Ada, and to grammars such as *Backus-Naur Form* (BNF). Application protocols describe their PDUs in terms of an abstract syntax.

The presentation layer communicates with the application layer in terms of this abstract syntax. The actual details of this communication are implementation-dependent and thus beyond the scope of the relevant standards. The presentation layer translates between the abstract syntax of the application layer and a transfer syntax that describes the data values in a binary form, suitable for interaction with the session service. The transfer syntax thus defines the representation of the data to be exchanged between presentation entities. The translation from the abstract syntax to the transfer syntax is accomplished by means of encoding rules that specify the representation of each data value of each data type.

Before a presentation connection can be used to exchange data, the two presentation protocol entities must agree on a transfer syntax. Each entity knows the abstract syntax of its user, and each has available one or more transfer syntaxes that are suitable for encoding. It is simply a matter of the two entities agreeing on a particular transfer syntax to use. Once this is done, the combination of abstract and transfer syntaxes is referred to as the presentation context that is being used for the exchange.

The ISO standards make no assumptions about the way in which abstract or transfer syntaxes are specified. The presentation service is general-purpose and is intended to support all application protocols and any appropriate syntaxes. However, Sec. 9.5 explains some tools that have been developed to be of general utility in syntax specification.

The fundamental requirement for selection of a transfer syntax is that it support the corresponding abstract syntax. In addition, the transfer syntax may have other attributes that are not related to the abstract syntaxes that it can support. For example, an abstract syntax could be supported by any one of four transfer syntaxes, which are the same in all respects except that one provides data compression, one provides encryption, one provides both, and one provides neither. The choice of syntax depends on security and cost considerations.

9.3   ISO PRESENTATION SERVICE

This section examines the presentation service that has been developed and standardized by ISO [DIS 8822].

Characteristics of the Presentation Service

The ISO presentation service provides two general categories of service. Its prime service, of course, is to handle the representation of application data in such a way that two application entities can successfully exchange data even if they use a different local representation of that data. To provide this service, the presentation layer has two functions that it carries out on behalf of presentation service users:

- *Negotiation of transfer syntaxes:* For any given type of user data, a transfer syntax is negotiated that is usable by each presentation entity for transforming to/from its user's data representation.
- *Transformation:* Data provided by the user is transformed into the transfer syntax representation for transmission; data received for delivery to the user is transformed from the transfer syntax representation to the user's representation.

In addition to these presentation services, the applications require the services provided by the session layer for dialogue management. Because of the layered architecture of OSI, applications do not have direct access to session services. Thus session-related service requests must be passed through the presentation layer to the session service (Fig. 9.2). We elaborate on this point, where appropriate, in the following discussion.

At any time during the life of a presentation connection, the presentation service is dealing with one or more presentation contexts. Each context specifies the abstract syntax of the user's data and the transfer syntax to be used in transmitting that user data. Two categories of contexts are employed. The *defined context set* consists of presentation contexts that have been defined by agreement between the two presentation users and the presentation service provider. The *default context* is a presentation context that is always known to the presentation provider and is used when the defined context set is empty. At the presentation service interface, the value of the user data parameter is structured as a list of typed data values; the type identifies the presentation context applicable to the data value and the syntactic description of the data value within that context.

As with the session layer, the presentation layer services are grouped into functional units for the purpose of negotiation at connection establishment time. These are listed in Table 9.3. Most of these are identical with those defined at the session layer. These are provided so that, at connection establishment time, a presentation user may request and negotiate the use of particular session services.

There are three presentation-related functional units. The presentation kernel functional unit is always available and supports information transfer on whatever session functional unit services are selected. If two applications are using a common representation for all data to be exchanged, then only the presentation kernel is needed, and the presentation layer becomes a virtually null service that merely passes requests and responses down to session and passes session indications and con-

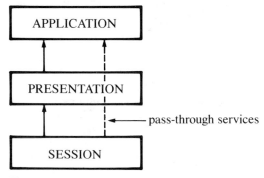

Figure 9.2. Pass-through services.

Table 9.3. **Presentation Service Functional Units**

Session Functional Units	Presentation Functional Units
Negotiated release	Presentation kernel
Half-duplex	Context management
Duplex	Context restoration
Expedited data	
Typed data	
Capability data exchange	
Minor synchronization	
Major synchronization	
Resynchronize	
Exceptions	
Activity management	

firms up to application. If two applications do not share a common representation, then the presentation layer performs the necessary transformation. If only the kernel functional unit is selected, then only the default context and the contexts negotiated as part of the defined context set at the time of connection establishment may be used. With the context management functional unit, it becomes possible to change the defined context set during the course of a presentation connection. Both additions to and deletions from the context set are permitted.

The context restoration functional unit is available to deal with the interaction between context management and session synchronization. If changes are made to the defined context set during the life of a connection, and a resynchronization occurs, then it becomes necessary to determine the state of the defined context set after the resynchronization. In general, we would like to make the defined context set conform to the change in dialogue that has taken place. How this is done is illustrated in Fig. 9.3 (compare Fig. 8.8), and can be summarized as follows, based on the resynchronization option selected:

- *Abandon:* The defined context set remains the same. Thus, we are abandoning the current dialogue, but the two sides remember the most recent context agreement between them.
- *Restart:* A restart moves the dialogue back to a previously defined synchronization point. The defined context set is set equal to the value it had when that synchronization point was originally defined. This is an appropriate action, as a restart is used to recover to a known point in the dialogue.
- *Set:* If the serial number for the set option falls into the range of the restart or abandon option, then the action indicated above for the corresponding option is taken. If the serial number is for some

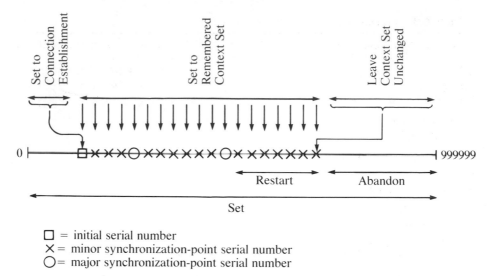

□ = initial serial number
✕ = minor synchronization-point serial number
○ = major synchronization-point serial number

Figure 9.3.   Effect of resynchronization on the defined context set.

other known synchronization point, then the defined context set is restored to that point. Otherwise, the defined context set is restored to the value negotiated at connection establishment time.

As with the other layers, the presentation service is defined in terms of primitives and parameters (Table 9.4). Note that all presentation primitives correspond to session layer primitives (see Table 8.5) of the same name, with the exception of the P-ALTER-CONTEXT primitives. The presentation parameters have the same meanings as in the session service, with the additions noted in the discussion below. The presentation primitives are grouped into five facilities, which we discuss in turn.

Connection Establishment Facility

A presentation connection is established using the P-CONNECT primitives. Connection establishment results in the establishment, on a one-to-one basis, of a session connection whose lifetime is identical to that of the supported presentation connection. Many of the parameters in the S-CONNECT.request primitive, such as quality of service and session requirement, are passed down unchanged to the session layer for use in setting up the session connection. The new parameters are as follows:

- *Multiple defined contexts:* A flag used to negotiate the availability of more than one context at a single time. If the flag is not set, the defined context set shall not have more than one member.
- *Context definition list:* This is a list of the presentation contexts to

Table 9.4.   ISO PRESENTATION SERVICE PRIMITIVES AND PARAMETERS

Connection Establishment Facility

P-CONNECT.request (calling PSAP, called PSAP, multiple defined contexts, context definition list, default context name, quality of service, presentation requirements, session requirements, serial number, token, session connection identifier, data)

P-CONNECT.indication (calling PSAP, called PSAP, multiple defined contexts, context definition list, context definition result list, default context name, default context result, quality of service, presentation requirements, session requirements, serial number, token, session connection identifier, data)

P-CONNECT.response (responding PSAP, multiple defined contexts, context definition result list, default context result, quality of service, presentation requirements, session requirements, serial number, token, session connection identifier, result, data)

P-CONNECT.confirm (responding PSAP, multiple defined contexts, context definition result list, default context result, quality of service, presentation requirements, session requirements, serial number, token, session connection identifier, result, data)

Connection Termination Facility

P-Release.request (data)

P-Release.indication (data)

P-Release.response (result, data)

P-Release.confirm (result, data)

P-U-Abort.request (context identifier list, data)

P-U-Abort.indication (context identifier list, data)

P-P-Abort.indication (reason, data)

Context Management Facility

P-ALTER-CONTEXT.request (context definition list, context deletion list, data)

P-ALTER-CONTEXT.indication (context definition list, context deletion list, context definition result list, data)

P-ALTER-CONTEXT.response (context definition result list, context deletion result list, data)

P-ALTER-CONTEXT.confirm (context definition result list, context deletion result list, data)

Information Transfer Facility

P-Typed-Data.request (data)

P-Typed-Data.indication (data)

P-Data.request (data)

P-Data.indication (data)

P-Expedited-Data.request (data)

P-Expedited-Data.indication (data)

Table 9.4   (continued)

P-Capability-Data.request (data)
P-Capability-Data.indication (data)

Dialogue Control Facility

P-Token-Give.request (tokens)
P-Token-Give.indication (tokens)

P-Token-Please.request (token, data)
P-Token-Please.indication (token, data)

P-CONTROL-GIVE.request
P-CONTROl-GIVE.indication

P-Sync-Minor.request (type, serial number, data)
P-Sync-Minor.indication (type, serial number, data)
P-Sync-Minor.response (serial number, data)
P-Sync-Minor.confirm (serial number, data)

P-Sync-Major.request (serial number, data)
P-Sync-Major.indication (serial number, data)
P-Sync-Major.response (data)
P-Sync-Major.confirm (data)

P-Resynchronize.request (type, serial number, tokens, data)
P-Resynchronize.indication (type, serial number, tokens, context identifier list, data)
P-Resynchronize.response (serial number, tokens, data)
P-Resynchronize.confirm (serial number, tokens, context identifier list, data)

P-U-Exception-Report.request (Reason, data)
P-U-Exception-Report.indication (Reason, data)

P-P-Exception-Report.indication (Reason)

P-Activity-Start.request (activity ID, data)
P-Activity-Start.indication (activity ID, data)
P-Activity-Resume.request (activity ID, old activity ID, serial number, old SC ID, data)
P-Activity-Resume.indication (activity ID, old activity ID, serial number, old SC ID, data)

P-Activity-End.request (serial number, data)
P-Activity-End.indication (serial number, data)
P-Activity-End.response (data)
P-Activity-End.confirm (data)

P-Activity-Interrupt.request (reason)
P-Activity-Interrupt.indication (reason)

Table 9.4   (continued)

P-Activity-Interrupt.response
P-Activity-Interrupt.confirm

P-Activity-Discard.request (reason)
P-Activity-Discard.indication (reason)
P-Activity-Discard.response
P-Activity-Discard.confirm

---

be placed in the initial defined context set. Each item in the list consists of an identifier, by which the context will be known, and an abstract syntax name, which specifies the syntax used by the application. It is up to the service provider to determine the transfer syntax to be used for each context.

- *Context definition result list:* This list contains an entry for each item in the context definition list, indicating acceptance or rejection.
- *Default context name:* The default context is automatically used in some contexts, for example, in the passing of expedited data. The default context name is supplied by the user if it wishes to identify explicitly the abstract syntax supported by the default context for future reference.
- *Default context result:* Has the value agreed or refused.
- *Presentation requirements:* Used to select the context management and context restoration functional units.

Connection Termination Facility

The P-Release provides access to the S-Release service available from the session layer. Similarly, P-U-Abort and P-P-Abort are passed down to session. In case of the P-U-Abort, a context identifier list is provided to specify the contexts that are used in the user data parameter.

Context Management Facility

The context management facility allows changes to be made to the defined context list. The requestor provides a list of contexts to be added to the defined context list, together with a list of contexts to be deleted. The service provider passes these to the other user, together with an indication of which proposed new contexts it can support. The user can either accept or reject each proposed change. Based on the provider's ability to support new contexts plus the response of the other user, the service provider confirms to the requesting user the resulting additions and deletions to the defined context set.

Information Transfer Facility

The information transfer facility provides the user with access to the information transfer facility of the session layer. In the case of data, typed data and capability data, the data parameter is passed between application entities using the defined context set, or in the default context if the defined context set is empty. In the case of expedited data, the data is passed using the default context. This convention is used because it is possible for an expedited data request to overtake an alter context request. Hence, the two sides may not agree on the defined context set at the time of arrival of the expedited data.

Dialogue Control Facility

All of the primitives in this facility provide access to the corresponding session layer primitives. There is no added value and none of the services of the session layer are lost.

9.4   ISO PRESENTATION PROTOCOL

The ISO standard for the presentation protocol [DIS 8823] specifies the following:

- The structure and encoding of presentation protocol data units (PPDUs) used for the transfer of data and control information.
- Procedures for the transfer of data and control information from one presentation entity to a peer entity.
- The means for selecting, by reference to functional units, the procedures to be used by the presentation entities.
- The linkages between the presentation protocol and (1) the presentation service and (2) the session service.

These points should become clear as the discussion proceeds.

Presentation Protocol Data Units

As with other standard protocols, the presentation protocol functions by means of the exchange of protocol data units (PDUs). Each PDU consists of a header, containing control information, and may also include a data portion, containing data passed down from the next higher layer or to be delivered to the next higher layer. The PDUs for the presentation layer, together with their parameters, are listed in Table 9.5. Two aspects of this list are noteworthy. First, the list is not very long; and second, many of the parameters (those marked with an asterisk) are identical with parameters found in comparable session PDUs (see Table 8.9). These two are manifestations of the same underlying concept: that there is tight linkage

Table 9.5. PRESENTATION PROTOCOL DATA UNITS AND PARAMETERS

PPDU	Parameters
Connect (CP)	Calling PSAP, Calling SSAP*, Called PSAP, Called SSAP*, Multiple defined contexts, Context list, Default context, Protocol version, Quality of service*, Presentation requirements, User session requirements, Revised session requirements*, Serial number*, Token assignment*, Session connection ID, User data
Connect Accept (CPA)	Called PSAP, Called SSAP*, Responding PSAP, Responding SSAP*, Multiple defined contexts, Context result list, Default context result, Protocol version, Quality of service*, Presentation requirements, User session requirements, Revised session requirements*, Serial number*, Token assignment*, Session connection ID*, User data
Connect Reject (CPR)	Called PSAP, Called SSAP*, Responding PSAP, Responding SSAP*, Context result list, Default context result, Quality of service*, Session requirements*, Session connection ID*, Provider reason, User data
Abnormal Release User (ARU)	Context identifier list, User data
Abnormal Release Provider (ARP)	Provider reason, Abort data
Alter Context (AC)	Context definition list, Context identifier deletion list, User data
Alter Context ACK (ACA)	Context definition result list, Context deletion result list, User data
Typed Data (TTD)	User data
Data (TD)	User data
Expedited Data (ED)	User data
Capability Data (CD)	User data
Capability Data ACK (TCC)	User data
Resynchronize (RS)	Type*, Serial Number*, Tokens*, Context identifier list, User data
Resynchronize ACK (RSA)	Tokens*, Context identifier list, User data

* = session-related parameters

between the presentation layer and the session layer. We have already referred to this linkage in our discussion of the presentation service (Fig. 9.2). Let us explore this linkage further.

Below the presentation layer, there is a direct relationship between layer N service primitives and layer N PDUs. Consider Fig. 8.7a. An S-CONNECT.request triggers the transmission of a Connect SPDU, which triggers an S-CONNECT.indication; in the other direction, an S-CONNECT.response triggers an Accept SPDU, which triggers an S-Connect.indication. In general, a confirmed session service causes the exchange of two SPDUs, and a nonconfirmed service causes a single SPDU to be transmitted. Each SPDU becomes user data in a transport-level data or expedited data TPDU. A similar set of statements can be made about lower layers. In some cases, more PDUs are exchanged for a given service (e.g., transport-level retransmission of lost TPDUs), but the principles remain the same:

1. Each layer N service is implemented by the exchange of layer N PDUs.
2. Each layer N PDU becomes user data and is encapsulated in a layer $(N - 1)$ PDU.

At the presentation layer (and, we shall see, also at the application layer), these principles do not apply. Not every presentation service requires presentation PDUs, and some of the parameters in some PPDUs do not appear as user data in SPDUs. To explain the motivation for these differences, we consider two presentation services: connection establishment and token passing.

As protocols for the upper three layers of the OSI model were being developed, it became evident that for the negotiation of connection options to work well, it would be useful to negotiate and establish the session, presentation, and application connections simultaneously. This, of course dictates a strict one-to-one relationship (no multiplexing) with coextensive lifetimes for the three connection types. This process is known as *embedding,* as the connection request and response PDUs of the three upper layers are carried one inside the other. Figure 9.4 shows how the Connect PPDU is embedded in the Connect SPDU. Embedding allows for connection establishment at the application level with the minimum number of PDU exchanges. Without embedding, a session connection must be established even when it turns out that a presentation connection cannot be established (e.g., lack of agreement on a transfer syntax), and both a session and a presentation connection must be established even if it turns out that an application connection cannot be established. These unnecessary connections would then need to be released, requiring additional PDU exchanges. In addition, the responding application entity could not specify values for negotiating presentation and

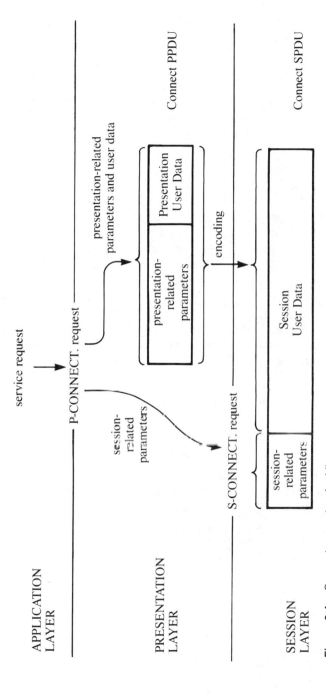

Figure 9.4. Connect request embedding.

session services, because the information needed for such a decision (i.e., the information in the connection indication primitive) would not be available until after the session and presentation connections had been established.

Now consider the P-Token-Give service. The presentation layer has nothing to do with this service. It does not add any value to the service, or impose any conditions on its use. Thus, when a P-Token-Give.request is issued by a presentation user, the presentation entity simply invokes S-Token-Give.request, with no user data (PPDU) parameter. The S-Token-Give triggers the transmission of a Give Tokens SPDU. When this is received by the other receiving session entity, it issues an S-Token-Give.indication to the receiving presentation entity, which issues a P-Token-Give.indication to the receiving presentation user. Thus, in the data exchanged between systems, there is no presentation header.

In Table 9.5, those parameters marked by an asterisk are included in the header of the session PDU that encapsulates the presentation PDU, and not in the PPDU header. The formats of PPDU headers are specified using an abstract syntax in the standard. Table 9.6 shows the relationship between presentation service primitives, presentation protocol data units, and session service primitives. Table 9.7 shows which PPDUs are needed to support each presentation functional units.

We now turn to an examination of the presentation protocol support for the presentation facilities.

Connection Establishment Facility

This facility has already been considered. Connection-related PPDUs are embedded in connection-related SPDUs, via the S-Connect primitives.

The multiple defined contexts parameter may be present in the CPA PPDU only if it was present in the CP PPDU. If it is not present in the CPA PPDU, then the option is not selected. The context list and context result list are used to negotiate the use of transfer syntaxes for each abstract syntax requested by the presentation user. Those syntaxes proposed by the initiator and accepted by the responder may be used. The presentation requirements consist of those functional units required by both users.

Connection Termination Facility

Orderly release of the connection is a session function. When the session connection is released, the presentation connection is also automatically released. Hence, there are no PPDUs for this service. When a presentation user aborts a connection, it may wish to pass some user-defined data, and this requires the context and user data information in the ARU PPDU. If a connection is aborted, but not by one of the users, then there

Table 9.6. **RELATIONSHIP AMONG PRESENTATION PRIMITIVES, PRESENTATION PDUs, AND SESSION PRIMITIVES**

Presentation Primitives	Presentation PDUs	Session Primitives
P-Connect	CP, CPA, CPR	S-Connect
P-Release	—	S-Release
P-U-Abort	ARU	S-U-Abort
P-P-Abort	ARP	S-U-Abort
P-P-Abort	—	S-P-Abort
P-Alter-Context	AC, ACA	S-Typed-Data
P-Typed-Data	TTD	S-Typed-Data
P-Data	TD	S-Data
P-Expedited-Data	TE	S-Expedited-Data
P-Capability-Data	TC, TCC	S-Capability-Data
P-Token-Give	—	S-Token-Give
P-Token-Please	—	S-Token-Please
P-Control-Give	—	S-Control-Give
P-Sync-Minor	—	S-Sync-Minor
P-Sync-Major	—	S-Sync-Major
P-Resynchronize	—	S-Resynchronize
P-Resynchronize	RS, RSA	S-Resynchronize
P-U-Exception-Report	—	S-U-Exception-Report
P-P-Exception-Report	—	S-U-Exception-Report
P-Activity-Start	—	S-Activity-Start
P-Activity-Resume	—	S-Activity-Resume
P-Activity-End	—	S-Activity-End
P-Activity-Interrupt	—	S-Activity-Interrupt
P-Activity-Discard	—	S-Activity-Discard

are two possibilities. One of the two presentation entities may initiate the abort; in that case the entity sends an ARP PPDU to the other presentation entity, with one of the following reasons:

- Unrecognized PPDU
- Unexpected PPDU
- Unexpected session service parameter
- Unrecognized PPDU parameter
- Reason not specified

The abort data parameter identifies the PPDU that triggered the abort procedure. When an ARP is received by a presentation entity, it issues a P-P-Abort.indication to its user. Note that the ARP is carried in an S-U-

Table 9.7.   ASSOCIATION OF PPDUs WITH FUNCTIONAL UNITS

Functional Unit	O/M*	PPDU Code	PPDU Name
Kernel functional unit	M	CP	Connect Presentation PPDU
		CPA	Connect Presentation accept PPDU
		CPR	Connect Presentation reject PPDU
		ARU	Abnormal Release-User PPDU
		ARP	Abnormal Release-Provider PPDU
		TD	Data PPDU
		TE	Expedited data PPDU†
		TTD	Typed data PPDU‡
		TC	Capability data PPDU§
		TCC	Capability data Ack. PPDU§
Context Management functional unit	O	DC	Alter Context PPDU
		DCA	Alter Context Ack. PPDU
		RS	Resynchronize PPDU
		RSA	Resynchronize Ack. PPDU
Context Restoration Functional Unit	O		No further PPDUs.‖

*O = Optional, M = Mandatory
†The session expedited functional unit must also have been selected.
‡The session typed data functional unit must also have been agreed by the presentation service users.
§The session capability data functional unit must also have been agreed.
‖The presentation context management functional unit must also have been selected.

Abort.indication. This is correct, as it is the session user that initiates the abort.

The other alternative is that the session entity aborts the session connection, which causes the simultaneous abort of the presentation connection. In this case, the presentation entity receives an S-P-Abort (which has no embedded PPDU), and issues a P-P-Abort to its user.

Context Management Facility

The P-Alter-Context service is a confirmed service. Hence, two PPDUs are involved: Alter Context (AC) and Alter Context ACK (ACA). This is a service that has nothing to do with session, and, therefore, there is no corresponding SPDU to use as a vehicle. Furthermore, it is desired that this facility not depend on data token control. Accordingly, the AC and ACK PPDUs are transmitted as typed data by session, allowing them to bypass token control.

Information Transfer Facility

The four types of data (normal, typed, expedited, and capability) are transferred using the corresponding session service. In each case, the only parameter is the presentation user data.

Dialogue Control Facility

All of the services in this facility are essentially session services. With the exception of the P-Resynchronize service, none of the services in this facility require that the presentation entities exchange data.

If the context restoration functional unit has been selected, then there is the possible need to restore a defined context set to a previous value. Accordingly, the presentation entity will remember the value of the defined context set at the time of each minor and major synchronization service. However, this function does not require the exchange of PPDUs.

The P-Resynchronize request and response primitives are handled in one of three ways:

1. If neither the context management nor context restoration functional units is selected, then the presentation entity issues a S-Resynchronize request or response.
2. If context management is selected but context restoration is not, then the presentation entity issues an RS or RSA in the user data parameter of a S-Resynchronize request or response. The context identifier list parameter refers to the current defined context set.
3. If both context management and context restoration are selected, then the presentation entity issues an RS or RSA, with the context identifier list parameter set to the appropriate restored defined context set.

The reception of an S-Synchronize indication or confirm is handled in the corresponding manner: A P-Synchronize indication or confirm is issued and context restoral, if required, is performed.

It should be clear why the RS and RSA PPDUs are not needed for case 1 above, and why they are needed for case 3. It is perhaps less obvious that they are also needed for case 2, as case 2 does not allow the restoration of a previous defined context set. The problem that case 2 addresses is this. Suppose one presentation entity is attempting to alter the context at about the same time that the other is trying to resynchronize the connection. The scenario of Fig. 9.5 could occur. User *A* issues a P-Alter-Context.request. User *B* receives the indication and issues a response that accepts the alteration. At this point, user *B* assumes that the new defined context set is in force. User *B* now issues a P-Resynchronize.request. This triggers an S-Resynchronize.request. The session pro-

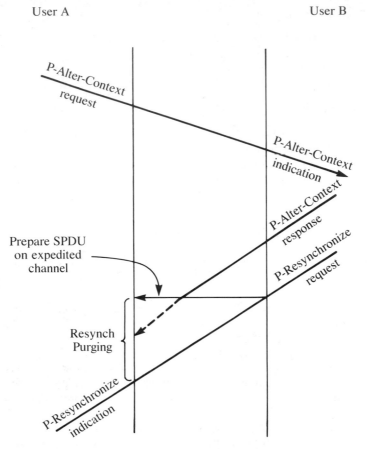

Figure 9.5.   Loss of defined context set consistency by resynchronization.

tocol entity will issue a Resynchronize SPDU, which will be carried by a data TPDU. But recall from Sec. 8.3 that the session protocol entity may also issue a Prepare SPDU, which is carried by an expedited data TPDU. If the expedited data TPDU overtakes the TPDU that is carrying the ACA PPDU, then that latter TPDU is discarded, and the ACA never gets through. Hence, user *A* never receives a P-Alter-Context.confirm, and assumes that the defined context set has not been altered. This would leave the two presentation entities with different opinions on the contexts of the defined context set. To avoid this possibility, the resynchronization activity results in the exchange of RS and RSA primitives to enforce agreement.

9.5   SYNTAX AND REPRESENTATION

Earlier in this chapter, we discussed the need for an abstract syntax and encoding rules to specify the representation for data types defined in the abstract syntax. These issues have been addressed by both CCITT and ISO. In recommendation X.409, CCITT defines a *standard notation* and a *standard representation* for data types and values [POPE84]. These terms correspond to the terms abstract syntax and encoding rules, respectively. ISO has issued separate documents for these two concepts, one is referred to as Abstract Syntax Notation One (ASN.1) [DIS 8824], and the other referred to as Basic Encoding Rules [DIS 8825]. The ISO specifications are compatible with those of CCITT, but include a few extensions. The descriptions below apply to both sets of standards.

Abstract Syntax

The abstract syntax (ISO ASN.1, CCITT standard notation) is based on the concept of the data type. This notion is the same as that used in many common programming languages. Typically, these languages have simple types, such as integers and Booleans, that are predefined, as well as facilities for combining these simple types in various ways to form more elaborate data structures. In Pascal, for example, the built-in types include integers, Booleans, and characters, and these may be combined to form arrays, records, and sets. Moreover, the methods of combination may be applied recursively to produce arbitrarily complex types. Similarly, these concepts may be used by applications to communicate data types to the presentation layer.

ASN.1 and X.409 refer to four classes of types:

- *Universal:* Generally useful, application-independent types and construction mechanisms; these are defined in the standard and are listed in Table 9.8.
- *Application-Wide:* Relevant to a particular application; these are defined in other standards.
- *Context-Specific:* Also relevant to a particular application, but applicable in a limited context.
- *Private:* Types defined by users and not covered by any standard.

Each type is distinguished by a tag, which specifies the class of type and identifies the particular type. For example, UNIVERSAL 4 refers to OctetString, which is of class UNIVERSAL and has ID 4 within that class.

The syntax is used both to define data types and to specify data values. The easiest way to describe the syntax is by example. We shall use an example taken from both the ISO and the CCITT documents, and reproduced as Fig. 9.6. The example defines the structure of a personnel record. Part a of the figure depicts the personnel record informally and gives an example of a specific record.

Table 9.8. UNIVERSAL CLASS OF DATA TYPES

Tag	Type
UNIVERSAL 1	Boolean
UNIVERSAL 2	Integer
UNIVERSAL 3	BitString
UNIVERSAL 4	OctetString
UNIVERSAL 5	Null
UNIVERSAL 6	Object Identifier
UNIVERSAL 7	Object Descriptor
UNIVERSAL 8	External
UNIVERSAL 9–15	Reserved for addenda
UNIVERSAL 16	Sequence and Sequence-of
UNIVERSAL 17	Set and Set-of
UNIVERSAL 18	NumericString (Character String)
UNIVERSAL 19	Printable String (Character String)
UNIVERSAL 20	TeletexString (Character String)
UNIVERSAL 21	VideotexString (Character String)
UNIVERSAL 22	IA5String (Character String)
UNIVERSAL 23	UTCTime
UNIVERSAL 24	GeneralizedTime
UNIVERSAL 25	Graphic String (Character String)
UNIVERSAL 26	Visible String (Character String)
UNIVERSAL 27	General String (Character String)
UNIVERSAL 28	Reserved for addenda

(a) Informal description of personnel record

The structure of the personnel record and its value for a particular individual are shown below.

Name: **John P. Smith**
Title: **Director**
Employee Number: **51**
Date of Hire: **17 September 1971**
Name of Spouse: **Mary T. Smith**
Number of Children: **2**

Child information
Name: **Ralph T. Smith**
Date of Birth: **11 November 1957**

Child Information
Name: **Susan B. Jones**
Date of Birth: **17 July 1959**

Figure 9.6. Example use of ASNI.

(b) Formal description of record structure

The structure of every personnel record is formally described below using the standard notation for data types.

PersonnelRecord :: = **[APPLICATION 0] IMPLICIT SET {**
    Name,
    title [0] IA5String,
    EmployeeNumber,
    dateOfHire [1] Date,
    nameOfSpouse [2] Name,
    [3] IMPLICIT SEQUENCE OF ChildInformation DEFAULT {}}

ChildInformation :: = **SET {**
    Name,
    dateOfBirth [0] Date}

Name :: = **[APPLICATION 1] IMPLICIT SEQUENCE {**
    givenName IA5String,
    initial IA5String,
    familyName IA5String}

EmployeeNumber :: = **[APPLICATION 2] IMPLICIT INTEGER**

Date :: = **[APPLICATION 3] IMPLICIT IA5String** -- *YYYYMMDD*

(c) Formal description of record value

The value of John Smith's personnel record is formally described below using the standard notation for data values.

{
    {givenName "John", initial "P", familyName "Smith"},
    title "Director",
    51,
    dateOfHire "19710917",
    nameOfSpouse {givenName "Mary", initial "T", familyName "Smith"},
    {
        {
            {givenName "Ralph", initial "T", familyName "Smith"},
            "19571111"},
        {
            {givenName "Susan", initial "B", familyName "Jones"},
            "19590717"}}}

Figure 9.6   (continued)

In part b, we see the formal description of the data type. In the notation, a type definition has the form:

$$<type\ name> ::= <type\ definition>$$

A simple example is

SerialNumber ::= INTEGER

There are no simple types defined in the example. A similar definition is

EmployeeNumber ::= [APPLICATION 2] IMPLICIT INTEGER

This makes use of the built-in type Integer, but the user has chosen to give the type a new tag. The use of the term [APPLICATION 2] gives the tag (class and ID) for this new type. The designation IMPLICIT has to do with the representation of values in the transfer syntax. With that term present, values of this type will be encoded only with the tag APPLICA-TION 2. If the designation were not present, then the values would be encoded with both the APPLICATION and UNIVERSAL tags. The use of the implicit option results in a compact representation. In other applications, compactness may be less important than other considerations, such as the ability to carry out type-checking. In the latter case, explicit tagging can be used (omit the term IMPLICIT).

The definition of the Date type is similar to that of Employee-Number. In this case the type is a character string consisting of characters from the standard character set known as IA5; this is essentially the same as the ASCII character set. The double hyphen indicates that the rest of the line is a comment; the format of values of the Date type will not be checked, other than to determine that the value is a IA5 character string.

The remaining types are more complex. Consider next the definition of Name. The basic type of Name is Sequence, which is defined to be an ordered series of other types. A Sequence is analogous to the record structure found in many programming languages, such as COBOL. The beginning and the end of a Sequence definition are marked by curly brackets. A Sequence consists of a series of elements, each specifying a type and, optionally, a name. Three forms of Sequence are allowed:

- A variable number of elements, all of one type (the designation SEQUENCE OF is used).
- A fixed number of elements, possibly of more than one type.
- A fixed number of elements, some of which are optional; all elements, including optional ones, must be of distinct types.

The example is of the second form, and consists of three character-string types, each of which is given a name.

Next, let us consider the definition of ChildInformation, which is of type Set. A Set is similar to a Sequence, except that the order of the elements is not significant. The elements may be arranged in any order when they are encoded into a specific representation. As with a Sequence, the three forms described above are allowed. In this example, the set contains two elements. The first is the data type Name, which is the defined Sequence just discussed. This is an example of the recursive capability to define types within types. Note that no name is given to the first element, but that the second element is given the name dateOfBirth. The second element is the data type Date defined elsewhere. This data type is used in two different contexts, here and in the definition of PersonnelRecord. In each context, the data type is given a name and a context-specific tag, [0] and [1], respectively.

Finally, the overall structure, PersonnelRecord, is defined as a Set with five elements. Associated with the last element is a default value of a null sequence, to be used if no value is supplied. Figure 9.6b is an example of a particular value for the personnel record.

The example just described shows the use of a representative sample of the types available with the syntax. As Table 9.8 indicates, there are others. Among the most important of these are:

- *BitString:* An ordered set of zero or more bits. Individual bits can be assigned names to indicate a specific meaning.
- *OctetString:* An ordered set of zero or more octets. Can be used to model binary data whose format and length are unspecified.
- *External:* A type whose values are unspecified and that can be defined using any well-specified notation. It is used for presentation service user data in the ISO presentation protocol.
- *Object Identifier:* A unique identifier for a particular object, encoded as a series of integers. Object identifiers are used to name abstract and transfer syntaxes.
- *Object Descriptor:* A human-readable text providing a brief description of an object designated by an object identifier.

Encoding Rules

The representation of a value of a data type consists of three components, and is shown in Fig. 9.7. The type field encodes the tag (class and number) of the type of the data value. The first two bits of the type field indicate to which of the four classes (universal, application-wide, context-specific, or private) this type belongs. The next bit indicates whether the form of the type:

- *Primitive:* The Contents field directly represents the value.
- *Constructor:* The Contents field is the complete encoding of one or more other data values. This is used for types such as Sequence and Set.

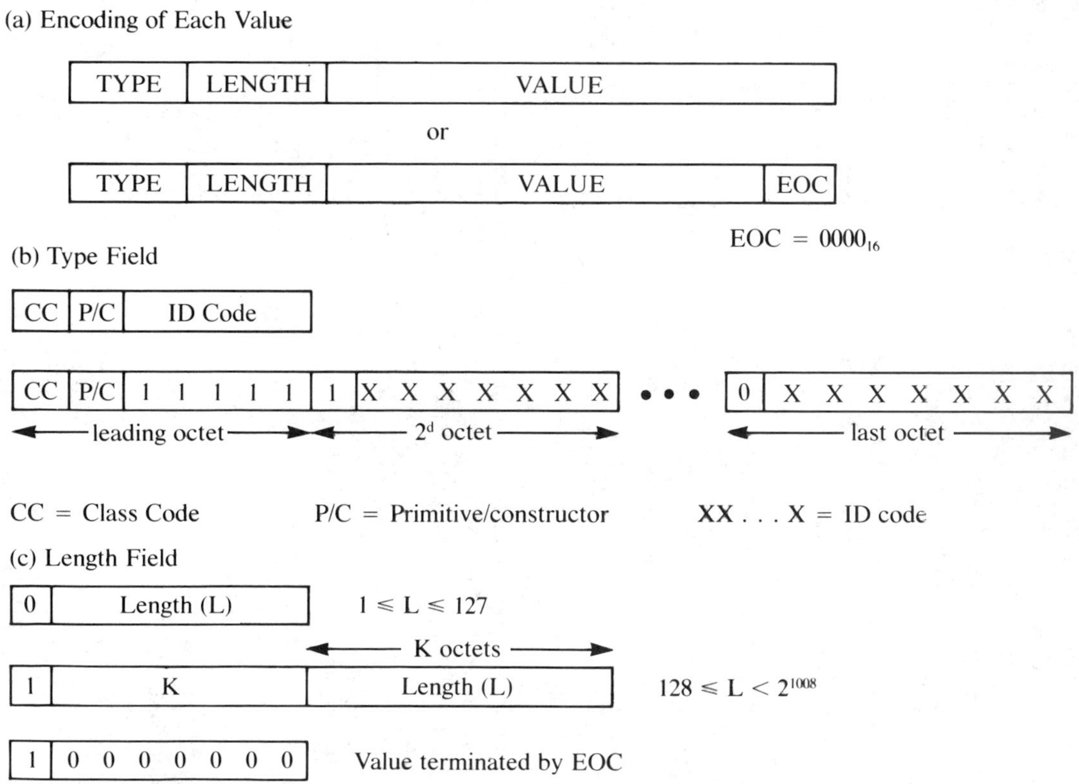

(a) Encoding of Each Value

TYPE	LENGTH	VALUE

or

TYPE	LENGTH	VALUE	EOC

$EOC = 0000_{16}$

(b) Type Field

CC	P/C	ID Code

CC	P/C	1 1 1 1 1	X X X X X X X	• • •	0	X X X X X X X

← leading octet → ← 2^d octet →   ← last octet →

CC = Class Code   P/C = Primitive/constructor   XX . . . X = ID code

(c) Length Field

0	Length (L)

$1 \leq L \leq 127$

← K octets →

1	K	Length (L)

$128 \leq L < 2^{1008}$

1	0 0 0 0 0 0 0

Value terminated by EOC

Figure 9.7. Encoding of values.

272

(The octet-level representation of the record value given in Figure 9.6 is shown below. The values of Identifiers, Lengths, and the Contents of Integers are shown in hexadecimal, two hexadecimal digits per octet. The values of the Contents of Octet Strings are shown as text, one character per octet.)

```
Personnel
Record    Length    Contents
60        8185

          Name      Length    Contents
          61        10

                              IA5 String    Length    Contents
                              16            04        "John"

                              IA5 String    Length    Contents
                              16            01        "P"

                              IA5 String    Length    Contents
                              16            05        "Smith"

          Title     Length    Contents
          A0        0A

                              IA5 String    Length    Contents
                              16            08        "Director"

          Employee
          Number    Length    Contents
          42        01        33

          Date of
          Hire      Length    Contents
          A1        0A

                              Date          Length    Contents
                              43            08        "19710917"
```

Figure 9.8. Encoding of Fig. 9.6.

273

	Length	Contents		Length	Contents		Length	Contents
Name of spouse A2	12							
		Name 61	10					
				IA5 String 16	04	"Mary"		
				IA5 String 16	01	"T"		
				IA5 String 16	05	"Smith"		
[3] A3	42							
		Set 31	1F					
				Name 61	11			
						IA5 String 16	05	"Ralph"
						IA5 String 16	01	"T"
						IA5 String 16	05	"Smith"
				Date of birth A0	0A			
						Date 43	08	"19571111"

Set	*Length*	*Contents*				
3	1F					
		Name	*Length*	*Contents*		
		61	11			
				IA5 String	*Length*	*Contents*
				16	05	"Susan"
				IA5 String	*Length*	*Contents*
				16	01	"B"
				IA5 String	*Length*	*Contents*
				16	05	"Jones"
		Date of birth	*Length*	*Contents*		
		A0	0A			
				Date	*Length*	*Contents*
				43	08	"19590717"

Figure 9.8 (continued)

The remaining five bits of the Type field can encode a numeric ID code that distinguishes one data type from another within the designated class. For tags whose number is greater than or equal to 31, those five bits contain the binary value 11111, and the ID code is contained in the last seven bits of one or more additional octets. The first bit of each additional octet indicates whether this is the last additional octet in the Type field.

The Length field specifies the length L in octets of the Contents field. For L less than 128, the Length field consists of a single octet beginning with a zero. If the length of the Contents field is not immediately known, but is greater than 127, the first octet of the Length field contains a seven-bit code that specifies the length of the Length field. The remaining octets of the Length field specify the length of the Contents field. If the length of the Contents field is not immediately known, then the Length field has the binary value 10000000, and the Contents field is terminated by an end-of-contents marker consisting of 16 zero bits.

Figure 9.8 shows the encoding of the example personnel record value.

chapter **10**

Application Layer

The application layer is at the boundary between the open systems environment and the application processes that use that environment to exchange data [BART83]. To support the wide variety of possible applications, the protocols and services potentially available in the application layer are many and varied. They include facilities of general utility to a wide variety of applications and facilities specific to distinct classes of applications. Because of this variety, the standards at this layer deserve, and will receive, an entire volume in this series. This chapter, after the usual examination of the OSI specification, examines the ISO standards for common application service elements: those elements of general utility.

10.1 OSI DEFINITION

As the top layer of the OSI model, the application layer exhibits some differences from the other layers. Specifically, the application layer does not provide services to a higher layer. Accordingly, there is no concept of an *application service access point* (SAP). The application layer does provide services, but these services are provided to application processes that lie outside the seven-layer architecture. The OSI document defines an application process as "an element within an open system which per-

277

forms the information processing for a particular application." The following examples of application processes are provided:

- A person operating a banking terminal is a manual application process.
- A FORTRAN program executing in a computer center and accessing a remote data base is a computerized application process; the remote database management systems server is also an application process.
- A process control program executing in a dedicated computer attached to some industrial equipment and linked into a plant control system is a physical application-process.

Application processes in different open systems that wish to exchange information do so by accessing the application layer. The application layer contains application entities that employ application protocols and presentation services to exchange information. It is these application entities that provide the means for application processes to access the OSI environment. We can think of the application entities as providing useful services that are relevant to one or more application processes.

Table 10.1 lists the services and functions of the application layer. Remember that, in this case, the services of the layer are provided to

Table 10.1.   SERVICES AND FUNCTIONS OF THE APPLICATION LAYER

Services
Information transfer
Identification of intended communications partners
Determination of the current availability of the intended communication partners
Establishment of authority to communicate
Agreement of privacy mechanisms
Authentication of intended communication partners
Determination of cost allocation methodology
Determination of the adequacy of resources
Determination of the acceptable quality of service
Synchronization of cooperating applications
Selection of the dialogue discipline including initiation and release procedures
Agreement on responsibility for error recovery
Agreement on the procedures for control of data integrity
Identification of constraints on data syntax

Functions
Functions that imply communication between open systems and are not already performed by the lower layers

application processes and not to a higher layer. As can be seen, the functions are not spelled out, as they will depend on the application. However, the OSI document suggests a grouping of functions that clarifies the task of the application layer and also serves as a guide to standardization efforts. This grouping is illustrated in Fig. 10.1 and consists of three types of elements:

- *User element:* That part of an application process specifically concerned with accessing OSI services. It does this by interfacing with application service elements, which are identifiable collections of functions that provide OSI services.
- *Common application service elements:* Provide capabilities that are generally useful to a variety of applications.
- *Specific application service elements:* Provide capabilities required to satisfy the particular needs of specific applications.

Examples of common application service elements are *association control* and *commitment, concurrency, and recovery.* Standards have been developed by ISO for both of these elements [DP 8649/1, DP 8650/1] and are described in this chapter. Examples of specific application service elements are file transfer, job transfer, message exchange, and remote

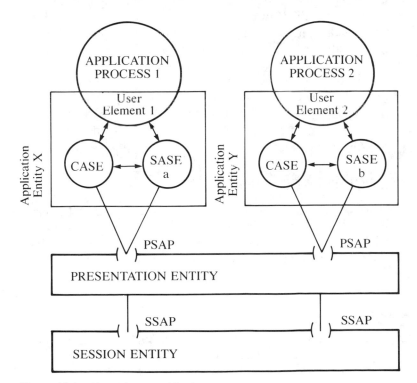

Figure 10.1.   Upper layer architecture.

terminal access. ISO and CCITT have developed and are continuing to develop standards in this category. Because of the variety and quantity of such standards, they are the subject of a separate volume in this series.

It should be emphasized that the common and specific application service elements do not form sublayers of the application layer, such as was found in the network layer. The common application service elements exist as peers with specific application service elements and provide a set of functions that would have to be present in each specific application service element if they were not provided separately.

Each application process is represented to its peer and exchanges data with that peer by means of an application entity. An application entity consists of one user element and a set of application service elements needed to support the particular application. Thus, application service elements are combined in different ways to support different applications. In the application, the user must implement a user element that knows how to access the services of those service elements required for the exchange.

Within an application entity, application service elements may call on each other and on presentation services. The user element does not directly deal with the presentation layer, but may only invoke services of the application service elements within the entity. Each application entity is unambiguously identified by means of a presentation service access point (PSAP), which is, in turn, mapped one-to-one onto an SSAP.

If two application entities wish to communicate in a connection-oriented manner, an application connection, referred to as an *association*, must be established. This association is mapped one-to-one onto a presentation connection. The association is used to exchange protocol information between application service elements in the two application entities. Thus, there may be more than one protocol using the single association (application connection).

10.2 ASSOCIATION CONTROL

One set of services that is a common requirement of almost all applications is that of establishing, maintaining, and terminating connections. Accordingly, ISO has developed service [DIS 8649/2] and protocol [DIS 8650/2] standards for this facility as part of the Common Application Service Elements.

Basic Concepts

Two concepts are essential to an understanding of the association control facility: application association and application context. DIS 8649/2 defines an *application association* as follows:

A cooperative relationship between two application entities, formed by their exchange of application protocol control information through their use of presentation services.

This concept needs to be contrasted with that of presentation connection. The OSI document defines an (N)-connection as an "association established by the (N)-layer between two or more (N + 1)-entities." The application association and the presentation connection are actually two different aspects of the same thing, namely, the relationship that exists between two application entities that are performing a shared task. From the point of view of the communication mechanisms needed to support information exchange, the relationship is a presentation connection. The presentation connection provides a *pipe* for the transfer of abstract data values with no constraints on the way these values are used. From the point of view of the information exchange itself, the relationship is an application association. The association supports agreed procedures and shared semantics for the use of the corresponding presentation connection.

The application association supports the meaningful cooperative exchange between application entities within a defined application context. An *application context* is defined as

An explicitly identified set of application service elements, related options, and any other necessary information for the interworking of application entities on an application association.

An application context, then, is a mutually agreeable relationship between application entities in different open systems. The relationship exists for a period of time during which a cooperative task is performed. The relationship includes an agreement as to which application service entities will be employed, and a definition of the semantics of all user information to be exchanged.

With these concepts in mind, we now turn to a description of the ISO standards for association control.

Association Control Service [DIS 8649/2]

Table 10.2 lists the primitives and parameters of the ISO application control service. Keep in mind that this service is a common application service element, and provides service to user elements and specific application service elements. The purpose of this service is to support the establishment, maintenance, and termination of application associations. Note that many of the parameters provided by a user are not used directly by the application association service, but are mapped directly into pa-

Table 10.2. ASSOCIATION CONTROL SERVICE PRIMITIVES AND PARAMETERS

A-ASSOCIATE.request (Calling application entity title, Called application entity title, Application context name, User information, Calling PSAP*, Called PSAP*, Single presentation context, Presentation context definition list, Default presentation context name*, Quality of service**, Presentation requirements*, Session requirements**, Serial number**, Tokens**, Session connection identifier**)

A-ASSOCIATE.indication (Calling application entity title, Called application entity title, Application context name, User information, Calling PSAP*, Called PSAP*, Single presentation context, Presentation context definition list, Presentation context definition result, Default presentation context name*, Default presentation context result*, Quality of service**, Presentation requirements*, Session requirements**, Serial number**, Tokens**, Session connection identifier**)

A-ASSOCIATE.response (Responding application entity title, Application context name, User information, Result, Responding PSAP*, Presentation context definition result, Default presentation context result*, Quality of service**, Presentation requirements*, Session requirements**, Serial number**, Tokens**, Session connection identifier**)

A-ASSOCIATE.confirm (Responding application entity title, Application context name, User information, Result, Responding PSAP*, Presentation context definition result, Default presentation context result*, Quality of service**, Presentation requirements*, Session requirements**, Serial number**, Tokens**, Session connection identifier**)

A-RELEASE.request (Reason, User information)

A-RELEASE.indication (Reason, User information)

A-RELEASE.response (Reason, User information, Result)

A-RELEASE.confirm (Reason, User information, Result)

A-ABORT.request (User information)

A-ABORT.indication (Abort source, User information)

A-P-ABORT.indication (Reason*, Data*)

* = Mapped directly to presentation service
** = Mapped directly to session service

rameters for the presentation or even the session service. As we discussed in Chap. 9, there is a relatively tight linkage among the three upper layers of the OSI model.

We examine each primitive type in turn, beginning with the A-ASSOCIATE service. This service is used to set up an application association. A one-to-one correspondence exists between an application association and a presentation connection, and therefore, between an application association and a session connection. The A-ASSOCIATE primitives are supported by the P-CONNECT primitives, and the parameters of those presentation primitives (see Table 9.4) are made available to the association control user. The *added value* of the association control service is reflected in these additional parameters:

- Calling, called, and responding application entity titles
- Application context name
- User information
- Single presentation context
- Presentation context definition list and result
- Result

Application entity titles identify application entities unambiguously. These titles are declared in the association control protocol as ASN.1 type EXTERNAL, meaning that the abstract syntax and transfer syntax are outside the scope of the standard. Other agreements or standards are needed to identify application entities. Application context names identify the context; the responder may propose a different application context than the requestor. The result of this negotiation is not defined in the standard but is application specific. Application context names are of ASN.1 type OBJECT IDENTIFIER. This allows names to be assigned to application contexts by standards organizations as part of the application-layer standards.

The single presentation context parameter, if present, specifies that the presentation multiple contexts facility is not to be used. If the parameter is not present, then the requestor may propose a list of presentation contexts to comprise the defined context set. This list is passed down to the presentation service, with the possible addition of a context to be used by the application control service provider. In the confirm primitive, the acceptance or rejection of each user-requested context is indicated.

The final new parameter in the A-ASSOCIATE service is Result. Only this and the application context name are mandatory; the others may be assumed to be set by prior agreement to simplify implementation. The result parameter is provided by the responding user or by the service provider, and takes one of the following values:

- Accepted
- Rejected by responder (reason not specified)
- Rejected by responder (transient)
- Rejected by responder (permanent)
- Rejected by responder (application entity title not recognized)
- Rejected by responder (application context not supported)
- Rejected by the association control service element
- Rejected by presentation service-provider (transient)
- Rejected by presentation service-provider (permanent)

If the association is accepted, then an application association is created simultaneously with the underlying presentation and session connections.

The A-RELEASE service is used for the orderly release of an association. If the session negotiated release functional unit was selected for the association, the responder may respond negatively, thus causing the unsuccessful completion of the release service and the continuation of the association. On the request and indication primitives, the reason parameter takes on one of the following values: normal, urgent, or undefined. On the response and confirm primitives, it takes on one of the following values: normal, not finished, or undefined. The result parameter indicates acceptance or rejection of the release request. If the release is successful, then the application association is released simultaneously with the underlying presentation and session connections.

The A-ABORT and A-P-ABORT cause the termination of the application association simultaneously with the underlying presentation and session connections. With A-ABORT, the abort source parameter indicates that the abort was initiated by either the association control service provider or by the other service user. With A-P-ABORT, the parameters are mapped directly from those of the P-P-ABORT service.

Association Control Protocol [DIS 8650/2]

The association control protocol is easily explained. Table 10.3 lists the application protocol data units (APDUs), together with their parameters. In keeping with the presentation in the standards documents, this table shows only those parameters that are actually part of the APDU and passed down to the presentation layer as presentation user data. In contrast, Table 9.5 listed PPDU parameters plus parameters that are passed directly to the session layer. There seems to be no particular significance to this stylistic change.

Table 10.4 shows how application primitives are mapped into presentation primitives via the APDUs. As with the presentation service, we

Table 10.3.   ASSOCIATION CONTROL PROTOCOL DATA UNITS AND PARAMETERS

APDU	Parameters
A-ASSOCIATE-REQUEST (AARQ)	Protocol version, Called application entity title, Calling application entity title, Application context name, User information
A-ASSOCIATE-RESPONSE (AARP)	Protocol version, Result, Responding application entity title, Application context name, User information
A-RELEASE-REQUEST (RLRQ)	Reason, User information
A-RELEASE-RESPONSE (RLRE)	Reason, User information
A-ABORT (ABRT)	Abort source, User information

Table 10.4. **RELATIONSHIP AMONG APPLICATION ASSOCIATION PRIMITIVES, APPLICATION ASSOCIATION APDUs, AND PRESENTATION PRIMITIVES**

Application Primitives	Application PDUs	Presentation Primitives
A-ASSOCIATE	AARQ, AARE	P-CONNECT
A-RELEASE	RLRQ, RLRE	P-RELEASE
A-ABORT	ABRT	P-U-ABORT
A-P-ABORT	—	P-P-ABORT

see the tight coupling from the application service down to the presentation service. For example, Fig. 10.2 expands on Fig. 9.4 to show the interrelationship between application, presentation, and session in the setting up of a connection between entities.

As with PPDUs, the format of APDUs is defined in terms of an abstract syntax.

10.3 COMMITMENT, CONCURRENCY, AND RECOVERY

The ISO service [DIS 8649/3] and protocol [DIS 8650/3] standards for the commitment, concurrency, and recovery (CCR) facility are quite different from those for association control. They are considerably more complex and they are more truly optional. With the exception of connectionless applications, virtually all applications need association control services, whereas the CCR services are applicable in a more limited context. Nevertheless, it is a context that encompasses a variety of applications, and therefore, it is appropriate to develop CCR as a common application service element.

Basic Concepts

In a simple protocol, an initiator requests an action and a responder either performs the action and acknowledges it or refuses the action and provides a reason for refusal. This protocol is adequate for a number of applications, but has two basic flaws to it:

- A system crash leaves the result ambiguous
- If multiple systems are involved, there is a lack of coordination that could produce an inconsistent result.

Let us examine these two cases in turn. Figure 10.3 shows the operation of the protocol. The protocol could be used to update a data base. For example, we wish to credit money to a banking account, by adding to the current total in the record of the relevant account holder. When the re-

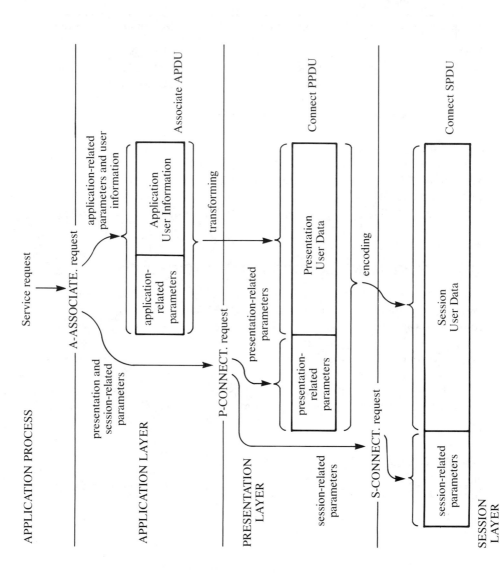

Figure 10.2. Associate and connect request embedding.

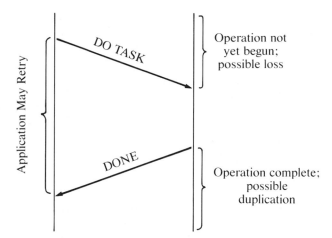

Figure 10.3. Protocol for a simple confirmed service.

sponder (system *B*) receives the update task, it *secures* the data by making the appropriate data base update. It then *releases* the task by sending an acknowledgment. If *B* crashes prior to performing its task, then no response is sent, and the sending system (system *A*) may repeat the transmission. However, it could happen that the task is performed by *B* and no ACK is received by *A*. This could occur for one of two reasons:

- An application entity failure: *B* completes the task and then fails before it can send the ACK.
- A communications failure: *B* completes the task and sends an ACK, but the OSI environment fails to deliver it. This can occur even if a reliable transport protocol is used, as even a reliable protocol cannot deliver data if physical connectivity is lost.

It is clear that if system *A* fails to receive an ACK, it cannot determine if the task occurred or not. If it retries the task, there is the potential for duplication; if it does not, there is the potential for loss.

The second flaw relates to the involvement of more than two systems in a task. For example, consider the transfer of funds from account *Y* to account *X* by an application entity *Z*. *Z* performs the two actions in some order (e.g., credit *X*, debit *Y*). The problem is that the global database is inconsistent for some period of time and could be left in an inconsistent state. Consider these two possibilities:

- Credit account *X* (accepted) followed by debit account *Y* (refused—insufficient funds)
- Debit account *Y* (accepted) followed by credit account *X* (refused—unknown account number)

In either of the above cases, if the network crashes after the first task is completed, then that work cannot be undone in a timely manner; the result is inconsistent.

To see how to overcome these two flaws, we need to introduce four concepts:

- Commitment
- Recovery
- Rollback
- Concurrency

Commitment and Recovery

Let us consider the case of Fig. 10.3 again. We will call the application entity that initiates the task, the master (A in this case) and the application entity that receives the request, the subordinate (B in this case). Figure 10.4 shows the CCR procedure. The master first asks the subordinate if it will offer to commit to a specific task; the task to be performed is given a unique identifier. The subordinate either agrees to perform the task or refuses. If it agrees, then the subordinate sends back an acknowledgment and retains the information about the requested task, but does not perform it. When the master receives the acknowledgment, it issues a commit, which instructs the subordinate to perform the task. The subordinate

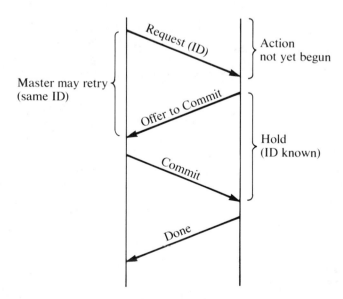

Figure 10.4. CCR procedure.

performs the task and sends an acknowledgment. Now, let us consider the possible problems:

- The master issues a request and then crashes prior to receipt of the offer to commit from the subordinate. The master has recorded (on disk) its request, so that when the master is reactivated, it retransmits the request with the same ID.
- The subordinate crashes after receiving the request but prior to offering to commit. The master times out and retransmits the request. If the subordinate is reactivated, it receives the request and may proceed.
- If the subordinate offers to commit, but the offer does not get through (because of application entity failure or communications failure), this may produce a retransmission, but this is recognized as a duplicate by the subordinate, which merely repeats its offer to commit.
- When the subordinate issues an offer to commit, it secures the information about the requested task on disk. If the subordinate crashes after the offer but before receiving a commit, then the master will get no acknowledgment and may retransmit the commit. Once the subordinate is active, it will recognize the commit, perform the action, and issue an acknowledgment.
- If the subordinate completes the task, but the final acknowledgment does not get through (because of application entity failure or communications failure), the master reissues the commit and receives a refusal with the diagnostic, *ID unknown,* which is interpreted to mean that the subordinate has completed the task.

Rollback

With no failures, the scenario of Fig. 10.4 indicates the successful completion of a task. There is another possible outcome known as rollback. In this case, the master sends a request to a subordinate, receives an offer to commit, and then orders a rollback. This causes the subordinate to delete the task request and to take no further action on the task.

When only two parties are involved, the rollback capability does not appear to be very useful. The master should not have asked for the offer to commit until it was ready to have the task performed. The utility of rollback is evident when more than two parties are involved. Using the earlier example of application entity Z ordering a transfer of funds from account Y (controlled by application entity N) to account X (controlled by application entity M), we have the following scenario:

1. Z requests that M credit account X. If M refuses (account unknown), Z terminates the action.
2. Z requests that N debit account Y. If N refuses (insufficient funds), Z performs a rollback on M and N and terminates the action.

3. If both *M* and *N* offer to commit, then *Z* issues a commit to both entities, and the desired action is undertaken.

If a crash occurs prior to step 3, no harm is done, as neither *N* nor *M* will perform the offered action until explicitly ordered to do so. If a crash occurs somewhere during step 3, it is possible that an inconsistent result will occur. However, at each step, the action is secured by storing state information on disk. Accordingly, once the crash is repaired, the master and subordinates can interact to complete the transaction.

The concept of commitment and rollback can be extended to an arbitrary number of application entities. The master may issue a request to one or more subordinates. One (or more) of the subordinates may need to involve other entities before it can offer to commit. In that case, the subordinate becomes a superior in relation to another subordinate, and requests an offer to commit from that subordinate before giving its offer to commit to the master. This process can be repeated at any point, resulting in a treelike structure of offers to commit. If all of the subordinates offer to commit to their part of the task, then the master eventually receives offers to commit from all of its immediate subordinates and may release the action (Fig. 10.5a). If one or more of the subordinates refuse, then that refusal percolates up the tree to the master, and the master issues rollbacks, which ripple down the tree to all subordinates (Fig. 10.5b).

It is important to distinguish rollback from recovery. Rollback is a CCR service, which allows a master to abort a task after the offer to commit but before the task has actually begun. Recovery is the process of determining the status of a task after an application or communication failure and taking appropriate action. The CCR service provides partial support for recovery; the actual recovery process is application-specific.

Concurrency

Closely associated with the concept of commitment is that of concurrency. Several requirements relate to concurrency:

- Once an application entity has offered to commit to an action, it must be possible for the entity to actually commit (perform the action). This means it should not be possible for some other entity to seize a needed resource and deny access to the entity that made the offer to commit.
- Once a task has begun, interference from other entities must be prevented. For example, a crash may temporarily leave a data base in an inconsistent condition. It must be possible to prevent access (read or write) until the task is brought to completion.

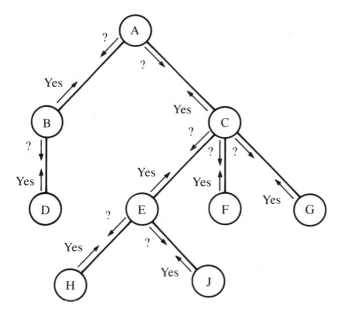

(a) No Refusals

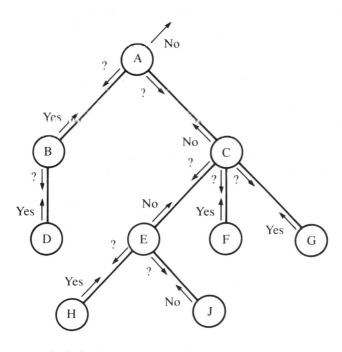

(b) Refusal

Figure 10.5. Atomic action trees.

The techniques associated with concurrency should become clear as we discuss the CCR service.

CCR Service

ISO defines the CCR service in DIS 8649/3. A number of terms are used in the standard, and these are listed and defined in Table 10.5. It is recommended that the reader study this table before proceeding with this section.

Table 10.5. GLOSSARY OF CCR TERMS

Application Failure	The failure of an application entity to meet its normal specification
Secure Data	Data that survives an application failure and is available to the application entity after local recovery procedures have restored it to normal operation
Communications Failure	The failure of a communication path to meet its normal specification. Examples: loss of data or of an application association that is visible to the application
CCR Relationship	A relationship between two or more application entities that survives both communications failure and an application failure and that is established and terminated using CCR service primitives
Atomic Action Data	Secure data used for the duration of a CCR relationship to maintain that relationship and the state of the relationship
Bound Data	Secure data that exists beyond the CCR relationship, but whose state is bound by the rules of the CCR to the state of the CCR relationship for the duration of the CCR relationship
Atomic Action	A sequence of operations performed by a distributed application with the following properties: a. the atomic action is directly or indirectly controlled by a unique application entity b. the atomic action progresses without interference from external actions c. the parts of the atomic action being undertaken by different application entities (possibly in different open systems) either (i) all complete successfully (ii) all terminate with no change to bound data, and with the controlling application entity having available one or more diagnostic messages supplied by the other application entities involved in this atomic action

Table 10.5 (continued)

Master	The unique application entity within the distributed application that directly or indirectly controls the entire activity for this atomic action
Subordinate	An application entity controlled directly (by protocol exchanges) by a superior
Superior	An application entity that directly controls (by protocol exchanges) one or more subordinates
Initial State	The state of bound data at the time of first use by an atomic action
Final State	The state of bound data produced as a result of the operations of the atomic action
Commitment (of an atomic action)	Termination of an atomic action with the release of bound data in the final state, and with termination of the CCR relationship
Rollback (of an atomic action)	Termination of an atomic action with release of bound data after returning it to the initial state, and with termination of the CCR relationship
An Offer of Commitment	A statement by a subordinate to a superior that the subordinate is ready for either commitment or rollback
Period of Use (of a datum used by an atomic action)	The time from the first use of the datum by any branch of the atomic action to the last use of that datum by the atomic action
Concurrency Control	Ensuring that an atomic action is not committed unless a. all atomic actions that have changed the value of a datum prior to its period of use by this atomic action have committed b. no change has been made to the value of a datum during its period of use, except by branches of this atomic action
Recovery Control	Ensuring the correct progress of an atomic action in the presence of application or communications failure
Restart	A facility by which the state of an application and the state of the communications are associated with resynchronization so as to return the state of the application (including its bound data) and the state of the communications to an earlier state associated with a previously communicated mark (session-defined synchronization point)

Secure Data

A key concept that emerges from Table 10.5 is that of secure data. The CCR service depends on the survival of secure data after an application failure. On present-day computer systems, secure data is generally equated with data written on disk, with the disk file closed and all associated directories and catalogues updated and written back. Because the update of secure data is relatively expensive, the CCR service and protocol are designed to minimize the frequency of secure data update.

It must be recognized that even secure data can be lost. For example, a disk crash could cause both an application failure and a loss of secure data. If secure data is lost, then the CCR service may not be able to provide recovery. However, it is assumed that the loss of secure data is infrequent compared with that of normal data.

Three categories of secure data are defined in the CCR standards:

- *Bound data:* Data that is to exist before and after the atomic action and that the user may manipulate during the atomic action. Because this data is subject to commitment and rollback, access by other users to this data during the atomic action must be subject to concurrency control. The identity of the data is determined by the user. For example, in a file transfer application, the file contents would be bound data, but the file attribute, "date last accessed," normally would not.
- *Atomic action data:* Data that exists only for the duration of the atomic action and that is in the nature of state information. This data allows the atomic action to be controlled by the CCR service, and is sufficient to enable the initial state of any bound data to be restored. The data needed and their use are implementation matters beyond the scope of the standards.
- *Other secure data:* This is data not of direct concern to the CCR service, and is not affected by rollback or restart. A typical example are the charges that are being accumulated as an action progresses.

Characteristics of the CCR Service

CCR is introduced in the document [DIS 8649/3] as have the following key characteristics:

- *Atomic action tree:* When more than two application entities are involved in an atomic action, then the CCR service can be modeled as a tree (Fig. 10.5). Each node of the tree is an application entity; each branch of the tree represents an application association.
- *Two-phase commitment:* In Phase I, the master determines whether subordinates are prepared to carry out (i.e., offer to com-

mit to) the action. In Phase II, all subordinates are ordered to commit or rollback.

- *Failure:* The CCR service takes into account the possibility that an application entity may fail at any time, by ensuring that secure data is not lost. After an application failure and the restoral of the failed application, the secure data and the CCR service primitives enable the atomic action to be successfully restarted. Any loss of transferred information is recovered by the CCR restart mechanism.
- *Concurrency control:* Each application entity involved in an atomic action makes changes to bound data in its own open system. Local mechanisms, such as locking, are used to provide concurrency control.
- *Restart and rollback:* Bound data used during an atomic action is capable, by local mechanisms, of being restored to its initial state at any time up to commitment, in response to restart and rollback requirements. The distinction between these two services is explained below.
- *CCR architecture:* With respect to the CCR service, the application layer architecture consists of CCR common application service elements (CASEs) and CCR users. The CCR CASE in an application entity may (1) service a user that is a superior and makes an association with a subordinate; (2) service a user that is a subordinate and makes an association with a superior; or (3) function in both roles. The role of the CCR CASE depends on the location of the application entity in the action tree.

Atomic Action

The CCR service is based on the concept of an atomic action. An atomic action is one that, to an outside observer, takes place as a single unit; either all the changes, on all systems, required by the action occur, or none of them occur (the action is rolled back by the master). To the direct user of the CCR service, however, the commitment and rollback functions needed to assure that the requested action is indeed atomic are visible.

The main features of an atomic action, as defined in DIS 8649/3, are:

- Commitment implies that the results produced by the atomic action have become permanent. No CCR recovery capability exists for undoing a committed action.
- A superior may order rollback to the initial state at any time prior to ordering commitment.
- A superior may not order a subordinate to commit unless it has received an offer of commitment from it.
- If a subordinate has offered commitment and has not been ordered to rollback, it may not subsequently refuse an order to commit.

- A subordinate may refuse commitment at any time up to making an offer to commit.
- The superior orders rollback for any subordinate that has refused commitment.

Service Primitives and Parameters

Table 10.6 lists the primitives and parameters that define the CCR service. Briefly, the service primitives provide the following functions:

- *C-BEGIN:* A request by a superior to a subordinate to offer a commitment
- *C-READY:* A subordinate's offer to commit
- *C-COMMIT:* A superior's order to a subordinate to commit
- *C-REFUSE:* A subordinate's refusal to commit
- *C-ROLLBACK:* A superior's order to a subordinate to rollback

Table 10.6. PRIMITIVES AND PARAMETERS OF THE CCR SERVICE

C-BEGIN.request (Atomic action identifier, Branch identifier, Atomic action timer, User data)

C-BEGIN.indication (Atomic action identifier, Branch identifier, Atomic action timer, User data)

C-PREPARE.request (User data)
C-PREPARE.indication (User data)

C-READY.request (User data)
C-READY.indication (User data)

C-REFUSE.request (User data)
C-REFUSE.indication (User data)

C-COMMIT.request
C-COMMIT.indication
C-COMMIT.response
C-COMMIT.confirm

C-ROLLBACK.request
C-ROLLBACK.indication
C-ROLLBACK.response
C-ROLLBACK.confirm

C-RESTART.request (Resumption point, Atomic action identifier, Branch identifier, Restart timer, User data)

C-RESTART.indication (Resumption point, Atomic action identifier, Branch identifier, Restart timer, User data)

C-RESTART.response (Resumption point, User data)

C-RESTART.confirm (Resumption point, User data)

- *C-PREPARE:* An optional service, used by a superior to indicate the end of this branch of the atomic action and to request the subordinate to issue a C-READY or C-REFUSE
- *C-RESTART:* Issued by a superior or a subordinate when it is necessary to return the state of this branch to an earlier known state

Figures 10.6 and 10.7 show the sequence of events for an atomic action that ends in commitment and that ends in rollback, respectively. Let us now examine each of the service primitives in more detail.

The C-BEGIN service initiates a new action or a new branch of an atomic action. In the latter case, it is adding a new subordinate to an existing atomic action. The C-BEGIN service defines a new CCR relationship. As can be seen, this is an unconfirmed service. As we shall discuss when we describe the CCR protocol, however, the C-BEGIN primitives map onto S-SYNC-MAJOR primitives, establishing a major synchronization point on the application association. Thus, the C-BEGIN service is effectively a confirmed service.

The parameters of the C-BEGIN primitives are these:

- *Atomic action identifier:* Unambiguously identifies the atomic action. It consists of the master's name (unambiguously identifies the application entity that is the master of this action), and the atomic action suffix, which unambiguously identifies this atomic action for this master.
- *Branch identifier:* Consists of the name of the superior of this particular branch, and a branch suffix, which identifies this branch among all branches of this atomic action with this superior.
- *Atomic action timer:* An optional parameter, which indicates how long the superior intends to wait before issuing a rollback to cancel the request.
- *User data:* Application specific

The use to which the timer is to be put is not specified in the standard, which simply says that the timer can be used by an application entity to make decisions affecting the atomic action. For example, suppose X issues a C-BEGIN to Y and, before Y can offer to commit, it attempts to establish an association with a subordinate to perform part of the action to be committed. If Y cannot establish the association because of network failure or remote system failure, it must decide whether to keep trying to establish the association or to try to organize the work another way (do it itself or find another subordinate). The atomic action timer from its superior helps in making that decision.

Once the C-BEGIN has been issued, there may need to be an exchange of application data to further define the requested action prior to the decision by the subordinate to offer to commit or to refuse the action. This activity is application-specific and employs application service prim-

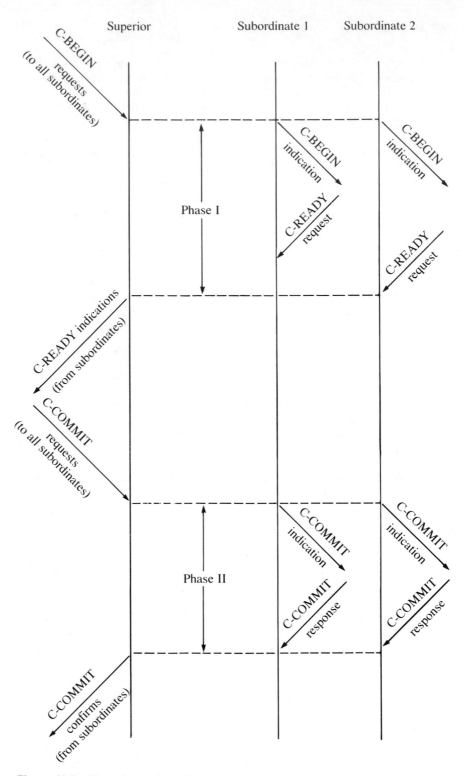

Figure 10.6. Normal commitment sequence.

298

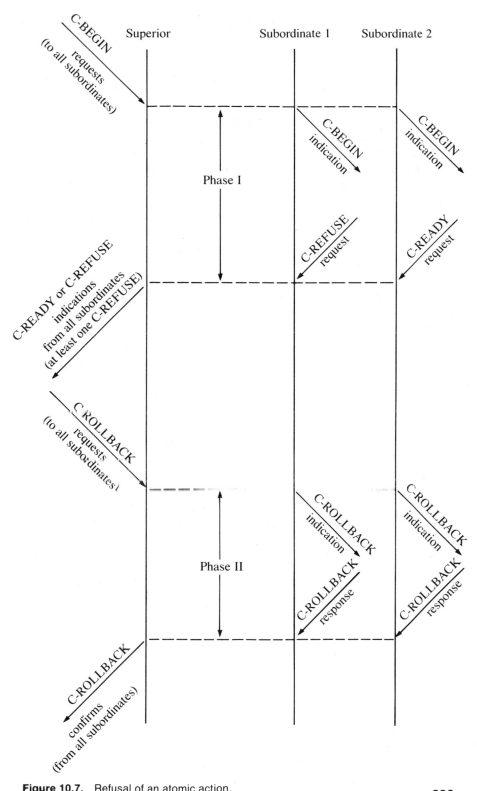

Figure 10.7. Refusal of an atomic action.

299

itives that are not part of the CCR service. Following this exchange, the superior expects the subordinate to reply with an offer to commit or a refusal. The end of this application-specific exchange may be implicit (known by the nature of the application-specific exchange) or may need to be explicit. In the latter case, the superior issues a C-PREPARE primitive to indicate the end of the exchange and to request the subordinate to issue a C-READY or C-REFUSE.

The C-READY primitive is used by the subordinate to offer to commit. From this point on, the subordinate is required to ensure that both commitment to the action and rollback are possible. It docs this by applying concurrency controls to all affected data and by securing the necessary data against the possibility of a crash. Alternatively, the subordinate may refuse the requested action with a C-REFUSE. This primitive may carry an application-specific diagnostic in the user data parameter.

C-COMMIT is an order to commit. The request can only be issued to subordinates from whom a C-READY has been received. This is a confirmed service. The subordinate will issue a C-COMMIT.response as the last event in the termination of the atomic action, following the release of all resources, and following local termination of the CCR relationship. These primitives also establish a major synchronization point on the application association.

At any time after issuing a C-BEGIN, but before issuing a C-COMMIT, a superior may issue a C-ROLLBACK. The subordinate will issue a C-ROLLBACK.response as the last event in the termination of the atomic action, following the release of all resources, and following local termination of the CCR relationship.

Once a C-BEGIN has been issued, a superior is required to complete the atomic action with a rollback or commit, so that the subordinate's resources can be released. Thus, following a crash by either a superior or a subordinate, the superior must attempt to recover so that the action can be completed. The purpose of the RESTART facility is to return the state of the CCR relationship to a known point from which recovery can proceed.

The C-RESTART.request can be issued by either a superior or a subordinate. The resumption point parameter in the request and indication primitives takes on the value ACTION, COMMIT, or ROLLBACK, to indicate that the action should be restarted at the beginning, or at the last commitment or rollback synchronization point, respectively. If the C-RESTART.request was issued by the superior, the resumption point parameter in the response and confirm parameters takes on one of the following values:

- *DONE*: Commitment or rollback is complete
- *RETRY-LATER:* Subordinate cannot proceed with the restart at this time. A typical case of this situation is when the subordinate

cannot establish an association with one or more of its subordinates.
- *REFUSE:* The subordinate refuses commitment. The superior will then issue a rollback.
- *ACTION:* Requests that action be restarted at the beginning.

If the C-RESTART.request was issued by a subordinate, then the only valid value of the resumption point parameter in the response and indication primitives is ACTION.

The atomic action and branch identifiers have the same form and value as those in the corresponding C-BEGIN primitives. The restart timer, if present, indicates to the subordinate that the superior has the intention of waiting that amount of time for a confirm primitive before relinquishing the association.

CCR Protocol

The CCR protocol provides a relatively straightforward support of the CCR service. Table 10.7 lists the CCR APDUs and their parameters. In most cases, there is a simple relationship between the service and the protocol. An APDU whose name ends with the letters RI is moving in the

Table 10.7.   CCR PDUs AND PARAMETERS

APDU	Parameters
C-BEGIN RI	Atomic action identifier, Branch identifier, Atomic action timer, User data
C-PREPARE RI	User data
C-READY-RI	User data
C-REFUSE-RI	User data
C-COMMIT-RI	
C-COMMIT-RC	
C-ROLLBACK-RI	
C-ROLLBACK-RC	
C-RESTART-RI	Resumption point, Atomic action identifier, Branch identifier, Restart timer, User data
C-RESTART-RC	Resumption point, User data
C-START-RI	
C-START-RC	
C-ABANDON-RI	
C-ABANDON-RC	
C-RESYNC-RI	
C-RESYNC-RC	

direction from the user that issued a request primitive to the user that will receive the indication primitive. An APDU whose name ends in RC is moving in the opposite direction (response issuer to confirm receiver). The parameters of the APDUs are direct mappings from those of the CCR service primitives.

The CCR protocol relies heavily on the session service. The presentation service is essentially transparent. To begin, an application association is required. In addition to any requirements of the specific application, the following session functional units are required by CCR:

- Kernel
- Typed data
- Major synchronize
- Resynchronize

The major/activity token shall be with the superior for the duration of a CCR atomic action.

Table 10.8 shows how CCR service primitives are mapped into session service primitives via CCR APDUs. The presentation service and PPDU involvement is not shown because it is essentially a pass-through (see Table 9.6). When a C-BEGIN.request is issued, the CCR protocol first acquires the major/activity token and then establishes a major synchronization point. It then uses the C-BEGIN-RI APDU to carry the parameters of the C-BEGIN.request and to deliver these in a C-BEGIN.indication. If a subordinate refuses to offer a commitment, then

Table 10.8. RELATIONSHIP BETWEEN CCR PRIMITIVES, CCR APDUs, AND SESSION PRIMITIVES

CCR Primitives	CCR APDUs	Session Primitives
C-BEGIN	C-START RI, C-START-RC and	S-SYNC-MAJOR
	C-BEGIN-RI	S-TYPED-DATA
C-PREPARE	C-PREPARE-RI	S-TYPED-DATA
C-READY	C-READY-RI	S-TYPED-DATA
C-REFUSE	C-ABANDON-RI, C-ABANDON-RC and	S-RESYNCHRONIZE
	C-REFUSE-RI	S-TYPED-DATA
C-COMMIT	C-COMMIT-RI	S-SYNC-MAJOR
C-ROLLBACK	C-ROLLBACK-RI	S-RESYNCHRONIZE
C-RESTART	C-RESYNC-RI, C-RESYNC-RC and	S-RESYNCHRONIZE
	C-RESTART-RI, C-RESTART-RC	S-TYPED-DATA

a resynchronization takes place back to the beginning of the atomic action (C-BEGIN). In this case, the abandon presentation resynchronization option is employed (the defined context set is unchanged). As with a refusal, a rollback involves resynchronization with the abandon option.

In the case of the C-BEGIN.request, a separate protocol exchange is used to define a major synchronization point and then the parameters of the C-BEGIN primitive are carried as user data in a typed data transmission. In the case of the C-COMMIT.request, a major synchronization point is established, but there are no parameters to transmit. Hence, only the S-SYNC-MAJOR session service is used.

Finally, the C-RESTART service involves resynchronization with the restart option (restore previously defined context set), followed by the use of typed data to transmit the C-RESTART parameters.

appendix A

Services and Functions of the OSI Layers

Services	Functions
Physical Layer	
Physical connections	Physical-connection activation and deactivation
Physical SDUs	
Physical connection endpoints	Physical SDU transmission
Data-circuit identification	Physical layer management
Sequencing	
Fault condition notification	
Quality of service parameters	
Data Link Layer	
Data-link connection	Data-link connection establishment and release
Data-link SDUs	
Data-link connection endpoint identifiers	Data-link SDU mapping
	Data-link connection splitting
Sequencing	Delimiting and synchronization
Error notification	Sequence control
Flow control	Error detection
Quality of service parameters	Error recovery
	Flow control

305

Services	Functions
	Identification and parameter exchange
	Control of data-circuit interconnection
	Data link layer management

Network Layer

Services	Functions
Network addresses	Routing and relayin
Network connections	Network connections
Network connection endpoint identifiers	Network connection multiplexing
Network SDU transfer	Segmenting and blocking
Quality of service parameters	Error detection
Error notification	Error recovery
Sequencing	Sequencing
Flow control	Flow control
Expedited NSDU transfer	Expedited data transfer
Reset	Reset
Release	Service selection
	Network layer management

Transport Layer

Services	Functions
Transport connection establishment	Mapping transport addresses onto network addresses
Data transfer	Multiplexing transport connections onto network connections
Transport connection release	Establishment and release of transport connections
	End-to-end sequence control on individual connections
	End-to-end error detection and any necessary monitoring of the quality of service
	End-to-end error recovery
	End-to-end segmenting, blocking, and concatenation
	End-to-end flow control on individual connections
	Supervisory functions
	Expedited TSDU transfer

Session Layer

Services	Functions
Session connection establishment	Session connection to transport connection mapping

Services	Functions
Session connection release	Session connection flow control
Normal data exchange	Expedited data transfer
Quarentine service	Session connection recovery
Expedited data exchange	Session connection release
Interaction management	Session layer management
Session connection synchronization	
Exception reporting	

Presentation Layer

Services	Functions
Transformation of syntax	Session establishment request
Selection of syntax	Data transfer
	Negotiation and renegotiation of syntax
	Transformation of syntax including data transformation, formatting, and special purpose transformations
	Session termination request

Application Layer

Services	Functions
Information transfer	Functions that imply communication between open systems and are not already performed by the lower layers
Identification of intended communications partners	
Determination of the current availability of the intended communication partners	
Establishment of authority to communicate	
Agreement of privacy mechanisms	
Authentication of intended communication partners	
Determination of cost allocation methodology	
Determination of the adequacy of resources	
Determination of the acceptable quality of service	
Synchronization of cooperating applications	
Selection of the dialogue discipline including initiation and release procedures	

Services	Functions
Agreement on responsibility for error recovery	
Agreement on the procedures for control of data integrity	
Identification of constraints on data syntax	

appendix B

Standards Cited in This Book

Table B.1.   ISO STANDARDS CITED IN THIS BOOK

OSI Reference Model	
ISO 7498	Open Systems Interconnection—Basic Reference Model
ISO 7498/DAD 1	Addendum 1: Connectionless Model
ISO 7498/PDAD 3	Addendum 3: Naming Including Addressing
Data Link Layer	
ISO 3309	High-Level Data Link Control Procedures—Frame Structure
ISO 4335	High-Level Data Link Control Procedures—Consolidation of Elements of Procedures
DIS 7478	Multilink Procedures
ISO 7809	High-Level Data Link Control Procedures—Consolidation of Classes of Procedures
DIS 8802/2	Local Area Networks—Part 2: Logical Link Control
DIS 8886	Data Link Service Definition for Open Systems Interconnection

Table B.1   (continued)

	Network Layer
ISO 8208	X.25 Packet Level Protocol for Data Terminal Equipment
DIS 8348	Network Service Definition
DIS 8348/DAD 1	Addendum 1: Connectionless-Mode Transmission
DIS 8348/DAD 2	Addendum 2: Covering Network Layer Addressing
DIS 8473	Protocol for Providing the Connectionless-Mode Network Service
DIS 8648	Inernal Organization of the Network Layer
DIS 8878	Use of X.25 to Provide the OSI Connection-Oriented Network Service
	Transport Layer
ISO 8072	Transport Service Definition
ISO 8072/DAD 1	Addendum 1: Connectionless-Mode Transmission
ISO 8073	Connection Oriented Transport Protocol Specification
ISO 8073/PDAD 2	Addendum 2: Operation of Class 4 Over Connectionless Network Service
DIS 8602	Protocol for Providing the Connectionless-Mode Transport Service
	Session Layer
DIS 8326	Basic Connection-Oriented Session Service Definition
DIS 8327	Basic Connection-Oriented Session Protocol Specification
	Presentation Layer
DIS 8822	Connection-Oriented Presentation Service Definition
DIS 8823	Connection-Oriented Presentation Protocol Specification
DIS 8824	Specification of Abstract Syntax Notation One (ASN.1)
DIS 8825	Specification of Basic Encoding Rules for Abstract Syntax Notation One (ASN.1)
	Application Layer
DP 8649/1	Definition of Common Application Service Elements—Part 1: Introduction
DIS 8649/2	Definition of Common Application Service Elements—Part 2: Association Control

Table B.1 (continued)

DIS 8649/3	Definition of Common Application Service Elements—Part 3: Commitment, Concurrency, and Recovery
DP 8650/1	Specification of Protocols for Common Application Service Elements—Part 1: Introduction
DIS 8650/2	Specification of Protocols for Common Application Service Elements—Part 2: Association Protocol
DIS 8650/3	Specification of Protocols for Common Application Service Elements—Part 3: Commitment, Concurrency, and Recovery

Table B.2. CCITT STANDARDS CITED IN THIS BOOK

	OSI Reference Model
X.200	Reference Model of Open Systems Interconnection for CCITT Applications
X.210	Open System Interconnection (OSI) Layer Service Definition Conventions

	Physical Layer
X.21	Interface Between Data Terminal Equipment (DTE) and Data Circuit-Terminating Equipment (DCE) for Synchronous Operation on Public Data Networks

	Data Link Layer
I.440	ISDN User-Network Interface Data Link Layer—General Aspects
I.441	ISDN User-Network Interface Data Link Layer Specification

	Network Layer
X.2	International User Classes of Service in Public Data Networks and ISDNs
X.25	Interface Between Data Terminal Equipment (DTE) and Data Circuit-Terminating Equipment (DCE) for Terminals Operating in the Packet Mode and Connected to Public Data Networks by Dedicated Circuit
X.75	Terminal and Transit Call Control Procedures and Data Transfer System on International Circuits Between Packet-Switched Data Networks
X.96	Call Progress Signals in Public Data Networks
X.213	Network Service Definition for Open Systems Interconnection for CCITT Applications

Table B.2 (continued)

Transport Layer	
T.70	Network Independent Basic Transport Service for the Telematic Services
X.214	Transport Service Definition for Open Systems Interconnection for CCITT Applications
X.224	Transport Protocol Specification for Open Systems Interconnection for CCITT Applications
Session Layer	
T.62	Control Procedures for Teletex and Group 4 Facsimile Services
X.215	Session Service Definition for Open Systems Interconnection for CCITT Applications
X.225	Session Protocol Specification for Open Systems Interconnection for CCITT Applications
Presentation Layer	
X.409	Message Handling Systems: Presentation Transfer Syntax and Notation

REFERENCES

BART83   Bartoli, P. The application layer of the reference model of open systems interconnection. *Proceedings of the IEEE,* December 1983.

BELL84   Bellchambers, W., J. Francis, E. Hummel, and R. Nickelson. The international telecommunication union and development of worldwide telecommunications. *IEEE Communications Magazine,* May 1984.

BERT80   Bertine, H. Physical level protocols. *IEEE Transactions on Communications,* April 1980.

BODS85   Bodson, D. The federal telecommunication standards program. *IEEE Communications Magazine,* January 1985.

BOGG80   Boggs, D., J. Shoch, E. Taft, and R. Metcalfe. Pup: An internetwork architecture. *IEEE Transactions on Communications,* April 1980.

BROD83   Brodd, W. HDLC, ADCCP, and SDLC: What's the difference? *Data Communications,* August 1983.

CALL83   Callon, R. Internetwork protocols. *Proceedings of the IEEE,* December 1983.

CANE86   Caneschi, F. Hints for the interpretation of the ISO session layer. *Computer Communication Review.* July/August 1986.

CERN84   Cerni, D. *Standards in Process: Foundations and Profiles of ISDN and OSI Studies.* National Telecommunications and Information Administration, Report 84–170, December 1984.

CHAP82   Chapin, A. Connectionless data transmission. *Computer Communication Review,* April 1982.

CHAP83   Chapin, A. Connections and connectionless data transmission. *Proceedings of the IEEE,* December 1983.

313

CONA83   Conard, J. Services and protocols of the data link layer. *Proceedings of the IEEE,* December 1983.

COS86   Corporation for Open Systems. *Prospectus.* Alexandria, VA, April 1986.

DALA81   Dalal, Y., and R. Printis. 48-Bit absolute internet and ethernet host numbers. *Proceedings, Seventh Data Communications Symposium,* 1981.

DALA82   Dalal, Y. Use of multiple networks in the Xerox network system. *Computer,* October 1982.

DARP81   Defense Advanced Research Projects Agency. *Internet control message protocol.* RFC: 792, September 1981.

DHAS86   Dhas, C., and U. Konangi. X.25: An interface to public packet networks. *IEEE Communications Magazine,* September 1986.

DOLA84   Dolan, M. A minimal duplex connection capability in the top three layers of the OSI reference model. *Proceedings, SIGCOMM '84,* June 1984.

EMMO84   Emmons, W., and H. Chandler. OSI session layer services and protocols. *Proceedings of the IEEE,* December 1983.

FARO86   Farowich, S. Communicating in the technical office. *IEEE Spectrum,* April 1986.

FLET82   Fletcher, J. An arithmetic checksum for serial transmissions. *IEEE Transactions on Communications,* January 1982.

FOLT80   Folts, H. A powerful standard replaces the old interface standby. *Data Communications,* May 1980.

FOLT81   Folts, H. Coming of age: A long-awaited standard for heterogeneous nets. *Data Communications,* January 1981.

FOLT82   Folts, H. A tutorial on the open systems interconnection reference model. *Open Systems Data Transfer,* June 1982.

HEFF86   Heffernon, H. Committee formed to serve federal OSI users. *Government Computer News,* September 20, 1986.

HELD86   Held, G. *Data Communications Networking Devices.* New York: Wiley, 1986.

HEMR84   Hemrick, C. The internal organization of the OSI network layer: Concepts, applications, and issues. *Journal of Telecommunications Networks,* Fall 1984.

HEMR85   Hemrick, C. *The OSI Network Layer Addressing Schemes, its Implications, and Considerations for Implementation.* National Telecommunications and Information Administration, Report 85–186, November 1985.

HUMM85   Hummel, E. The CCITT. *IEEE Communications Magazine,* January 1985.

KAMI86   Kaminski, M. Protocols for communicating in the factory. *IEEE Spectrum,* April 1986.

LOHS85   Lohse, E. The role of the ISO in telecommunications and information systems standardization. *IEEE Communications Magazine,* January 1985.

MCCL83   McClelland, F. Services and protocols of the physical layer. *Proceedings of the IEEE,* December 1983.

MCQU78   McQuillan, J., and V. Cerf. *Tutorial: A Practical View of Computer Communications Protocols.* Silver Spring, MD: IEEE Computer Society Press, 1978.

MEIJ82   Meijer, A., and P. Peeters. *Computer Network Architectures*. Rockville, MD: Computer Science Press, 1982.

NSPA79   National Standards Policy Advisory Committee. *National Policy on Standards for the United States*. 1979. Reprinted in [CERN84].

PETE61   Peterson, W., and D. Brown. Cyclic codes for error detection. *Proceedings of the IRE*, January 1961.

PISC84   Piscitello, D., and L. Chapin. An international internetwork protocol standard. *Journal of Telecommunication Networks*, Fall 1983.

PISC86   Piscitello, D., A. Weissberger, S. Stein, and A. Chapin. Internetworking in an OSI environment. *Data Communications*, May 1986.

POPE84   Pope, A. Encoding CCITT presentation transfer syntax. *Computer Communication Review*, October 1984.

POST80   Postel, J. Internetwork Protocol approaches. *IEEE Transactions on Communications*, April 1980.

RUTK86   Rutkowski, A. An overview of the forums for standards and regulations for digital networks. *Telecommunications*, October 1986.

SELV85   Selvaggi, P. The development of communications standards in the DOD. *IEEE Communications Magazine*, January 1985.

SHEL82   Sheltzer, A., R. Hinden, and M. Brescia. Connecting different types of networks with gateways. *Data Communications*, August 1982.

SHER86   Sherr, S. ANSI and information systems. *Proceedings, Computer Standards Conference*, May 1986.

STAL84   Stallings, W. A primer: Understanding transport protocols. *Data Communications*, November 1984.

STAL85   Stallings, W. Can we talk? *Datamation*, October 15, 1985.

STAL87   Stallings, W. *Local Networks, Second Edition*. New York: Macmillan, 1987.

STAL88   Stallings, W. *Data and Computer Communications, Second Edition*. New York: Macmillan, 1988.

TOML75   Tomlinson, R. Selecting sequence numbers. *Proceedings, ACM SIGCOMM/SIGOPS Interprocess Communication Workshop*, 1975.

WARE83   Ware, C. The OSI network layer: Standards to cope with the real world. *Proceedings of the IEEE*, December 1983.

YANO81   Yanoschak, V. Implementing the X.21 interface. *Data Communications*, February 1981.

ZHAN86   Zhang, L. Why TCP timers don't work well. *Proceedings, SIGCOMM '86 Symposium*, August 1986.

INDEX